TELEPEN
KV-733-048

Youth policy in the 1990s

Despite its importance, youth policy is an often ignored area of Government planning and legislation, and policy initiatives seem to lack any guiding theme or relevance to the needs of young people. In *Youth Policy in the 1990s* John C. Coleman and Chris Warren-Adamson have brought together prominent experts in key areas of youth policy. They provide a critical review of the major issues which implicitly or explicitly affect the world of adolescents and examine to what extent they paint a picture of existing youth policy. The aim is to provide a baseline for a policy on youth in the 1990s.

The book recommends the introduction of a Minister for Young People and the use of youth impact statements at national and local level and seeks to provide information and argument for those seeking to plan policy for young people from a corporate or inter-agency perspective.

The contributors are all recognized experts in their fields. They tackle their topic first by examining the historical perspective, with a special concentration on the past decade. Each has paid regard to particular themes – ethnicity, class and gender, and where possible, has brought in material from other countries and cultures. They have then put forward suggestions for future policy.

John C. Coleman is Director of the Trust for the Study of Adolescence, Brighton, and Editor of the *Journal of Adolescence*. **Chris Warren-Adamson** was formerly Associate Director of the Trust for the Study of Adolescence and is an Adviser to the National Council of Voluntary Child Care Organisations.

Youth policy in the 1990s

The way forward

Edited by
John C. Coleman and
Chris Warren-Adamson

London and New York

First published in 1992
by Routledge
11 New Fetter Lane, London EC4P 4EE

Simultaneously published in the USA and Canada
by Routledge
a division of Routledge, Chapman and Hall Inc.
29 West 35th Street, New York, NY 10001

Typeset by Selectmove Ltd, London
Printed and bound in Great Britain by
Mackays of Chatham PLC, Chatham, Kent

British Library Cataloguing in Publication Data
A Catalogue record for this book is available from the British Library.

Library of Congress Cataloging in Publication Data

Youth policy in the nineteen nineties: the way forward / edited by John Coleman and Chris Warren-Adamson.
p. cm.
Includes bibliographical references and index.
1. Teenagers – Government policy – Great Britain. 2. Teenagers – Great Britain. I. Coleman, John C. II. Warren-Adamson, Chris, 1946– III. Title: Youth policy in the 1990s.
HQ799.G7Y59 1992
305.23'5'0941–dc20 91–21386
CIP

ISBN 0–415–05835–X (hbk)
ISBN 0–415–05836–8 (pbk)

Contents

Figures and tables

FIGURES

TABLES

Abbreviations

AHA	Area Health Authority
APSA	Association for the Psychiatric Study of Adolescents
BMRB	British Market Research Bureau
BSA	Building Societies Association
CBI	Confederation of British Industry
CHC	Community Health Council
CHE	Community Home with Education
COS	Charity Organization Society
CTC	City Technology College
CYPA	Children and Young Persons Act
DC	detention centre
DES	Department of Education and Science
ERA	Educational Reform Act
ESRC	Economic and Social Research Council
FE	further education
GP	general practitioner
HAS	Health Advisory Service
HEA	Health Education Authority
HEC	Health Education Council
HMI	Her Majesty's Inspector
IT	Intermediate Treatment
JCHPT	Joint Committee on Higher Psychiatric Training
LEA	Local Education Authority
LMS	Local Management of Schools
MSC	Manpower Services Commission
NACYS	National Advisory Committee for the Youth Service
NAYPIC	National Association of Young People in Care
NCVQ	National Council for Vocational Qualifications
NEDO	National Economic Development Office
NHS	National Health Service
PIC	Private Industry Council
PSE	personal and social education
RCPsych	Royal College of Psychiatrists

Scotvec	Scottish Vocational Education Council
SSD	social services department
TEC	Training and Enterprise Council
TVE	Technical and Vocational Extension
TVEI	Technical and Vocational Education Initiative
WHO	World Health Organization
YCS	youth custody centre
YOP	Youth Opportunities Programme
YTS	Youth Training Scheme

Editors' note

This book originated from discussions between the editors when they were both employed by the Trust for the Study of Adolescence in its very early stages. The Trust, based in Brighton, is an independent research organization and registered charity, which was established in 1988. Its primary aims are: 'The advancement of knowledge concerning adolescence and the promotion of public and professional education in respect of this stage of human development.'

The Trust has a particular commitment to issues of youth policy, and to representing the needs of young people. Major research concerns include the impact of family breakdown, the parenting of adolescents, sexual development, leaving care, teenage parenthood, and altruism in young people.

Contributors

Michael Banks joined the MRC/ESRC Social and Applied Psychology Unit, University of Sheffield, in 1978, previously having been Lecturer in Social Psychology at St Thomas's Hospital Medical School. He has published widely on youth topics, including health education, unemployment, training, and economic socialization. Recent books include (with P. Ullah) *Youth Unemployment in the 1980s: Its Psychological Effect* (Croom Helm, 1988) and Banks et al. *Careers and Identities* (1991).

Christopher R. Brannigan is Deputy Director of the Centre for Advanced Studies in Education, and Manager of Birmingham Polytechnic's Student Satisfaction Project. A behavioural psychologist and former Chair of the British Association for Behavioural Psychotherapy, he has contributed to, and is the editor of, several journals. He has also directed research and evaluation projects on TVEI and TRIST and recently advised the DES on the development of Post-16 education in CTCs.

John C. Coleman is Director of the Trust for the Study of Adolescence in Brighton, and Editor of the *Journal of Adolescence*. He has a longstanding interest in and involvement with adolescence. His published works include *The Nature of Adolescence* (2nd edition, Routledge, 1990).

Nick Frost is currently Development Officer (Child Care) for Wakefield Community and Social Services Department. He was formerly a social worker and Lecturer in Applied Social Studies. He has published on various aspects of social work and social policy, and is co-author of *The Politics of Child Welfare* (1989).

Leo B. Hendry is Professor and Head of the Department of Education, University of Aberdeen. Before taking up a University appointment in the early 1970s he was a school teacher in Scotland and England and a College of Education Lecturer in London and Leeds. He has published over sixty research papers, ten book chapters and is author or co-author of ten books, including *The Nature of Adolescence* (1990) with John C. Coleman.

Damian Killeen is Director of the Strathclyde Poverty Alliance. His previous posts have included working for Shelter (Scotland) as Young

Persons' Housing Worker, co-ordinating the work of the Stopover Hostel for homeless young people in Edinburgh and directing the work of the 'First Aid' advice and information service for young people in Doncaster. He has served as Chairperson of the National Association of Young People's Counselling and Advisory Services and has a background in community arts, community work, and intermediate treatment. In 1988 Shelter published Killeen's report 'Estranged' – a study of the impact of the withdrawal of entitlement to welfare benefits from 16 and 17 year olds.

Janet Paraskeva is the Director of the newly established National Youth Agency. She was previously Director of the National Youth Bureau, one of the organizations whose functions have been merged within the new single Agency. Her previous posts have included five years as an HMI and a spell with the ILEA Inspectorate as well as working in other national and voluntary youth organizations, chairing the British Youth Council, and establishing the European Confederation of Youth Clubs. Her early experiences include time as a secondary teacher, teaching Science and Maths in two Birmingham schools, and as a part-time youth worker with mentally disabled young people in Bromsgrove and in a mixed youth club in North Warwickshire.

John Pitts is Reader in Applied Social Science at the West London Institute of Higher Education. He has worked as a practitioner, researcher, and consultant in juvenile justice. In 1983–4 he chaired the London IT Association. He is author of *The Politics of Juvenile Crime* (1988), *Working with Young Offenders* (1990), and editor, with John Dennington, of *Developing Services for Young People in Crisis* (1991).

Ian Skeldon is a Consultant Child and Adolescent Psychiatrist who is employed by the South Western Regional Health Authority. He works in the Child and Family Psychiatry Service provided by Frenchay Health Authority in Bristol. This service has a multi-disciplinary orientation and Ian Skeldon works as a member of a busy team of professionals which provides a wide range of services within the District. He works in both the community and the hospital components of the service which provides resources to the specialized child and adolescent neurosurgery, plastic surgery, and burns and neuropaediatric services.

Mike Stein is Senior Lecturer in the Department of Adult Continuing Education at the University of Leeds. He is author of *Leaving Care and the 1989 Children Act, the Agenda?* (1991), *Living Out of Care* (1990), (with Nick Frost) *The Politics of Child Welfare* (1989), and (with Kate Carey) *Leaving Care* (1986). He is currently Research Director of 'A Study of Leaving Care Schemes, 1990–4', a four-year research project funded by the Department of Health. He has been an adviser to NAYPIC and has worked in both probation and social services.

Fiona Stewart holds BA (Hons) and MA degrees in Social Sciences from the University of London. She joined the Henley Centre in 1984 and is now Associate Director in the Social Futures Group. Her particular research interest lies in demographic and social change and its impact on business marketing. She is a frequent commentator in the media and at conferences on all aspects of social change, especially those relating to women.

Sylvia Tilford is currently a Senior Lecturer in Health Education at Leeds Polytechnic. Her main teaching contributions are to an international MSc in Health Education and Health Promotion. Current research interests include intersectoral collaboration in health promotion, curriculum development of health education in the UK and overseas and patient education. Prior to involvement in health education she was at various times a science teacher in comprehensive schools, playgroup leader, outreach worker in a psychiatric hospital, and lecturer in psychology in adult and further education.

Philip H. Walkling is Professor in Education and Dean of the Faculty of Education at Birmingham Polytechnic. He is an educational philosopher, with a particular interest in educational responses to cultural diversity.

Chris Warren-Adamson was formerly Associate Director of the Trust for the Study of Adolescence. He is an Adviser to the National Council of Voluntary Child Care Organisations and has spent his career in work with children and young people. Among his books are (with W. Stone) *Protection or Prevention – A Critical Look at the Voluntary Child Care Sector* (1988).

Richard Williams is a Consultant Child and Adolescent Psychiatrist employed by the United Bristol Healthcare Trust. He is an Honorary Clinical Lecturer in Mental Health to, and an examiner for, the University of Bristol. He is also examiner for the Royal Colleges of Psychiatrists and Physicians. He is a past Chairman of the Association for the Psychiatric Study of Adolescence. The *Journal of Adolescence* is published for the Association and Richard Williams is an Assistant Editor.

1 Dear Minister . . .

Chris Warren-Adamson

Our primary motive for bringing together this collection is to hurry along that which is already gathering momentum, the idea of a minister for young people, and the inevitable tool which is implied by such a post, the application of a youth impact statement.

So, Minister, we offer in these pages a preliminary reader to inform your early portfolio. There are many dimensions of youth – we chose eleven – and invited contributors who are prominent and respected in their field to evaluate youth policy. We asked each contributor to tackle his or her topic by examining the historical perspective, with a particular concentration on the past decade. They were asked to have regard to particular themes – ethnicity, class, and gender – and where possible to enhance their material with reference to other countries and cultures. And lastly, they were asked to give some indication of future trends.

There are of course some difficulties in using the term 'youth impact statement'. Why not 'family impact statement'? We are after all firmly committed to the view that promoting young people and intervening with them and on their behalf involves supporting their parents, extended family and friends, and their communities. We keep the focus on youth because that is self-evidently the mood abroad – that, after the last decade, Britain urgently needs to invest in its young people and urgently needs to like its young people.

We are not proposing a particular line. Rather, we want these pages to speak for themselves. Suffice to say that, on the whole, it is not a happy tale. It is a picture of contradictions: new curricula and promising legal frameworks (Chapters 7 and 9) operating with seriously diminished services and bruised and unhappy work-forces, just plain decline (Chapter 6), a paranoia about a 'dependent' young people leading to a tale of homelessness which takes your breath away, the perplexing interaction between the imperatives of the market-place and young people as consumers (Chapter 3), the complexities of inclusion and exclusion (Chapters 1 and 8), and a nation facing persistent unemployment where the numbers of young people are disproportionately high.

John Coleman's chapter, 'The nature of adolescence' (Chapter 2), reviews theories of adolescence; then discusses matters of civil status of young people and how legal ambiguity can add pressure to the world of the young person; and finishes by reminding us of a check-list of needs for young people. Coleman's theory review is an important starting point to this reader because it becomes evident within these pages that myth and stereotype can contribute significantly to policy formation. We learn that psychoanalysis and sociology, while providing helpful frameworks for the understanding of disturbance in adolescence, are given little support by research. Yet the emphasis on threatening behaviour has become assimilated into our traditional view of adolescent behaviour and may be given undue prominence, for example in the development of policy. Coleman modestly does not describe his own focal theory of adolescence, which is part of a more promising direction in theory and research which links with the wider ecological or interactionist perspective. This trend is important because it emphasizes competency and adaptive behaviour and works towards assembling a theory of adolescent normality. Hence, it links with and informs the empowerment perspective in intervention which is given strong support in several chapters. Coleman also discusses the Gillick principle, which he argues still leaves room for doubt, caution, and ambiguity. He argues that the legal framework for young people is seriously ambiguous and indeed, powerful examples emerge from recent war commentary: 'You can lose your life for your country but you can't vote!' (February 1991 re the Gulf War).

Leo Hendry in 'Sport and leisure: the not-so-hidden curriculum?' (Chapter 5) reminds us early on of a stereotype which resurfaces consistently in these chapters. Referring to Davis (1990) '. . . themes of rebellon, delinquency, moodiness, energy, aggression and excitement still have currency in the public consciousness, and, reinforced by the media, in creating stereotypic pictures of youth today'. Thus, Hendry evaluates the recent history of sport and recreational provision as not only reflecting the needs of a particular group but also reflecting a concern to integrate and control young people. The historical perspective reveals a surprising number of deliberations on the recreational needs of young people and we note the evolution of leisure participation over the last twenty-five years as an expression of mass culture and the domination of the notion of 'sport for all' (European Sports Charter 1975). But the main thrust of Hendry's chapter, and the basis of much of his research, is to record the subtle and interacting features which serve to exclude or make young people exclude themselves from sport and recreational activity. 'It is possible to propose therefore that a "hidden agenda" of values operates within sports which impinges upon, and influences, young people in a way that facilitates the sports involvement of some but constrains the regular participation of many.' He develops for sport what is a well-known critique of the formal education system, the presence of a 'hidden curriculum' whose range of subliminal messages ensures the inclusion of some and the exclusion or self-exclusion of others. His argument gives a vivid account of the self-reinforcing circle of achievement in school which ensures that participation in sport at school and afterwards has a class and gender bias. The chapter ends with the theme of empowerment, to which a number of contributors return, implicitly and explicitly, and which is an approach that demands an examination of needs across a range of levels and that consumers should be actively involved in planning their services.

Damian Killeen's chapter, 'Leaving home' (Chapter 11), underlines a societal concern about the independence of youth. Killeen examines recent housing and social-security policy and we are pressed to conclude that current policy towards those young people who face the challenge of independence is based on the motive actively to discourage a 'dependency culture'. Whatever the political perspective there is no doubting that we have a problem and Killeen documents acknowledgement by Government of the connection between its policy and homelessness through attempts to soften the impact of some policies. One view suggests Britain is near the top of the league in terms of the young homeless: 'numbers of young beggars to be found in London and other major British cities would not disgrace some parts of South America and Africa'. It is argued that the plight of the young homeless is rooted in the combination of a policy since 1985 to limit financial support for young people living away from their parents' home and a housing policy where the move towards private-sector provision has proved inadequate to the task of providing social housing. Killeen argues for policy towards this age group to be reframed in terms of 'interdependence' and that we are ill-served by concepts of independence or fear of dependence. Killeen reminds us of the use of the youth impact report in Denmark and Sweden and urges that Britain adopt the same.

Mike Stein and Nick Frost in 'Empowerment and child welfare' (Chapter 9) make empowerment a central part of their chapter. They provide an important political perspective on childhood (as opposed, for example, to a biological or psychological perspective) and place power at the centre of their analysis of childhood. They argue that 'generation' should be added to our list of perspectives on inequality – ethnicity, gender, disability, and class. Stein and Frost offer a widely held view of the Children Act 1989, applauding its so-called Gillick principle which finally lays to rest the idea of children as their parents' chattels. Moreover, the combination of the (qualified) duties to provide family support, the promotion of contact for the child with extended family and friends, the explicit duty to consult the child, those with parental responsibility and significant others, and the presumption of no order coupled with a duty to take reasonable steps to avoid care proceedings, all make up the corner-stones of an empowering approach. At the same time many argue that the Act is spoilt by the inclusion of the definition of 'in need' and the way much of the legal provision is qualified by these two words. Thus, we are reminded that this legislation reveals a motive of social policy we find in several of these chapters, the attempt to target, to aim state intervention at the few while ensuring that caring for the majority of children is privatized.

John Pitts in 'Juvenile-justice policy in England and Wales' (Chapter 10) describes a transformation in juvenile-justice ideology and intervention in the last twenty years, from (quoting Booker) 'The utopian belief that through drastic social and political reorganisation, aided by the greater use of state planning, we should be able to create a new kind of just, fair, and equal society', through to radical non-intervention which

> told workers in the juvenile justice system that in their attempts to act in what they presumed to be a young offender's best interest they could actually be disadvantaging them further [Schur 1974]. It enjoined them instead, wherever and whenever possible, to 'leave the kids alone'.

Pitts identifies a 'success' for juvenile justice by systems management, which is an attempt to change the behaviour of those who make decisions to ensure that penalties imposed on young offenders are minimized so that fewer children and young people are committed to care and custody. But Pitts's account of the 1980s in particular echoes a theme of several of the other chapters. Whatever the short-term gains of specific interventions they were made against a backcloth of a growing and increasingly marginalized section of the youth population. Some special lessons stand out. The French experience, for example, reminds us that politically committed, broad-based strategies aimed at and enlisting communities in partnership offer tough but realistic advantages over quick and simple interventions. Pitts summarizes:

> In the sphere of crime and justice, the 1980s was the decade of simple solutions and increasingly complicated problems . . . By the end of the decade, many politicians, criminologists and senior police officers were agreed that more policing and the seemingly endless manipulation of penalties could do little to contain what was essentially a social and economic problem.

In so far as 'we adopt conceptions of health that define it as multi-dimensional' then Sylvia Tilford's chapter, 'Health matters' (Chapter 7), is in many ways central to the reader. This broad perspective underpins the development of the Health Promotion movement, but it is in concept only. Tilford quotes Friedman (1989):

> policies and legislation in the many different sectors that have an impact on young people's health – education, employment, social services, youth, culture and sport – as well as health care are rarely co-ordinated in such a way as to provide a systematic approach to young people's health.

Tilford concentrates on health care and education sectors. When health concerns of youth are discussed we return to a theme identified in Hendry's chapter. Matters of control and stereotypical concerns may be as important as the accurate identification of need. Tilford writes:

> Society's wishes to control those behaviours of young people who are defined as threatening can be more influential than narrow health concerns in defining policy actions . . . sexual behaviour and illicit drug use are examples where social control has clearly been an important consideration.

Tilford's chapter provides substantial data on the health concerns of young people. It is also a telling critique of health-promotion strategies and the relative strengths and weaknesses of the education and health-care sectors. Radical, preventive, and empowerment models are discussed, and the power of intervention on a broad front is underlined. Tilford's prescription for greater health promotion parallels themes from other chapters. In particular she calls for healthy public policies, creating supportive environments, strengthening community action, developing personal skills, avoiding the narrow consumerist approach of the NHS White Paper, and instead requiring full dialogue, elicitation of community needs as well as professionally defined ones, and effective formal democratic structures.

Richard Williams's and Ian Skeldon's chapter, 'Mental health services for adolescents' (Chapter 8), is especially commended to students and others as a detailed and critical introduction to mental-health services for young people. For example, you will find here an account of the child-guidance system, which has been decimated in recent years. In passing, the authors also reject, as do Coleman, Banks, and Hendry and many others, that adolescence is a period of widespread emotional turmoil: 'There still exists a traditional view that adolescence is a time of inevitable emotional turmoil. . . . This can therefore be held out to be the characteristic and normal state and the term "adolescence" thereby comes to have a pathological implication.' In concept, the high water mark for adolescent services is expressed in the publication *Bridges over Troubled Waters* (NHS Health Advisory Service, 1986), which recommended comprehensive and integrated services for disturbed young people, and the excellent idea of local resource centres. The authors' analysis of the non-implementation of the report serves as a summary in overall terms of a declining service. These are: cuts or little growth in expenditure, the dissemination of services into the community, substantial changes in Health Service management and administration, and a contention that originators of such services themselves came to retirement age at a crucial time. The reader is left with a picture of a declining service poorly responding to or ill-served by the Health Service structure and culture designated by the NHS and Community Care Acts.

Michael Banks's 'Youth employment and training' (Chapter 4) stated aim is to trace the state of affairs whereby Britain has been so widely criticized for its apparent lack of investment in the practice of employing 16–18 year olds. This document draws on substantial data in its documentation of the impact of unemployment on young people, emphasizes young people's special vulnerability to unemployment and points to the disproportionate representation of young people in the overall unemployment figures. Banks's historical analysis of youth labour patterns and expectations connects with the current poor level of delivery of training available. Banks traces the evolution of the Youth Training Scheme (YTS), a programme which has been greatly amended in its course. Some of the early problems concerned low take-up, inequalities in earnings for ex-YTS trainees in jobs, and a question-mark as to the scheme's potential for leading to lasting employment. Banks's own conclusions are tentative about the capacity of current programmes to bring about the necessary sea change in training delivery.

'The adolescent as consumer' (Chapter 12) is not to be linked to the theme of democratic participation of other chapters. Fiona Stewart's account concerns the adolescent as potential spender, consumer of goods. Her chapter is full of unusual and important data about the significance of adolescents in the market-place, the complex interaction between consumption, image, and life-styles. Figures which describe vividly those who can spend and those who cannot find similar expression in the theme of marginalization in other chapters. What are the implications of being excluded from the consumption process? Stewart's chapter is the only one explicitly to mention individualism, the political philosophy of the decade. She makes sense of it in two ways: first, in terms of the move away from mass consumption, and the idea of buying things that not many other people will have; and second, she quotes Stuart Hall: 'greater fragmentation and pluralism, the weakening of older collective solidarities and block identities and the emergence of new identities associated with greater work flexibility, and the maximisation of individual choices through personal consumption'. And, according to Gardner and Sheppard, the weakening or loss of received identities has left a gaping hole where class, association, or region once was. Consumption has filled this perceived gap.

Early on in their chapter, 'Secondary education' (Chapter 3), Phil Walkling and Chris Brannigan write: '. . . the educational radicalism of the two main parties since 1944 never reaches the point of bringing together a clear vision of educational goals with the resources likely to achieve them'. The inability to match the radicalism of ideas with resources is an enduring theme of this reader. This is a despairing chapter; it makes you understand why unlikely people increasingly opt for private school. It attempts to analyse the course of the radicalizing policies of the 1980s and is a forceful account of change. Many themes emerge and four in particular find parallels in other chapters. First, accountability is an increasingly complex notion where teachers must weave a path between trying to meet the perceived needs of the children, their children's parents as managers, and the direct agenda of industry. Here consumerism does not appear to equate with the broad-based participation which many of the contributors call for. Second, there appears to be a contradiction between the rhetoric of opportunity and the consistent exclusion of young people from suitable opportunities. Third, there is the challenge to and suspicion of professional self-interest. Those on the receiving end of this face a dilemma. It should be a principle of professional practice to be wary of the immediate and institutionalized ways in which self-interest can mean poor attention to the needs of clients, here meaning children. Yet the fear is that the consistent bruising delivered to professionals seriously undermines their ability to sustain good standards. Walkling and Brannigan are at pains to assert the existence of high standards of practice despite such scepticism. Fourth, there is the tendency to ignore the results of evaluation of policy or to act in advance of findings.

Radicalism, ill-matched by resources, is no less a theme for the Youth Service. But Janet Paraskeva's account of the evolution of the Youth Service through to the establishment of the new National Youth Agency (April 1991) is less despairing ('Youth work and informal education', Chapter 6). Quality assurance and other principles of the decade may have worked to give the Youth Service a tighter definition and a core curriculum. But it may well be a different service:

> With increased centralisation a core curriculum for the service and the possibility of a core curriculum for training – a unified structure leading to possible degree status with a variety of access points, modular organisation and credit accumulation of transfer – all in the context of educational reform, the possible demise of the education authority, and certainly local management of resources, could see a radical change in what we now know as the youth service.

The recommended Statement of Purpose for the Youth Service (Ministerial Conference 1990, unpublished) is one which would do justice to the overall intention of this reader: '. . . to redress all forms of inequality, to ensure equality of opportunity for all young people to fulfil their potential as empowered individuals and members of groups and communities; and to support young people during the transition to adulthood'.

2 The nature of adolescence

John C. Coleman

WHAT IS ADOLESCENCE?

This book is concerned with policy relating to young people in society. The term 'youth policy' is used to describe not only government initiatives and legislation, but a set of attitudes which determine the ways in which adults and young people interact. Underlying questions about youth and youth policy are more fundamental questions to do with, on the one hand, our values about children and the family, and on the other, our understanding of the nature of childhood and adolescence. It seems sensible, therefore, to introduce this book by including a chapter which addresses some of these more fundamental questions.

In seeking to understand adolescence we are brought face to face with a variety of puzzling issues. In the first place no one is entirely sure when adolescence begins, and when it ends. It may be convenient to use the teenage years – from 13 to 19 – as one definition, but it hardly fits the facts. At one end puberty may commence at 10 or 11, and parents or teachers may describe the behaviour of a boy or girl as 'adolescent' well before they reach the age of 13. At the other end those remaining in higher education, or still living at home in their early twenties, may be manifesting confrontational or dependent behaviour which is strikingly similar to a typical 16 year old.

We have only to consider current legislation to do with young people to see that age is a deeply confounding factor. Is adulthood reached at 16, 17, or at 18? Is a 10 year old a child or a young person? When do parental responsibilities cease? Asking such questions simply brings us face to face with the anomalies of our legal system, anomalies which have a profound effect on young people themselves. I shall return to this issue below. The fact is that chronological age, although giving us a broad indication of the adolescent stage, cannot be a precise definition. Around the edges, and particularly at either end, the definition of adolescence remains uncertain, and this itself reflects an important feature of the phenomenon.

The second problem associated with adolescence has to do with the possibility that it is a stage which is to some extent artificially created. Many were influenced by Margaret Mead's classic book *Coming of Age in Samoa* (1928). In this book she describes a society in which individuals pass from childhood to adulthood with no trauma or stress. The existence of rites of passage enable boys and girls to be clear about when and how they should assume adult roles and responsibilities, and this clarity ensures that the long transition and the ambiguity of status are not experienced. Although it is generally agreed now that Mead viewed Samoan society through rose-coloured spectacles, none the less the sense continues to linger that western society, through its emphasis on continued education and the prolonged economic dependence of young people on their parents, encourages adolescence to be a difficult period.

Indeed, Fiona Stewart's chapter in this book (Chapter 12) underlines the important place the teenage consumer has in an industrial economy. The spending power of those who have as yet no adult responsibilities is formidable, and advertising and the media have devoted much of their energies to ensuring that this market not only remains in place, but is expanded as far as possible. Such pressures undoubtedly play a part in creating younger and younger adolescents whose needs – for music, fashion, and so on – can only be met by new products.

None the less, this argument can only be taken so far. While it is certainly true that teenage consumers are an important element in western economies, that does not necessarily mean that our economic system – capitalism – has created adolescence. Adolescence has existed in one form or another since the Greeks, as we know from the writings of Plato. Two thousand years ago youth was seen as the political force most likely to challenge the status quo, and even in Elizabethan times, according to Shakespeare, the young were more likely to be 'wronging the ancientry' and 'getting wenches with child' than doing anything useful. A recent study by Montemayor (1991) analysed relationships between parents and adolescents in two historical periods – the 1920s and 1980s. He was able to show not only that issues of disagreement remained remarkably similar over the two periods, but, even more important, that levels of conflict within families were almost exactly the same. Clearly, therefore, in spite of enormous social and economic changes in the twentieth century, the phenomenon of adolescence has changed little. It is often said that the concept 'the teenage years' came about after the end of the Second World War, and came to public notice in the 1950s with films such as James Dean's *Rebel without a Cause*. Montemayor's research shows this not to be true – it may be that the term 'teenager' came into our vocabulary at that time, but adolescence itself has been around for very much longer. In fact the first substantial study of the psychology of adolescence was written by G. Stanley Hall; the date – 1904.

While adolescence is quite clearly affected by social and economic factors, and may manifest itself differently depending on the cultural and historical context, some form of transitional stage is common to most societies. The period of the transition will obviously vary both between and within societies. Thus, for example, in Britain work opportunities, housing, entry into further education, and family circumstances will all affect the way adolescence shades into adulthood, and the length of time the transitional stage is allowed to continue.

Irrespective of when the stage ends, however, in most western countries there are particular characteristics of adolescence which are of general relevance. There seems little doubt, for example, that almost all young people experience ambiguity of status. Between the ages of 15 and 17 uncertainties about their rights, and lack of clarity about where they stand in relation to the authority of their parents, are issues which will be familiar to many teenagers. 'When do I become an adult?' is a tricky question to answer, and is likely to lead to confusion, not least because a different answer would be given by a policeman, a doctor, a teacher, a parent, and a social worker.

From the point of view of the young person, another feature of adolescence which is especially wearing is the stereotyping which exists, and which devalues and belittles this generation. In a classic study published twenty-five years ago the Eppels put it well:

> The picture that has emerged of this group of young working people (15–17 years of age) is that most of them regard themselves as belonging to a generation handicapped by distorted stereotypes about their behaviour and moral standards. Many feel this so acutely that they believe whatever goodwill they may manifest is at best not likely to be much appreciated and at worst may be misinterpreted to their disadvantage. The view was repeatedly expressed or implied that the behaviour of a delinquent or antisocial fringe had unfortunately been extended to characterise their whole generation.
>
> (Eppel and Eppel 1966: 213)

Current research shows that, sadly, little has changed. So, what is adolescence?: a complex stage of human development, having some common features, but also involving enormously wide individual variations. In the sections below I shall be outlining some well-known theories of adolescence, as well as reviewing the results of some of the major research studies. I shall be concentrating on the common features of adolescence, but we should not lose sight of the fact that a stage which lasts for a minimum of six years cannot possibly be encapsulated in a few pages, and generalizations need to be treated with some care.

TRADITIONAL THEORIES

There is general agreement by all who have written about adolescence that it makes sense to describe the stage as being one of transition. The transition, it is believed, results from the operation of a number of pressures. Some of these, in particular the physiological and emotional pressures, are internal; while other pressures, which originate from peers, parents, teachers, and society at large, are external to the young person. Sometimes these external pressures carry the individual towards maturity at a faster rate than he or she would prefer, while on other occasions they act as a brake, holding the adolescent back from the freedom and independence which he or she believes to be a legitimate right. It is the interplay of these forces which, in the final analysis, contributes more than anything to the success or failure of the transition from childhood to maturity.

So far two classical types of explanation concerning the transitional process have been advanced. The psychoanalytic approach concentrates on the psycho-sexual development of the individual, and looks particularly at the psychological factors which underlie the young person's movement away from childhood behaviour and emotional involvement. The second type of explanation, the sociological, represents a very different perspective. While it has never been as coherently expressed as the psychoanalytic view, it is none the less of equal importance. In brief, this explanation sees the causes of adolescent transition as lying primarily in the social setting of the individual and concentrates on the nature of roles and role conflict, the pressures of social expectations, and on the relative influence of different agents of socialization. Let us now look more closely at each of these explanations.

Psychoanalytic theory

The psychoanalytic view of adolescence takes as its starting point the upsurge of instincts which is said to occur as a result of puberty. This increase in instinctual life, it is suggested, upsets the psychic balance which has been achieved by the end of childhood, causing internal emotional upheaval and leading to a greatly increased vulnerability of the personality. This state of affairs is associated with two further factors. In the first place, the individual's awakening sexuality leads him or her to look outside the family setting for appropriate 'love objects', thus severing the emotional ties with the parents which have existed since infancy. This process is known as disengagement. Second, the vulnerability of the personality results in the employment of psychological defences to cope with the instincts and anxiety which are, to a greater or lesser extent, maladaptive. An excellent review of recent psychoanalytic thinking as it applies to adolescence may be found in Lerner (1987).

Regression, a manifestation of behaviour more appropriate to earlier stages of development, and ambivalence are both seen as further key elements of the adolescent process. According to the psychoanalytic view, ambivalence accounts for many of the phenomena often considered incomprehensible in adolescent behaviour. For example, the emotional instability of relationships, the contradictions in thought and feeling, and the apparently illogical shift from one reaction to another reflect the fluctuations between loving and hating, acceptance and rejection, involvement and non-involvement which underlie relationships in the early years, and which are reactivated once more in adolescence.

Such fluctuations in mood and behaviour are indicative also of the young person's attitudes to growing up. Thus, while freedom may at times appear the most exciting of goals, there are also moments when, in the harsh light of reality, independence and the necessity to fight one's own battles become a daunting prospect. At these times childlike dependence exercises a powerful attraction, manifested in periods of uncertainty and self-doubt, and in behaviour which is more likely to bring to mind a wilful child than a young adult.

A consideration of ambivalence leads us on to the more general theme of non-conformity and rebellion, believed by psychoanalysts to be an almost universal feature of adolescence. Behaviour of this sort has many causes. Some of it is a direct result of ambivalent modes of relating, the overt reflection of the conflict between loving and hating. In other circumstances, however, it may be interpreted as an aid to the disengagement process. In this context if the parents can be seen as old fashioned and irrelevant then the task of breaking the emotional ties becomes easier. If everything that originates from home can safely be rejected then there is nothing to be lost by giving it all up.

Non-conformity thus facilitates the process of disengagement although, as many writers point out, there are a number of intermediate stages along the way. Baittle and Offer (1971: 35) illustrate particularly well the importance of non-conformity and its close links with ambivalence:

> When the adolescent rebels, he often expresses his intentions in a manner resembling negation. He defines what he does in terms of what his parents do not want him to do. If his parents want him to turn off the radio and study this is the precise time he keeps the radio on and claims he cannot study. If they want him to buy new clothes, 'the old ones are good enough'. In periods like this it becomes obvious that the adolescent's decisions are in reality based on the negative of the parents' wishes, rather than on their own positive desires. What they do and the judgements they make are in fact dependent on the parents' opinions and suggestions but in a negative way. This may be termed the stage of 'negative dependence'. Thus, while the oppositional behaviour and protest against the parents are indeed a manifestation of rebellion and in the service of emancipation from the parents, at the same time they reveal that the passive dependent longings are still in force. The adolescent is in conflict over desires to emancipate, and the rebellious behaviour is a compromise formation which supports his efforts to give up the parental object and, at the same time, gratifies his dependence on them.

To summarize, three particular ideas characterize the psychoanalytic position. In the first place adolescence is seen as being a period during which there is a marked vulnerability of personality, resulting primarily from the upsurge of instincts at puberty. Second, emphasis is laid on the likelihood of maladaptive behaviour, stemming from the inadequacy of the psychological defences to cope with inner conflicts and tensions. Examples of such behaviour include extreme fluctuations of mood, inconsistency in relationships, depression, and non-conformity. Third, the process of disengagement is given special prominence. This is perceived as a necessity if mature emotional and sexual relationships are to be established outside the home.

Sociological theory

As has been indicated, the sociological view of adolescence encompasses a very different perspective from that of psychoanalytic theory. While there is no disagreement between the two approaches concerning the importance of the transitional process, it is on the subject of the causes of this process that the viewpoints diverge. Thus, while the one concentrates on internal factors, the other looks at society and to events outside the individual for a satisfactory explanation. For the sociologist, socialization and role are the two key concepts. By socialization is meant the process whereby individuals in a society absorb the values, standards, and beliefs current in that society. Some of these standards and values will refer to positions, or roles, in society, so that, for example, there will be expectations and prescriptions of behaviour appropriate to roles such as son, daughter, citizen, teenager, parent, and so on. Everyone in a society learns through the agents of socialization, such as school, home, the mass media, and so on, the expectations associated with the various roles, although these expectations may not necessarily be clear-cut. Furthermore, socialization may be more or less effective, depending on the nature of the agents to which the individual is exposed, the amount of conflict between the different agents, and so on. During childhood the individual largely has his or her roles ascribed by others, but as he or she matures through adolescence greater opportunities are available, not only for a choice of roles, but also for a choice of how those roles should be interpreted. As will become apparent, it is implicit in the social-psychological viewpoint that both socialization and role assumption are more problematic during adolescence than at any other time.

Why should this be so? First, features of adolescence such as growing independence from authority figures, involvement with peer groups, and an unusual sensitivity to the evaluations of others all provoke role transitions and discontinuity, of varying intensities, as functions of both social and cultural context. Second, any inner change or uncertainty has the effect of increasing the individual's dependence on others, and this applies particularly to the need for reassurance and support for one's view of oneself. Third, the effects of major environmental changes are also relevant in this context. Different schools, the move from school to university or college, leaving home, taking a job, all demand involvement in a new set of relationships which in turn leads to different and often greater expectations, a substantial reassessment of the self, and an acceleration of the process of socialization. Role change, it will be apparent, is thus seen as an integral feature of adolescent development.

While role change may be one source of difficulty for the adolescent, it is certainly not the only one. Inherent in role behaviour generally are a number of potential stresses such as role conflict. Here the individual occupies two roles, let us say son and boy-friend, which have expectations associated with them which are incompatible. The individual is thus caught in the middle between two people or sets of people, who expect different forms of behaviour. Thus, in the case of son and boy-friend, the teenage boy's mother might put pressure on him to behave like a dutiful child, while his girl-friend will expect him to be independent of his parents and to care for her rather than for anyone else. Such a situation is one which few young people can avoid at some time or another.

Next there is role discontinuity. Here there is a lack of order in the transition from one role to another. Many years ago, Ruth Benedict (1938) drew attention to the fact that primitive cultures provided more continuity in training for responsibilities, sexual maturity, and so on than western societies, and the situation has hardly improved today. Role discontinuity is said to occur when there is no bridge or ordered sequence from one stage to the next, or when behaviour in the second stage necessitates the unlearning of some or all of that which was learned earlier. One only has to think of the problem of transition for the young unemployed or the grossly inadequate preparation for parenthood in our society to appreciate the point. Third, there is role incongruence. Here the individual is placed in a position for which he or she is unfitted; in other words the role ascribed by others is not the one that the individual would have chosen. Good illustrations from adolescent experience would be parents who hold unrealistically high expectations of their teenage children, or who, alternatively, fight to maintain their adolescent sons and daughters in childlike roles. Implicit in these theoretical notions is the view that the individual's movement through adolescence will be very much affected by the consistent or inconsistent, adaptive or maladaptive expectations held by significant people in his or her immediate environment.

Up to this point our discussion has concentrated on the features of role behaviour which lead sociologists and social psychologists to view adolescence not only as a transitional period, but as one which contains many potentially stressful characteristics. However, the process of socialization is also seen by many as being problematic at this stage. In the first place the adolescent is exposed to a wide variety of competing socialization agencies, including the family, the school, the peer group, adult-directed youth organizations, the mass media, political organizations, and so on, and is thus presented with a wide range of potential conflicts, values, and ideals. Furthermore, it is commonly assumed by sociologists today that the socialization of young people is more dependent upon the generation than upon the family or other social institutions. Marsland goes so far as to call it 'auto-socialization' in his description of the process:

> The crucial social meaning of youth is withdrawal from adult control and influence compared with childhood. Peer groups are the milieu into which young people withdraw. In at least most societies, this withdrawal to the peer group is, within limits, legitimated by the adult world. Time and space is handed over to young people to work out for themselves in auto-socialisation the developmental problems of self and identity which cannot be handled by the simple direct socialisation appropriate to childhood. There is a moratorium on compliance and commitment and leeway allowed for a relatively unguided journey with peers towards autonomy and maturity.
>
> (Marsland 1987: 12)

Both the conflict between socialization agencies and the freedom from clearly defined guidelines are seen as making socialization more uncertain, and causing major difficulties for the young person in establishing a bridge towards the assumption of adult roles. Brake (1985), in his discussion of youth subcultures, makes similar points, and it is a common assumption among those writing from the sociological point of view that the social changes of the last twenty years or so have created ever-increasing stresses for young people.

In particular it should be noted that most writers see little of value in what they believe to be the decline of adult involvement and the increasing importance of the peer group. Among such writers the adolescent peer group is frequently described as being more likely to encourage antisocial behaviour than to act as a civilizing agent, and though it is accepted that the effects of peer involvement depend on the standards and activities of the peer group, there is undoubtedly a general feeling that when young people spend a considerable amount of time with individuals of their own age, more harm than good is likely to come of it. While, on the one hand, there is clearly some logic in the view that the adolescent who is deprived of adult company is at a disadvantage in the transition towards maturity, on the other hand research does not bear out the myth of the all-powerful peer group, and it is still very much an open question as to what effect increasing age segregation has on the socialization process.

To summarize, the sociological or social-psychological approach to adolescence is marked by a concern with roles and role change, and with the processes of socialization. There can be little doubt that adolescence, from this point of view, is seen as being dominated by stresses and tensions, not so much because of inner emotional instability, but as a result of conflicting pressures from outside. Thus, by considering both this and the psychoanalytic approach, two mutually complementary but essentially different views of the adolescent transitional process have been reviewed. In spite of their differences, however, the two approaches share one common belief, and that is in the concept of adolescent 'storm and stress'. Both these traditional theories view the teenage years as a 'problem stage' in human development, and it is important therefore to see whether this view is borne out by the research evidence.

THE RESEARCH EVIDENCE

Broadly speaking, research provides little support for these traditional theories, and fails to substantiate much of what both psychoanalysts and sociologists appear to believe. To take some examples, while there is certainly some change in self-concept, there is no evidence to show that any but a small minority experience a serious identity crisis. In most cases, relationships with parents are positive and constructive, and young people do not in large part reject adult values in favour of those espoused by the peer group. In fact, in most situations peer-group values appear to be consistent with those of important adults rather than in conflict with them (Coleman and Hendry 1990). Fears of promiscuity among the young are not borne out by the research findings, nor do studies support the belief that the peer group encourages antisocial behaviour, unless other factors are also present. Lastly, there is no evidence to suggest that during the adolescent years there is a higher level of psychopathology than at other times. While a lot still needs to be learned about the mental health of young people, almost all the results that have become available so far indicate that, although a small minority may show disturbance, the great majority of teenagers seem to cope well and to show no undue signs of turmoil or stress.

Support for this belief may be found in every major study of adolescence that has appeared in recent years. Most would agree with the views of Siddique and D'Arcy (1984) who, in summarizing their own results on stress and well-being in adolescence, write as follows:

> In this study some 33.5 per cent of the adolescents surveyed reported no symptoms of psychological distress, and another 39 per cent reported five or fewer symptoms (a mild level of distress). On the other hand a significant 27.5 per cent reported higher levels of psychological distress. For the majority the adolescent transition may be relatively smooth. However, for a minority it does indeed appear to be a period of stress and turmoil. The large majority of adolescents appear to get on well with adults and are able to cope effectively with demands of school and peer groups. They use their resources to make adjustments

with environmental stressors with hardly visible signs of psychological distress.

(1984: 471)

There would appear to be a sharp divergence of opinion, therefore, between theory and research. Beliefs about adolescence that stem from traditional theory do not in general accord with the results of research. We need now to consider some of the reasons for this state of affairs. First, as many writers have pointed out, psychoanalysts and psychiatrists see a selective population. Their experience of adolescence is based primarily upon the individuals they meet in clinics or hospitals. Such experience is bound to encourage a somewhat one-sided perspective in which turmoil or disturbance is overrepresented. For sociologists, on the other hand, the problem is often to disentangle concepts of 'youth' or 'the youth movement' from notions about young people themselves. As a number of commentators have observed, youth is frequently seen by sociologists as being in the forefront of social change. Youth is, as it were, the advance party where innovation or alteration in the values of society are concerned. From this position it is but a short step to use youth as a metaphor for social change, and thus to confuse radical forces in society with the beliefs of ordinary young people (Brake 1985).

Another possible reason for the divergence of viewpoint is that certain adolescent behaviours, such as vandalism, drug-taking, and hooliganism, are extremely threatening to adults. The few who are involved in such activities therefore attain undue prominence in the public eye. The mass media play an important part in this process by publicizing sensational behaviour, thus making it appear very much more common than it is in reality. One only has to consider critically the image of the teenager portrayed week after week on the television to understand how, for many adults, the minority comes to be representative of all young people. All three tendencies mentioned so far lead to an exaggerated view of the amount of turmoil that may be expected during adolescence, and thus serve to widen the gap between research and theory.

One other factor needs to be considered in this context. In general social scientists responsible for large-scale surveys have tended to neglect the possibility that individual adolescents may be either unwilling or unable to reveal their innermost feelings. Much depends on the way the study is carried out, but it is important to remember how very difficult it is for anyone, let alone a shy or resentful teenager, to share fears, worries, or conflicts with a strange interviewer. Inhibition of this sort may well result in a bias on the part of those writing from the research point of view, and cause an underestimation of the degree of stress experienced by young people. Problems of method, therefore, may also be playing their part in widening the gap between theory and research, not by exaggerating the amount of inner turmoil, but by doing just the opposite – namely, causing research workers to miss the more subtle indications of emotional tension. The divergence of opinion referred to earlier can thus be seen to be the result of a number of factors. Both methods and theories have their weaknesses, and the fault cannot be said to lie exclusively with one side or the other.

Obviously the two traditional theories have some value, and it would be wrong to leave the impression that neither is any longer relevant. Perhaps the most important contribution made by these theories is that they have provided the foundation for an understanding of young people with serious problems and a greater knowledge of those who belong to minority or deviant groups. In this respect the two major theories have much to offer. However, it must be recognized that today they are inadequate as the basis for an understanding of the development of the great majority of young people. The fact is that adolescence needs a theory, not of abnormality, but of normality. Any viable theoretical viewpoint put forward today must not only incorporate the results of empirical studies, but must also acknowledge the fact that, although for some young people adolescence may be a difficult time, for the majority it is a period of relative stability.

In recent years psychologists have turned away from the question 'Is adolescence inevitably a period of stress and turmoil?' and directed their attention towards issues of coping and adjustment. This current focus is undoubtedly a more productive one, leading to an interest in why some young people run into difficulties while others do not, and a concentration on the characteristics of those who do experience undue stress during the teenage years. Unfortunately research still has some way to go before clear answers can be given to these questions, but at least the questions are being asked. One example of exciting work in this field comes in the recently published *Coping and Self-Concept in Adolescence* by Bosma and Jackson (1990) where a variety of adaptive coping strategies are outlined, and initial attempts are made to relate these strategies to behavioural outcomes.

In the next two sections of this chapter I wish to examine two major concerns which have affected adolescents and their relationships with adults in society. I shall be looking at the generation gap and status ambiguity in order to reflect on the adolescent's place in society.

THE GENERATION GAP

The concept of a generation gap has a long history in psychology. It is also continuously popular with television, the press, and other media for it has a certain sensational quality about it. In this respect it has strong affinities with other concepts such as 'storm and stress' and 'identity crisis'. There is no clear consensus as to the exact meaning of the phrase, but most agree that it implies at least two things: a discrepancy or divergence of viewpoint between adults and teenagers and, partly as a result of this, a degree of conflict between the generations. In fact some writers have gone so far as to describe a completely separate youth culture, isolated to a large extent from the adult world, and possessing its own norms and values. Recent writing, such as that of Brake (1985), perpetuates the idea of a youth subculture, and in the same year a book for parents of teenagers was published with the actual title *The Generation Gap* (McCormack 1985), giving further currency to the idea of a divide between young and old in our society.

In fact, however, a wide variety of studies have provided evidence of generally positive relationships between adolescents and their parents. Douvan and Adelson in their book *The Adolescent Experience* (1966) were among the first to illustrate this point. They reported the results of interviews with over 3,000 teenagers across the USA. The results indicated a general picture of minor conflicts between parent and adolescent, focusing especially on issues such as make-up, dating, leisure activities, music, and so on. As far as major values were concerned, however, very little difference emerged. On issues of morality, political or religious beliefs, and sexual attitudes, the divergence of opinion was minimal. In fact the vast majority of teenagers, far from despising or rejecting their parents, actually looked up to them and valued their advice.

Studies carried out in the UK and Europe portray a very similar picture. In Fogelman's (1976) report of the work carried out by the National Children's Bureau, entitled *Britain's 16-year-olds*, findings on relationships within the family corroborate all that has been said so far. In this study the parents were given a list of issues on which it is commonly thought adults and young people of this age might disagree. The results indicated a situation which was, from the parents' point of view, a relatively harmonious one. The two most commonly reported areas of disagreement – dress or hair-style, and the time of coming in at night – are what might be expected, but even here only 10 per cent of parents said that they often disagreed over these things.

The young people questioned in this study confirmed the attitudes of their mothers and fathers. They agreed that appearance and evening activities were sometimes issues of disagreement in the home, but otherwise they reported an atmosphere free from major conflict. It is of interest to note that about two-thirds of those with brothers and sisters said they quarrelled between themselves, yet 'many wrote a qualifying note to the effect that although they might often quarrel with a brother or sister, or disagree with their parents, this did not mean there was anything wrong with the underlying relationship' (Fogelman 1976: 36)

The work of Rutter and colleagues (1976) should also be mentioned in this context. In this wide-ranging survey of all 14 year olds on the Isle of Wight, parents, teachers, and young people themselves were extensively interviewed. As one aspect of the study Rutter examined the degree of alienation between the generations as experienced either by the adolescents or by their parents. The results showed that in only 4 per cent of the total group did the parents feel an increase in alienation at this stage of adolescence, while amongst the young people themselves only 5 per cent reported actual rejection of their parents. A further 25 per cent expressed some degree of criticism.

This is not to deny that conflicts exist, and there are many factors which will determine the extent of family conflict during the adolescent years. One obvious variable is age, and numerous studies have shown that conflict is likely to reach a peak at a particular age – usually around 15 for girls and somewhat later for boys. Similarly both culture and social class will have their effects too. Communication is also important as far as the sharing of values is concerned. First, if limited communication exists it is difficult to know what the other person's attitudes are. Where contentious issues such as sex or drugs are concerned, it is easy to assume that the parent or the teenager has stereotyped, rather than individual, views if there is no discussion about these issues. Second, if there is no communication there can be very little reciprocal influence. This means that on topics where there is limited communication, values between the generations are likely to be further apart because there is no chance of the one side influencing or being influenced by the other. Research shows interestingly that opinions in families are closer on topics which can readily be discussed, such as politics, than on topics such as sex which are very rarely discussed.

In considering relationships between parents and teenagers one interesting focus has been on the differences between the two groups in the way these relationships are perceived. Research shows that neither adolescents nor parents perceive the influence of social relationships accurately. Teenagers perceive their parents to be less influential than they really are, while adults perceive that they are more influential than they actually are. Furthermore, young people, in assessing the magnitude of the differences between the generations, appear to over-emphasize the extent of these differences, while conversely, parents underestimate such differences. In addition, parents are generally more satisfied with family cohesion and adaptability than are adolescents.

How, it may be asked, can all these findings be fitted into a coherent picture? Perhaps the first thing to say is that while on the one hand the notion of a full-scale generation gap is obviously not sustained by the research evidence, on the other hand it cannot simply be dismissed as a complete fiction. One important reason for the confusion which exists lies in the difference between attitudes towards close family members, and attitudes to more general social groupings, such as 'the younger generation'. Thus, for example, teenagers may very well approve and look up to their own parents while expressing criticism of adults in general. Similarly, parents may deride 'punks', 'drop-outs', or 'soccer hooligans' while holding a favourable view of their own adolescent sons and daughters. Another fact that needs to be stressed is that there is a difference between feeling and behaviour. Adolescents may be irritated or angry with their parents as a result of day-to-day conflicts, but issues can be worked out in the home and do not necessarily lead to outright rejection or rebellion.

Furthermore, too little credit is given to the possibility that adults and young people, although disagreeing with each other about certain things, may still respect each other's views, and live in relative harmony together under the same roof. Thus, there seems to be little doubt that the extreme view of the generation gap, involving the notion of a war between the generations, or the idea of a separate adolescent subculture, is dependent on a myth. It is the result of a stereotype which is useful to the mass media, and given currency by a small minority of disaffected young people and resentful adults. However, to deny any sort of conflict between teenagers and older members of society is equally false. Adolescents could not grow into adults unless they were able to test out the boundaries of authority, nor could they discover what they believed unless given the opportunity to push hard against the beliefs of others. The adolescent transition from dependence to independence is almost certain to involve some conflict, but its extent should not be exaggerated.

STATUS AMBIGUITY

Reference has already been made to the impact upon young people of not having a clearly defined status in society. There are a number of implications of this. First, it is intensely frustrating for adolescents themselves. A feeling of not knowing where you stand, of not knowing exactly how you are going to be treated – as a child or as an adult – can be very difficult to cope with. If society does not have a framework and clear bench-marks to tell you when you have reached adulthood, how can the individual young person work it out for him- or herself? The second implication of status ambiguity is that adults feel confused about adolescence. Not just parents, but teachers, social workers, and others all have to play a game in which the rules are being made up as they go along. In this game the institutional framework, such as the law, school rules, and so on, are of little help. Third, the uncertainty of status often serves to place young people in positions where they have very little power, and where damaging stereotypes can flourish easily.

Sexuality may be taken as one example of this, for here stereotypes of 'promiscuity' and 'permissiveness' interfere in the way adults perceive young people, and reduce the chances that boys and girls will receive the support, the education, and the medical care that they need. Sexuality is a particularly good illustration of status ambiguity in the UK because of what has come to be known as the Gillick case. The 1969 Family Law Reform Act set the age of medical majority at 16, thus indicating that a person of 16 or over is regarded as medically adult, having the right of confidentiality and being able to decide what information, if any, should be passed to his or her parents. As far as teenagers under 16 are concerned, it has been up to the individual doctor to decide whether to provide contraceptive advice and treatment.

These principles were set out in 1980 in a Department of Health and Social Security statement. Mrs Gillick, a mother of ten, challenged the statement on the grounds that it deprived her of her parental rights. She sought an assurance from her local health authority that no contraceptive advice or treatment would be given to her daughters without her knowledge and consent. The Health Authority would not give such an assurance, and the case went all the way to the House of Lords. Judgement was finally given in October 1985. By a three to two majority the Law Lords ruled that:

> A girl under 16 of sufficient understanding and intelligence may have the legal capacity to give valid consent to contraceptive advice and treatment including necessary medical examinations.
>
> Giving such advice and treatment to a girl under 16 without parental consent does not necessarily infringe parental rights.
>
> Doctors giving such advice in good faith are not committing a criminal offence of aiding and abetting unlawful intercourse with girls under 16.

The Law Lords further ruled that the decision of a doctor to give contraceptive advice and/or treatment to under-age girls should be guided by the following precepts:

(1) that the girl (although under 16 years of age) will understand his or her advice;
(2) that the doctor cannot persuade her to inform her parents or to allow him or her to inform the parents that she is seeking contraceptive advice;
(3) that she is very likely to begin or to continue having sexual intercourse with or without contraceptive treatment;
(4) that unless she receives contraceptive advice or treatment her physical or mental health or both are likely to suffer;
(5) that her best interests require the doctor to give her contraceptive advice, treatment, or both without parental consent.

Doctors ought not, the Law Lords ruled, to regard this as a licence to disregard the wishes of parents.

At first sight it may appear that this judgement left the situation unchanged, the individual doctor still having the right to treat someone under 16 without necessarily informing the parents. For at least two reasons, however, the Gillick case has in fact made the position of the under 16s worse rather than better. First, the complexity of the case, and the legal wrangles surrounding it, have left teenagers confused and uncertain where they stand. Second, the publicity accorded to Mrs Gillick, as well as the tightening up of definitions, has left doctors with less room to manoeuvre and has caused almost all medical practitioners to exercise greater caution than before.

Quite apart from the effect of all this on teenage sexual behaviour the issue is of considerable interest because it relates to one of the key issues of adolescence: at what point an individual ceases to be a child and starts to become an adult. One by-product of the Gillick case was that the Law Lords were forced to consider this question – a question usually considered more appropriately answered by a psychologist rather than a lawyer. Lord Fraser addressed the question as follows:

> . . . parental rights to control the child existed not for the benefit of the parent but for the child. It was contrary to the ordinary experience of mankind, at least in Western Europe in the present century, to say that a child remained in fact under the complete control of his parents until he attained the definite age of majority, and that on attaining that age he suddenly acquired independence.
>
> In practice most wise parents relaxed their control gradually as their child developed and encouraged him to become increasingly independent. Moreover, the degree of parental control actually exercised over a particular child did in practice vary considerably according to his understanding and intelligence. It would be unrealistic for the courts not to recognise those facts. Social customs changed, and the law ought to and did in fact have regard to such changes when they were of such major importance.
>
> (*The Times Law Reports*, 18 October 1985)

Lord Scarman agreed, adding this rider:

> If the law should impose upon the process of growing up fixed limits where nature knew only a continuous process, the price would be artificiality and a lack of realism in an area where the law must be sensitive to human development and social change.
>
> (ibid.)

The implications of such a statement are very far-reaching, not least because they contain a recognition of the limitations of the use of chronological age as a bench-mark for the determination of maturity. Some of the principles expressed by the Law Lords in the Gillick case have been incorporated into the Children Act 1989. A central tenet of this Act has been the change from the notion of parental rights to one of parental responsibilities. This has largely seemed to be a positive move, both for parents and young people, although unfortunately the concept of responsibility has been distorted in the White Paper *Crime, Justice and Protecting the Public* (1990) to which I shall refer below. Gillick has also had an effect on a range of other issues, for example the Children Act indicates that young people under the age of 16 can choose their own religion, change their name, give consent to surgery, seek confidential counselling, and so on, so long as *they have the maturity to understand the implications of the decision or request*. This is obviously an important step forward in recognizing the rights of young people. It may in practice, however, prove extremely difficult to define 'maturity to understand', and only time will tell how the courts will interpret this.

A further problem with the Children Act is that sadly, no attempt has been made to clear up the ambiguities relating to other aspects of civil status. Thus, for example, can it be right that an adolescent of 17 can join the army and be killed fighting in war, and yet does not have the vote? To take some further illustrations, at 16 you can marry, join a trades union, and live in a brothel, yet you cannot be tattooed, own a house or a flat, or use a pawn shop. At 17 you can drive most vehicles, buy a firearm, and hold a pilot's licence, yet you cannot vote, you cannot serve on a jury, or make a will. The law illustrates only too clearly our overall confusion about the status of young people. We do not know how to define adulthood, nor do we see it as a priority to clarify the situation for the sake of this group in society. Adult ambivalence is reflected in legislative ambiguity.

Recent government proposals concerning criminal justice legislation provide a further example of confusion over the status of young people. In the White Paper *Crime, Justice and Protecting the Public* (1990) it is suggested that parents should be made responsible for the criminal behaviour of their sons and daughters. A distinction is drawn between 10–15 year olds on the one hand, and 16–17 year olds on the other. For 10–15 year olds it is proposed that parents should have a large measure of responsibility for their children's actions. This involves parents attending court, taking into account the means of the parents in determining fines, and in some cases requiring parents to pay the fines. The White Paper recognizes that 16–17 year olds may be fully independent, but:

> in dealing with young offenders of this age, courts should not be required to involve parents when their children are living away from home, but they should have a power to do so when they consider it necessary. When the young people are living in their parents' home and still in full time education, then their parents must be involved, as they would be with younger juveniles.
>
> (1990: 44)

In an excellent review of this policy entitled 'Punishing the parents', Allen (1990) sets out some of the pitfalls implicit in these proposals. He mentions the fact that many parents of young offenders may themselves be struggling to cope with problems, with inadequate housing, and with disrupted family relationships. The chances that they are likely to 'mend their ways' and suddenly start to teach their children morality and good behaviour seems improbable. Even more important is the effect on such parents of forcing them to attend court, and thereby bringing them within the criminal justice system. Research already indicates that such an outcome is viewed with great anxiety by parents, yet few would have the resources to cope and to exercise greater 'control' over their youngsters.

These proposals may be altered as the Criminal Justice Bill passes through the House of Commons. None the less the proposals themselves reflect unfortunate attitudes among politicians and the judiciary to issues concerning the status of young people. Surely we want our 16 and 17 year olds to be more responsible, not less responsible for themselves? The message of this proposed legislation is that young people are dependent, and continue to be the 'property' and responsibility of their parents until 18. Nothing could be more designed to ensure a delay in the development of mature adult behaviour in our adolescents.

THE NEEDS OF YOUNG PEOPLE

One of the most striking features of much, although not all, youth policy is that it seems to be constructed more to meet the needs of adults than of young people. There appears among politicians to be a singular lack of awareness or understanding of the nature of adolescence. The Children Act 1989 is a notable exception, with its emphasis on the giving of children and young people the right to have their views taken into account. None the less, evidence will be presented in almost every chapter of this book to document the limited grasp that the adult world has of the reality of being a young person in Britain today. It seems useful, therefore, to conclude with a look at the needs of young people, so that these can be borne in mind by readers as they consider youth policy in its different manifestations.

The first area to which attention should be drawn is the young person's need for respect. One of the most common complaints of adolescents is that they are simply not taken seriously by the adults around them. They believe their views are rejected as immature even before they have had a chance to express them, and that there is a general attitude among adults which does not allow proper weight to be given to the opinions and ideas which stem from young people. This issue is very much bound up with status. If young people retain the status of children, then they are not taken seriously, and adults can retain power and decision-making responsibilities. It is true that to give up these things and to be willing to share power with young people requires courage and openness. Yet unless this can be achieved, teenagers will continue in an unsatisfactory state of limbo, feeling resentful and hostile because they are not accorded the status they deserve.

The second need is for both information and support. One of the more damaging stereotypes of youth is that because they are seeking independence, they have no further need of the adults around them. Nothing could be further from the truth. All teenagers need support, not only from their parents but from other adults as well. Of course if this is not available adolescents will turn to the peer group, but it has to be remembered that this only occurs when relationships with adults are poor, or are seen to be damaging. Furthermore, young people need information, and they need to have this provided in a responsible manner. Information about sexuality is a good example. It is only the adult world that can provide the comprehensive sexual information that young people need, but if this information is mixed up with value-laden messages, or is presented in an 'adult knows best' container, it will be of little help. Once again adults can be of most use if they can accept that they do not have all the power, and if they can come to terms with the fact that young people need gradually increasing autonomy in order to become adult.

Throughout this chapter I have mentioned the problems associated with ambiguous civil status. The contradictory definitions of adulthood exemplified by current legislation, and the confusion generated by the problem of medical confidentiality for under-16s, are both reflections of an unsatisfactory state of affairs. Young people need to have their civil status clarified and properly defined. We owe it to youth to provide such clarity. In addition to this, however, one has to conclude that the adult world gets the adolescents it deserves. If status is ambiguous, and the messages about maturity are mixed, the behaviour of young people will reflect this confusion. Can anyone be surprised that adolescent behaviour is sometimes childish and sometimes mature, at times caring and at times hostile, both responsible and irresponsible, if the legal framework has exactly these confusions within it? I think not.

Another central need for the most vulnerable young people is the need for protection. This is a subject to which a number of authors in the book draw attention, and it is an important one. While most adolescents will be living in family settings where they are well cared for, a minority will be exposed to risk or danger. It has seemed, particularly over the last decade, that this group – those in care, the runaways, and the homeless – have been poorly served by society. Indeed, it is clear that some aspects of social-security legislation have led to an increased number who are at risk. This should not be allowed to happen in a civilized society, and it is profoundly to be hoped that the 1990s will see a more caring and protective attitude on the part of our legislators towards the most vulnerable young people.

From what has been said already it will be clear that gradually increasing independence is not only a need, but should be a right for all adolescents. However hard it is, adults have to recognize that with adolescence comes an urgent necessity for a re-evaluation of the balance of the relationship between young and old, or at least between young and middle-aged. Decision making has to be shared, responsibilities have to be more evenly apportioned, and greater and greater freedom has to be allowed. Some adults will give total independence too early, while others may hang on, inevitably leading to conflict in the end. The task for adults is not easy, but unless the need for increasing autonomy is met, relationships will deteriorate and the opportunities for adults to remain influential in the lives of their youngsters will diminish.

Finally, there is, without doubt, a need for adults to be better informed about adolescents. In large part adults find this stage a puzzling and confusing one. Many talk of 'dreading the teenage years', and it is in this sort of atmosphere that stereotypes take hold. The situation is not made any easier by a marked paucity of good-quality information about adolescence. While much attention is given to babyhood and early childhood, those who want to learn about the adolescent stage of development have to hunt far and wide for the right book or set of training materials. Professionals in the youth field could undoubtedly do more to provide better training and assistance to enable adults to understand this stage more clearly. Ignorance breeds anxiety, but it also leads to poor parenting and relationship skills. Young people need adults to be better informed about adolescence because it is only in that way that their parents, the teachers, social workers, and others can give them the most effective support.

REFERENCES

Allen, R. (1990) 'Punishing the parents', *Youth and Policy* 31: 17–20.

Baittle, B. and Offer, D. (1971) 'On the nature of adolescent rebellion', in F.C. Feinstein, P. Giovacchini, and A. Miller (eds) *Annals of Adolescent Psychiatry*, New York: Basic Books.

Benedict, R. (1938) 'Continuities and discontinuities in cultural conditioning', *Psychiatry* 1: 161–7.

Bosma, H. and Jackson, S. (1990) *Coping and Self-Concept in Adolescence*, Berlin: Springer Verlag.

Brake, M. (1985) *Comparative Youth Subcultures*, London: Routledge & Kegan Paul.

Coleman, J.C. and Hendry, L. (1990) *The Nature of Adolescence*, 2nd edn, London and New York: Routledge.

Douvan, E. and Adelson, J. (1966) *The Adolescent Experience*, New York: John Wiley.

Eppel, E.M. and Eppel, M. (1966) *Adolescence and Morality*, London: Routledge & Kegan Paul.

Fogelman, K. (1976) *Britain's 16-year-olds*, London: National Children's Bureau.

Hall, G.S. (1904) *Adolescence*, New York: Appleton.

Lerner, R.M. (1987) 'Psychodynamic models', in V.B. Van Hasselt and M. Hersen (eds) *Handbook of Adolescent Psychology*, Oxford: Pergamon Press.

McCormack, M. (1985) *The Generation Gap: The View from Both Sides*, London: Constable.

Marsland, D. (1987) *Education and Youth*, London: The Falmer Press.

Mead, M. (1928) *Coming of Age in Samoa*, New York: Morrow.

Montemayor, R. (1991) 'Parents and adolescents in conflict: all families some of the time and some families most of the time', in P. Noller and V. Callan (eds) *The Adolescent in the Family*, Routledge: London.

Rutter, M., Graham, P., Chadwick, O., and Yule, W. (1976) 'Adolescent turmoil: fact or fiction', *Journal of Child Psychology and Psychiatry* 17: 35–56.

Siddique, C.M. and D'Arcy, C. (1984) 'Adolescence, stress and psychological well being', *Journal of Youth and Adolescence* 13: 459–74.

White Paper (1990) *Crime, Justice and Protecting the Public*, London: HMSO.

3 Secondary education

Phil Walkling and Chris Brannigan

SETTING THE SCENE

The structure of mass education in any state may be described in terms of its principles. Are the chief considerations equality or selection? Does the state wish (within its limited resources) to provide as high a level of development as possible for all citizens, or to concentrate, for economic or political reasons, on the production of elites? How is the competition for resources to be organized? Are geography, access, and the size of communities important factors? Who are the interested parties? Are the Churches to have a role in education in partnership with the state? What controls are to be placed upon voluntary schools?

From this kind of view, British secondary education seems to have been lost in the struggle of conflicting interests and traditions. Any survey of British educational policy is bound to conclude that the current state of affairs is chaotic. While clear lines of historical development can be traced, British education for children from the age of 11 can not be seen as having any clear structure. No doubt, this is because the educational radicalism of the two main parties since 1944 never reaches the point of bringing together a clear vision of educational goals with the resources likely to achieve them.

Discussions of the recent history of education in England and Wales commonly start from the Butler Act of 1944, which is treated as marking a clear break with what had gone before. The social legislation at the end of the war is often seen as signalling an end of the old order, as the cataclysm of the war was to mark a new start in world affairs. Just as we now know that the war ended not in 1945 but in 1989 with capitalism's victory in the Cold War, so we can, with the easy clarity of hindsight, see an event such as the 1944 Act as merely another stage in developments begun before the war and continuing after it.

Especially clear now is the fact that, despite the rhetoric of justice and equality in a newly free world, the old traditions of English education remained firmly in place. The majority of children continued to be educated in what were really elementary schools. The designation 'secondary-modern school' made little difference to life in those schools, which sought to develop habits of life suitable to those who would carry on the repetitive tasks thought necessary in the smug world of post-war industry. A few education authorities established technical schools for the middle-range of 'abilities' but these schools never made much impact and became lost with comprehensivization. The flagships of the state system remained the grammar schools, with curricula determined by entry into Higher Education via the traditional Ordinary and Advanced Level examinations, with their knowledge-based approach to learning. The allocation to (and within) these schools was (and is) heavily influenced by the social class of pupils, and there is no reason to believe that the secondary-modern schools were ever intended to be 'equal in esteem' in other than rhetoric.

The egalitarian justification for having a selective system which reserved intellectual education for only 20 per cent or so of children was the misuse of a misunderstood, and in any case erroneous, psychology. The view that there is something unambiguous called 'intelligence' which is the key factor in educational success, largely fixed at birth and certainly by 11, which can be accurately quantified in a fair competition, and which is a reliable basis for the allocation of educational resources, was freely used in the reports which prepared the way for the 1944 Act. Each of these propositions is very doubtful, and certainly insufficient evidence on which to base a gold, silver, and bronze education system.

The true reason for their acceptance in the Spens and Norwood Reports, on which the Act was based, was that a selective system in which 20 per cent went to grammar schools and most of the rest to a kind of revamped upper Elementary system, would not cost too much to implement because it was not that different from the opportunities already existing in many boroughs. The current structure of education in many parts of England reflects that history all too clearly.

If we take Birmingham as an example, we will see that every variety of educational provision for children aged over 11 which has been available since the Second World War can still be identified. There are small 11–16 comprehensives which in their shabby, inadequate buildings and low aspirations are no more than secondary moderns. There are large 11–18 comprehensives (often the result of merging grammar and secondaries) successfully offering the full range of courses across the whole spectrum of needs. Single-sex 'foundation' grammar schools sit near single-sex and mixed LEA and church comprehensive schools. Sixth-form colleges (some secular, some religious) run under school regulations, offer courses which may overlap those of large FE colleges which try to get as close to offering 'tertiary' provision as possible. In one area of the city, a system of middle and upper schools, inherited during local-government reorganization, can still be found. There are 'opted-out' community schools, and the first City Technology College sits just over the border in Solihull.

From one point of view, this represents an enviable range of choices for young people at 11 and 16. The reality is an astonishing range of quality of provision, resources, and physical conditions, between which few effective choices can be made. In the past, catchment-area boundaries prevented much choice, with middle-class parents accepting that they paid their school fees in their mortgages. With the removal of geographical constraints on recruitment, many schools are moving to aggressive marketing: it is at least an open question whether this will lead to an improvement in parents' and children's ability to make well-advised choices.

In her recent book *Secondary Education*, Maureen O'Connor (1990) has argued convincingly that the question of the right structure for education has so fascinated politicians, educationalists, the Press, and parents that it for a long time prevented effective discussion of anything else. Good education, she points out, can be possible independently of the structures within which it takes place. This is certainly true, within limits. The best secondary moderns acted as true community schools, and brought many children consigned to failure at 11+ to comparable educational standards in some subjects to those achieved in the grammar schools. Again, in some areas, particularly in Wales, exceptionally large numbers of children were received into grammar schools. Comprehensive schools took a variety of forms, with much heated debate about internal structures – streaming, setting, banding, and so on. The consequences in some cases allowed for easy movement between groups so that children were able to progress at rates which ignored the largely arbitrary classification at 11+. Of course, in other cases, curricular and institutional arrangements meant that the comprehensive was little more than a secondary modern, a technical high and a grammar school which happened to be in one building. Once in one stream, movement after the first few terms was practically impossible. On the other hand, the debate about structure is really a battle over wider issues, particularly social equality. Already in 1944, the legal framework permitted comprehensive solutions to the problems of providing sufficient places, and some areas found the single all-ability school the right way forward. Even within the streamed school, where competition for the examination streams could be quite fierce, there ought not to be such clear reinforcement of social divisions as could be produced by putting children in physically separated premises. The resources available for the education of the different groups could be more easily shared, thus avoiding the depressing drabness so often evident in the secondary-modern school.

TORY IDEOLOGY

Margaret Thatcher's governments have had eleven years in which a particularly vigorous ideology has been applied to, among other things, education. Why has no clear direction emerged?

The answer is that there is a tension between two key aspects of the radicalism of the Thatcher governments which has had important consequences for education policy. On the one hand, their free-market ideology as applied to education has given an emphasis to choice for the consumers of education and training. This has resulted in attacks on what are seen as vested interests. These include the teacher unions and the profession itself whose educational principles and methods of working are seen as restrictive practices designed to protect the interests of the education professions rather than to promote the interests of their customers. There have been similar robust attacks on Local Education Authorities (LEAs), on traditional cosy arrangements between employers, colleges, and training Quangos in the provision of vocational education, and even on the Olympians of Her Majesty's Inspectorate of Schools. Any group which might be seen as standing between the consumers and the suppliers of education and training is potentially in restraint of trade and fair game for a crusading government which believes that it knows the true wants and needs of the customers. (Just who the customers might be we shall consider later.) It is from this crusading zeal that the tension arises: unfettered trade in education requires the maximum of local, even individual, autonomy. Thus, there has been an unprecedented torrent of legislation intended to dismantle the consensual commonwealth of education as part of the welfare state and replace it with a larger and more varied range of options. Such legislation and the accompanying determination to build the changes into systems which cannot subsequently themselves be changed requires a growth in the power of the centre: a consequence apparently at odds with free-market principles. For example, the Education Reform Act (ERA) (1988) is said to have given the Secretary of State 365 new powers – one for every day of the year. Some of these powers are in respect of new permanent bodies such as the National Curriculum Council, institutions such as grant-maintained schools and City Technology Colleges (CTCs), and methods of operating the system such as Local Management of Schools (LMS). In these and similar cases it cannot be argued that these powers are designed merely to introduce changes which, once established, can run their own course while the powers wither away. These are permanent powers of a centralized state and in stark contrast to an ideology of free competition in which the state should act only as referee. The reason for the contradiction is that the real customers in the educational grocer's shop are not young people and their parents as we might naively assume. In free-market economics the unfettered consumer is assumed to know his or her own best interests. But in education the pattern of choices that people might make will affect the direction in which social and economic change moves. That is, of course, the professional business of politicians, and so there can never be a free market in education for the apparent customers because their choices must be constrained into directions dictated by the political and economic imperatives which drive government policy. The real customers are elsewhere.

Most investigations, including our own, demonstrate that there is no particular 'product' identified by the employer. The identifiable characteristics are usually very general and add up to little more than that young people should be numerate, literate, and socially skilled. We have yet to meet a school teacher who does not want young people to enter, let alone leave, secondary school literate, numerate, and socially skilled.

CONSERVATIVE PRACTICE

Sir Keith (now Lord) Joseph was one of the intellectual leaders of Thatcherism, with a particularly strong belief in monetarism and the innate rightness of the operation of a free market. His very clear vision included the view that education was not primarily to be seen as a means of social engineering for the achievement of equality. Rather, he saw it as his duty to rid the system of the influence of political (that is, socialist) ideas, which were thought to be particularly strong in the big cities and in the educational 'establishment', particularly the teaching profession.

As Secretary of State from 1981–6, Joseph instituted a series of measures to establish tendencies which have become strong lines of development. Thus, for example, his White Papers on the curriculum showed a willingness to venture into this 'secret garden', previously permitted to be the preserve of the education professionals, and to begin to direct it, particularly in respect of the new GCSE syllabuses, in ways which culminated in Kenneth Baker's Education Reform Act in 1988. Her Majesty's Inspectors of Schools (HMI) were encouraged to reduce their independence and sense of identity of interest with the education professions, and to act more like other civil servants in their active promotion of government policy. Joseph's interventions in teacher training reduced the powers of the universities, the Council for National Academic Awards, and the LEAs by central prescription in the content of both initial and in-service courses.

Joseph also began the process of alienating teachers and their unions by so mishandling a series of disputes over teachers' pay and conditions throughout his period of office that after 1986 his successor was able to suspend their negotiating rights altogether and to break the national power of both the unions and the LEA employers. These rights will not be restored until 1991, when it is likely that the increasing numbers of grant-maintained and other schools independent of LEAs will have some ability to fix pay scales locally. With his monetarist belief in the essential rightness of the idealized 'free market', Joseph sought to introduce the 'enterprise culture' into schools and colleges. Since the education professions were unwilling to go along with this, he observed with interest the arrival in schools of the Manpower Services Commission (MSC) from the Department of Trade and Industry. However, as a Secretary of State who was the head of a spending department, he made no effort whatsoever to fight for cash in cabinet. Indeed, as Mrs Thatcher's intellectual mentor he was one of the leading proponents of the view that public-sector resources were by their nature too lavish and that all changes could therefore be encompassed at the same time as resources were being cut. This of course led to hypocrisy in schools as they sought to use MSC funds ostensibly for such things as the Technical and Vocational Education Initiative (TVEI) in ways which enabled them to use the resources in maintaining their normal programme. Joseph's failure to fight for the resources necessary for his department was his greatest failure. Although a cultivated man personally, it signalled his intellectual shallowness, his lack of nerve, and his coldness: while capable of agonizing interminably over decisions, he never showed that he cared about their consequences for the people concerned. Because Joseph had presided over the origins of the crisis in our state schools, his successor Kenneth Baker was able to exploit the consequential alienation and weakness of the education professions.

While gradually developing the powers of the Secretary of State and encouraging the intervention of the centre in the professional and local affairs of schools and colleges, Joseph also began the trend towards increasing the responsibility of governing bodies, with limits on teacher representation and more parent governors. This trend reaches its culmination in the Baker legislation, which devolves all resource management to school level, either through LMS or through the increased availability of grant-maintained status via the 'opting-out' procedures. In the ideology of market responsiveness, the devolution of management should go as close as possible to the unit providing the service to the customer. The unit then has to suffer the consequences of how it is perceived by the customer. To aid the development of this 'free' market, Joseph began the process of removing geographical and other constraints on recruitment to popular schools. This has been reinforced in the ERA by the determination that parents will have information relating to the performance of the school against the testing requirements of the National Curriculum. A direct consequence of these moves has been the growth in schools of a marketing approach, with the glossy brochures and extravagant claims common in such matters. The once-powerful LEAs are being reduced in relation to schools to providers of inspectorate services. The advisory and support services are in the process of becoming self-financing, with the clear implication that, if their provision does not meet the needs or the budgets of schools, then schools might dispense with them or go elsewhere. John MacGregor recently warned LEAs that they must reduce the amount of money retained from school budgets for the provision of central services, thus signalling that, despite his reputation as an emollient Secretary of State (he had significantly reduced the assessment and administration demands of the National Curriculum on teachers), this central, ideological aspect of government policy would continue. In November 1990, as this chapter is being written, Kenneth Clarke, the latest Secretary of State, has joined the attack, supporting a lengthy *Daily Mail* diatribe against the 'teacher-bureaucrats' of the local authorities, whose operations deprive schools of funds and teachers (*Daily Mail*, 13 November 1990). In other quarters they are criticized for promoting fanciful educational theories which damage the nation's educational performance. As a main source of opposition to opting-out and the proper operation of LMS, the education professionals in the support and advisory services are the kind of target the present government likes: an apparently close-knit group of specialists who can be presented as using their secret knowledge to feather their own nests at the expense of their clients. Even the Government's own creature, the National Curriculum Council, is attacked for ignoring the clear will of the people that their children should be taught real knowledge, and allowing the theorists to protect their vested interest in keeping education much as it was before the Baker reforms.

From the 'Great Debate' to the present, education has remained high on the political and public agenda. There is no longer any possibility of it becoming once again the preserve of the professionals. Parental involvement in school governing bodies, with their increased powers, and the widespread view that the 'world of work' has a legitimate place in the curriculum, have created an openness to change in education that will not easily disappear in future.

It would be an interesting experiment to take a head teacher who retired in the late 1970s back into his or her old school to see how much of the work of the 1990s head teacher is recognizable. Much of this chapter has been about change. It is perhaps in the secondary school that change is most evident. With falling rolls it is possible that the 1970s head teacher's school has 250 semi-detached houses built on the site. Even if the school is still there it is likely to have been amalgamated, its name changed and a new high-tech CDT (Craft, Design, and Technology) block built on the old playing field. The pupils do not need the playing field because there are few teachers prepared under their imposed contracts to organize sports teams in their 'own time'.

EDUCATION THROUGH THE MARKET-PLACE

Of the changes in secondary schools which have already been discussed, one in particular is worth considering in more detail: the Government's renewed emphasis on training, enterprise, and economic and industrial awareness which has been imposed on schools in a variety of ways. An early sign of things to come was with the introduction of the Technical and Vocational Educational Initiative (TVEI) and subsequently that well-known acronym of an acronym, TRIST (TVEI Related In-Service Training). Both were presented packaged with money. The desperate lack of resources in most secondary schools meant that it was a very unusual head teacher and/or the increasingly influential Governing Body who would turn down such a generous offer. The strings attached to the package by the MSC became more obvious once the ink was dry on the contracts. To schools and heads who had been used to a considerable degree of academic freedom, 'cheque-book education' came as something of a surprise. Perhaps because so many not only adapted to the new regime but also managed it to the advantage of their own school, the Initiative became watered down into a very limited 'Extension'. The funding of TVEI also marked a distinct change in the relationship between LEAs and those supplying the money. The degree of accountability and extent of the external monitoring was enough to make even the most laid back of managers paranoid. It was difficult to turn around in some schools without falling over yet another observer with a note-pad and carefully sharpened phrase.

Somewhat unusually for educational initiatives, a comprehensive national and local evaluation process was funded and put into place. This was additional to the more familiar monitoring by local advisors/inspectors and HMI. Unfortunately, most of the local initiatives were approved and running before evaluators were appointed locally and nationally. Perhaps we will never know the truth of the rumour that the whole scheme was originally written on the back of an envelope in a 'gents' toilet' somewhere in the bowels of the Palace of Westminster. Many of the local external evaluators were members of institutions of higher education. Some monitored and evaluated one or two initiatives near to themselves, in areas of which they considered that they had special knowledge. Other institutions went into the business in a big way, evaluating several LEAs at the same time. People have elsewhere recorded the ensuing culture shock when careful, methodologically sound educational researchers met industrialists and elected officers whose experience, if any, of research and development was sometimes at considerable odds with the evaluators. Opinion rather than evidence had been the theme of the 'Great Debate' with its emphasis on education and work. Similarly, it was opinion rather than evidence that was presented by Margaret Thatcher when she announced the launch of TVEI in October 1982. And now despite an expensive monitoring and evaluation being put into place, a rush to a particular judgement seemed often to be the order of the day. In the end it did not seem to matter too much because in July 1986 plans for the extension of TVEI into a national scheme were announced before most evaluations had reported – indeed, before the third phase LEAs had completed their first year of pilot. The national scheme was to become known as TVE: Technical and Vocational Extension. This was again to be funded through the MSC, soon to become the TA (the Training Agency).

It was a new experience for educational researchers to be told that they were witnessing in education the arrival of industrial/commercial methods of research and development. The use of anecdotal evidence to support and develop an existing set of preconceived ideas, and pressure on evaluators to encourage a particular methodology by which certain factors or variables would be investigated rather than others, are far from the best, or even normal, traditions of market research and product development. The cynics were left to assume that contract researchers were not always allowed to be the seekers after truth that educational researchers would normally wish to be: alas for the mythological golden age of the freedom of education from politics! There was a great temptation for the evaluators to go native on the methodology and adopt the apparent cheap and cheerful rush to judgement that was apparently being asked for. For some researchers, to have access to their reports restricted and an executive summary of a synopsis being written by someone else was a new experience. Perhaps like the novelist whose careful work is bought up by a Hollywood studio and changed out of all recognition for the film script, the evaluator/researchers lost ownership. The cynics who believe in conspiracy theory may view the whole episode with suspicion. Opinion rather than evidence had been the theme of the 'Great Debate'. Similarly, it was opinion rather than evidence that was presented to prove the success of TVEI.

Once it was clear that contracts had been given to schools who were using allocated money with skill to support their educational programme, and that this was being evaluated by researchers who were experienced at objective data collection and analysis, there was a need to develop 'son of TVEI' before TVEI was old enough or mature enough to be a parent. The newborn TVE was a much slimmer child who was expected to spread itself thinly over all schools and across all aspects of the curriculum. The undernourished, underdeveloped child is almost invisible, unless of course the paymasters wish to visit it. At such times the child is reassembled, 'fed up', and presented for the kindly aunts and uncles, who pay the school fees, to inspect.

From out of such enthusiastic evaluations came a decision to invent a new sort of school that would have none of the disadvantages of being grafted on to an existing school. So came the City Technology Colleges (DES 1986). To many observers they seemed reminiscent of the Technical High Schools (for training the silver children to become the draughtsmen in the 1950s). We are already seeing reports in the Press strongly suggesting that no more CTCs will be opened, and the funding arrangements for the fifteen already opened, or planned, are under urgent review. Was it inevitable? The vast sums of money that commerce and industry were expected to pour into CTCs were not forthcoming. The CTCs' philosophy of partnership between education and industry could not be developed without financial support from the private sector. Where was the market research that indicated to the Secretary of State for Education that such money would be made available? What would happen to a school if they missed their financial targets by such enormous margins?

Kenneth Baker had publicly announced that a network of twenty CTCs would be opened, outside local-authority control and equally funded by industry and the DES. The CTCs would serve the Government's policy of reducing public expenditure by encouraging industry to cover the shortfall. When, where, and why it was decided that basic 11–18 education should become the responsibility of the private sector is not clear. With hindsight we might now assume that the target benefactors were not adequately consulted.

On a wave of euphoria some enthusiasts claimed that as many as one in four schools would be CTCs. Perhaps some of the excitement was due to the realization that a quarter of secondary schools in the UK would become directly responsible to the DES rather than an LEA. This was opting out before 'opting out' had been invented. The Inner London Education Authority (ILEA) had already been broken up and here was an opportunity to attack other LEAs. As CTCs were by definition planned for the inner cities it was likely to be Labour-controlled LEAs that would be most affected. Some Labour authorities responded by refusing to co-operate. When Birmingham was 'unable' to find a suitable inner-city site, the first CTC was placed some 400 yards outside the Second City's boundary in Solihull. To the citizens of Birmingham this was all the more amusing as Solihull is always viewed as the 'posh part' where everyone lives in big houses and has three cars. The reality of the site of Kingshurst CTC is considerably different to the myth – but myths make good stories.

A version of reality was that children and redeployed teachers from a 'redundant' school were able to watch 'their school' being gutted and arising phoenix-like at a cost of millions of pounds to the taxpayer. Less than 20 per cent came from private 'investors'. There was no doubt that the facilities in the first CTC were lavish when compared to other local secondary schools. It looked particularly lavish to visitors viewing it in its first year of operation when only the first of the seven years were on roll. The College will not be fully operational until 1995. There are some excellent staff, committed to education, full of ideas; but then so are other teachers in Solihull and Birmingham. They are working in much less favourable conditions with all children, not with a selected group who are considered to be motivated and to have motivated parent(s). The pupils at a CTC were to be selected on the basis of their

> . . . progress and achievement in primary school: on their readiness to take advantage of the type of education offered in CTCs; on their parents' commitment to full-time education or training up to the age of 18, to the distinctive characteristics of the CTC curriculum and the ethos of the CTC . . .
>
> (DES 1986)

Many LEA head teachers might envy such control over admissions.

Even if this apparently expensive experiment has failed the intention was and is clear. The educational message of the 1980s was that industry knows best. Education is run by a bunch of idiots who do not know what the real world is about and are not providing what employers want. People who have no particular training or experience of education, except that they themselves went to school, have children who went to school, and the worst of all those who sleep with a teacher by accident of marriage, or some other arrangement, are suddenly educational experts. This has led to evidence being presented of the following kind: 'my wife who was a primary teacher used to say . . .'; 'the school that a friend of one of my children went to used to . . .'. One hopes that industrialists make decisions in their 'day jobs' with a little more evidence being made available to them. It has become the flavour of the decade that all schools need industrialists to help develop curriculum, management skills, industrial and economic awareness, enterprise, appraisal, and particularly the government of schools. The ERA had given school governors enormous powers and responsibilities, especially with LMS and 'opting-out'.

Such involvement, or intervention, has frequently been justified by the suggestion that it is these people who employ the product of education and therefore not only know what they want but should have a strong voice in 'product development'. One might assume, from the limited data available, that the customer of education is not as we suggested earlier the pupil or his or her parents but the potential employer. Perhaps if unemployment was not officially around three million, the buyer's market might not be so influential.

The arguments that have been heard could have been reruns of the 'education for work' row between Snedden and Dewey that attracted so much attention in 1915 and has recently been reviewed by Corson (1990). What evidence is there that schools can in any way create new jobs? It is much more likely that they are able to increase the likelihood of one school leaver, with a particular range of profiled experiences and examination results, obtaining a job in preference to another school-leaver with a different set of experiences.

WHO ARE SCHOOLS FOR?

Much writing in 'educational theory' takes for granted that the customers are children. This is also the preferred view of teachers: their customers are their clients. The influence of this view – certainly in England and Wales – has given a very particular flavour to compulsory education. Not least in significance is the pre-eminently 'pastoral' view which English teachers take of their role, and the 'child-centred' movement in primary education, seen internationally as receiving its clearest expression in England in the 1960s and 1970s.

A consequence of this client-oriented view is that teachers have often felt that it is their duty to keep other interested parties (such as parents) at arm's length. Children certainly often do need protecting from the inappropriate expectations and prejudices of parents, potential employers, politicians, Churches, self-appointed 'community leaders', and so on. However, teachers have two problems in seeing children as the customers of education. First, as a customer group their immaturity means that they cannot always be assumed to know their own best interests, and so it is tempting for teachers to see their professional stock-in-trade as the special knowledge which allows them to be the true interpreters of children's educational needs. Second, compulsory education's customers do not pay the teachers' salaries. In all the public services, education is almost unique in this respect. Even in services catering for those made dependent, the clients might have paid taxes in the past, may still be taxpayers, and are in any case usually voters. Children have no votes and pay no taxes. The education vote is exercised by parents, who (in England at any rate) have historically had a low opinion of teachers, which has worsened in recent years.

If we add to this the English (not Welsh or Scottish) suspicion of intellectuals (probably a healthy trait) and the widespread acceptance of social class as a part of the natural order, it is easy to understand why there was for so long the acceptance of a system which presented many perfectly ordinary children at the age of 11 with the self-fulfilling prophecy that they were educational failures, while the remainder – the 'lucky' ones in the grammar schools – risked alienation from the culture of home and community.

However, on any account of education, there has to be some acknowledgement of the needs and rights of children as guiding the practice of professionals, so it is reasonable to ask how teachers have served them. From some points of view the picture looks good. The best schools are welcoming, businesslike places with programmes designed to meet the varied needs of pupils, including the special needs of some children with learning difficulties or disabilities. To ensure that the personal and emotional difficulties of pupils are not allowed to disrupt their educational progress too severely, and to promote good relations with other members of the school's internal and external community, pastoral roles for teachers are built into every level of the school's normal management structure. Meeting time for pastoral and other groups is part of the programme, so that the voice of the pupils can be heard. Each pupil is encouraged and expected to develop educationally to his or her fullest potential, and the achievement of full potential is not readily accepted. Teacher expectations based upon stereotypes of class, gender, race, or other irrelevant differences are recognized and resisted, often through the adoption of positive measures. The curriculum is full and demanding, with easy movement between levels and considerable care is exercised in the design of each pupil's programme. Pupil and parents are fully involved, along with teachers, in all important decisions affecting the pupil's progress. Assessment and the regular monitoring of achievement provide accurate and useful information to inform all parties to those decisions and to keep the professionals aware of their own successes and failures. All members of the school community are expected to promote values of co-operation and mutual support. Persons and property are protected.

It is important to make this statement of some of the features of the best schools given the current climate of hostility in some quarters to the education service as a whole. Such schools exist in large numbers, and an even larger number of schools have some of these features and aspire to the rest despite resource constraints and widespread indifference. Many teachers see their educational duty as countering social injustice by promoting opportunity for the least advantaged. Their professional satisfaction lies in the successes of their pupils. However, it is also true that schools like other institutions reflect the societies which produce them and have the added force that they can be very effective as reproducers of those societies. Thus, for example, racism in a school is not simply the evil which it can be in, say, the work-place: if tolerated or supported it becomes part of the formation of the pupils since that formation is the whole purpose of the institution. Thus, there is nothing in or about an educational establishment which is not a part of the curriculum.

For this reason, there has been in recent years considerable attention paid in schools to issues of social justice in terms of equality of opportunity. Typically, this has concentrated on issues to do with gender, with race and ethnicity, and with disability.

Issues to do with opportunities for women are complex (Acker 1990). If measures of examination results are used to identify inequalities, then women seem to be doing well, with broad equality across the nation in Advanced level examination results and the greater tendency of women over men to leave school with some examination successes. There is still evidence of their underrepresentation in certain subject areas and their concentration in vocational courses for 'servant' occupations such as secretarial and caring work. It may be that the National Curriculum and the reform of vocational qualifications will have some influence in breaking the gender relations of certain option choices. More important, perhaps, since everything in the school is a part of the curriculum, are the ways children learn about gender from their everyday experience in the classroom and playground. Schools are increasingly aware of the peer-group pressure in matters of sexuality to which girls can be subjected, and most have policies to counteract harassment. Women teachers have been responsible for raising consciousness in schools to increase opportunities for women pupils, and there is no doubt that feminist arguments are now broadly accepted and that teachers' expectations are changing. The elimination of sexist language from educational texts and teachers' discourse continues. These changes are, of course, slow and patchy in their distribution. The most influential change would result from the change in role model for boys and girls if larger numbers of women occupied senior managerial roles in schools and colleges. As with some other professions, there are very large numbers of women in the basic grades, in this case as classroom teachers, but they are not represented in anything like the same proportion in senior positions.

Race relations in schools and the place of antiracist and multicultural approaches in the curriculum have a much higher public profile than issues of women's equality. There are two closely related questions here. There is the issue of the place of the cultural heritage of the British ethnic minority communities in the curriculum. There is also the question of the opportunities presented to black children through education. Again, since everything in the school is a part of the curriculum, the messages given by the answer to the first question (what is in and what is out?) are seen by many as having a direct bearing on the second, especially because presence in the official curriculum is a sign of esteem. If the school ignores the culture of the home, then this can be a contributory factor to the alienation of the child from the values and processes of mainstream society. This was a matter much commented upon in the 1960s in relation to the poor educational achievement of working-class children.

The Swann Report is the leading policy document in a field which is rife with conflicting approaches. Practice in LEAs and schools has also been very varied. Some urban authorities have attempted positive training in antiracism for teachers and the adoption of antiracist practices in schools. These have very often had the result of provoking a hostile response from some teachers who do not relish being dubbed 'racist' simply because they are white. More sensible have been approaches aimed at curricular reform. They have been most noticeable in the primary phase of schooling, but have also influenced practice in secondary schools in the arts, religion, history, geography, social studies, and literature. The National Curriculum will have an unpredictable effect. In so far as it is a curriculum of general entitlement with levels of attainment clearly indicated, it should work against low expectations of teachers towards children, especially Afro-Caribbean, and should ensure that parents are given non-patronizing, reliable and comparative information of their children's progress. However, there are complaints that the detailed content of individual subjects is heavily eurocentric. The syllabus of religious education is particularly objectionable, with its emphasis, introduced in the House of Lords, on Christianity and the necessity for regular acts of worship. Many Muslims already use supplementary schools to give their children a grounding in Koranic studies and Urdu, just as Sunday Schools exist for children of Christian families. The reassertion of the special role of Christianity in state schools, given the cultural diversity of Britain and the increasingly secular character of its society, is a very unfortunate development for which the Anglican Bishops must take a particular responsibility. Just as we can expect many non-Christian parents to exercise their right to withdraw their children from religious education and worship, so the new legislation gives an opportunity for illiberal and fundamentalist Christians to bring pressure upon schools and LEAs to promote this particular religion. The scene is set for religious conflict in schools, which could result in the end of worthwhile religious education in which such great strides had been made since the war.

The nature of British secular society and the liberalism of its morality is unacceptable to some Muslim parents, and the new opting-out and 'direct grant' legislation has encouraged attempts to create state-funded Muslim schools, so far without success. Given that Christian and Jewish schools already have such status, it is difficult to see how the refusal can be anything other than racist in the eyes of the appellants.

The educational achievement of black children in British schools has been the subject of exhaustive study, which shows that the differences between groups of children are both marked and subtle. The summary research carried out for the Swann inquiry is the best comprehensive source (Taylor 1981; Taylor and Hegarty 1985). It seems clear that children of the Afro-Caribbean working class are likely to do markedly worse at school than their fellows, and that this is a reflection of a number of factors of which the clearest is the racist attitude of rejection to which their communities are subject in society in general.

Young people with disabilities have in recent years found a much greater willingness on the part of LEAs and schools to accept that so far as possible they should be educated in mainstream schools. For those with motor disabilities, it is increasingly recognized that, although many schools are poorly adapted to their needs, their disability is irrelevant to their educational performance. Parents can still have battles in resisting the prejudices of some education bureaucrats, but it is ever more widely recognized that the educational advantages for all pupils of the presence in the school of people with disabilities far outweigh the expense of necessary adaptations. Some sensory handicaps can also be catered for with a little ingenuity and goodwill. The decade started with promise for young people with special educational needs resulting from severe learning difficulties, psychiatric illness, mental handicaps, or severe emotional or behavioural problems. The Warnock Report (Department of Education and Science 1978) and the subsequent 1981 Education Act, despite their shortcomings, did seem to be about ensuring that schools would be normally expected to integrate children with special needs into mainstream schools. While there were always ways around integration they did seem to be positive moves towards a system that would cater for special needs rather than a pupil with special needs having to deal with an often inflexible, under-resourced and sometimes unwelcoming system.

Towards the end of the decade came the ERA, of which Dyson (1988) was prompted to suggest that: 'Having special needs is no longer about what the education service can provide for the individual, but how the child matches up to the expectations of the service.' A sorry development from a promising initiative. One mechanism which is central to the dilemma of children with special needs is 'statementing'. Statementing is a process, supported by Warnock, which was intended to ensure the legal entitlement of special needs children to the resources that would ensure effective education. Unfortunately, the ERA could be read to suggest that statemented children could be exempt from the requirements of the National Curriculum, and so may serve to negate their previously stated legal entitlement to effective education. This is the opposite to what many thought that statementing had been set up to achieve. Again the cynics might suggest that schools wishing to maintain their 'averages' may seek to have some children statemented who would otherwise pull their averages down.

Children with special needs may be further disadvantaged as a consequence of LMS. To mainstream children with special needs may have financial implications for the school in that they may require special equipment, access, specialist teaching, and perhaps small-group teaching. It will be difficult for schools to fund such things.

SUMMARY AND POSSIBLE WAYS FORWARD

The future for secondary education is very much dependent upon the outcome of the various political options. A new Labour government will restore the role of the LEAs by handling back opted-out schools to local-government control. The continuation of Conservative policy in whatever form will, through a combination of LMS and opting-out, result in a further weakening of the role of local authorities, in particular the specialist advisory and staff development services. One policy option currently being discussed would shift the main burden of educational expenditure to central government. Whatever happens, however, there are some changes which are irreversible. There will continue to be a National Curriculum, justified on all sides as representing the minimum entitlement for all children and therefore an important element of a policy of equal opportunity. Whether the rationale is given in terms of manpower supply or individual development, there will continue to be an increase in the numbers staying on for full-time education after 16 and a growth in the opportunities for further and higher education: demographic changes and labour shortages will require this.

There are clear signs that, as the supply of school-leavers declines, employers are competing directly with further and higher education for their attention. Recruiters assert, as the Armed Forces have done for some years, that to work for and be trained by them is preferable to higher education. After all, the advertiser implies, why have more of the same when one could be paid to train for a career? The effect of student loans and possible top-up fees on the participation of young people in further and higher education has yet to be seen, but there will certainly be an increase in the collaboration between education and employers and a growth in part-time award-bearing courses. At school level, there is an increased interest in compacts. These are agreements between a pupil (aged 14+) and an employer or tertiary education institution. Both parties agree goals which they will seek to fulfil and which are justified as being primarily in the interest of the pupil. If the goals are achieved, the pupil is guaranteed either a job (with training) or a place in education. The pupil's goals might be traditionally educational (examination passes), personal (diligence, attendance), or a programme of community or job-related experiences. There is no commitment of a contractual type on the pupil's part. Schools and employers nominate staff to deliver their part of the compacts, which are arranged through consortia. It remains to be seen whether this development works to the advantage of pupils. There are some educators who suspect that the effect might be to reduce pupil choice by tying them in to an employer too early and thus to reduce their legitimate expectations. For this reason, it is essential to organize such programmes through a proper agency and to monitor carefully the role of the employers, who must in any case form a large and varied group. On the plus side is the possibility that certainty of employment with a creditable employer committed to providing training will act as a motivation for education success in terms of goals set for each individual pupil.

We will always remember where we were when we heard that Margaret Thatcher had resigned. We were writing this chapter. The demise of Thatcherism had been discussed ever since she became Prime Minister. Whether it will outlive her period of office remains to be seen. The implications of the ensuing changes for education in the 1990s are again a matter for the political fortune-tellers. We have already seen a second Secretary of State taking office since the 'Education Reform Act', and with that some of the practices and policies of the 1980s are under threat, or at least 'subject to revision'. Perhaps there will now be a major rethink of policy and practice in education. Many of the issues that we have discussed in this chapter have become so entrenched within education and educators that they will be with us for a long time to come.

REFERENCES

Acker, S. (1990) 'Gender issues in schooling', in Noel Entwistle (ed.) *Handbook of Educational Ideas and Practices*, London: Routledge.

Corson, D. (1990) 'Introduction: Linking education and work', in David Corson (ed.) *Education for Work*, Philadelphia: Multilingual Matters Ltd.

DES (1978) *Special Educational Needs* (The Warnock Report), London: HMSO.

DES (1981) *Education Act 1981 – Special Educational Needs*, London: HMSO.

DES (1986) *City Technology Colleges: A New Choice of School*, London: HMSO.

DES (1988) *Education Reform Act*, London: HMSO.

Dyson, A. (1988) 'Outcasts and failures', *Times Educational Supplement* 29 April.

O'Connor, M. (1990) *Secondary Education*, London: Cassell Educational.

Taylor, M.J. (1981) *Caught Between: A Review of Research into the Education of Pupils of West Indian Origin*, Windsor: NFER-Nelson.

Taylor, M.J. and Hegarty, S. (1985) *The Best of Both Worlds. . . .? A Review of Research into the Education of Pupils of South Asian Origin*, Windsor: NFER-Nelson.

4 Youth employment and training

Michael H. Banks

HISTORICAL BACKGROUND TO THE YOUTH LABOUR MARKET AND TRAINING POLICY

> The practice of employing 16–18 year olds without training leading to nationally recognised qualifications must stop . . . the skills gap can no longer be ignored. The economic and social costs of doing so are unacceptable. A revolution in the expectations, standards and the delivery of training must take place.
>
> (CBI 1989)

It is the aim of this chapter briefly to trace the steps by which we have come to the apparent state summarized so neatly in the above CBI statement. This will be achieved with reference to the history of youth in the labour market, to more recent changes in unemployment levels and employment opportunities, to government training policy initiatives, to international comparisons of youth training, and finally to current policy developments.

We might remind ourselves initially of what the term 'youth' has come to mean, especially in relation to the world of work. Of course the term itself is a modern invention, and in Britain at least has come to be used more or less synonymously with adolescence, perhaps extending somewhat into what was previously called early adulthood. And in turn the psychosocial concepts of adolescence have varied greatly over time (Aries 1962; Kett 1977). The term 'adolescence' was rarely used prior to the eighteenth century, and although the characteristics of puberty were well recognized, little psychological significance was attached to them (Rutter 1979). The reaching of adulthood was determined largely by the acquisition of economic independence, regardless of when physiological maturity was reached. There is a convincing argument that the discovery of adolescence in the nineteenth century can be attributed to the middle classes (Gillis 1974). It was mainly the better-off families who could afford to do without the income, and therefore the work, of their children. Then by the turn of the century beliefs about the vulnerability of teenagers ushered in a sequence of protective legislation that was increasingly to affect all social classes. Consequently, during the early part of the twentieth century educational participation increased and more and more young people were effectively being removed from the labour market. These wide-ranging trends coincided with the articulation of the image of the teenage years as tumultuous, disturbing, and generally requiring guidance.

Some of the earliest work that would pass as research on young people in the labour market was carried out during the late Victorian period, when the problem was defined as one of 'boy labour'. The trends during this period, investigated by social and economic historians such as Beveridge and Tawney, can be characterized as follows. First, there was believed to be an excess demand for juvenile labour in certain 'blind alley' occupations. Second, juveniles were recruited straight from school and discharged from employment after two or three years, without training, to join the reserve army of unskilled labour, while their places were taken by a new cohort of school-leavers. Third, unemployment among 14 to 17 year olds was not considered a problem; the difficulty arose in the late teens if the youngster failed to make the transition to more secure and skilled employment. The position was well summarized by Beveridge:

> . . . it is clear that a great many boys and girls on leaving school enter occupations in which they cannot hope to remain for more than a few years and in which they are not fitted for any permanent career. With the . . . development of trades and processes to which apprenticeship has never been applied, there has come a break-up in the continuity of industrial life. The principle of apprenticeship was that people should enter in early youth the craft in which they would remain to the end. At the present time . . . some (industries) use far more boys than they can possibly find room for as men . . . They are the blind alley occupations which have to be abandoned when man's estate is reached . . . (The boys) enter, not as learners, but as wage earners, doing some work too simple or too light to require the services of grown people. When, therefore, they themselves grow up and begin to expect the wages of grown people, they must go elsewhere to obtain these wages. They leave or are dismissed and their places are taken by a fresh generation from the schools. They find themselves at eighteen or twenty without any obvious career before them, without a trade in their hands, and with no resources save unskilled labour. They go therefore – very likely after a period of military service – to overcrowd that already crowded market.
>
> (Beveridge 1909: 125–6)

Similarly, in his study of Glasgow, R.H. Tawney describes in considerable detail the contrasting early careers of tradesmen as compared with unskilled workers, noting particularly the frequent job changing and frictional unemployment of this latter group (Tawney 1909).

Other social surveys of that era included the famous Rowntree survey of York in 1910, in which, somewhat to the authors' surprise, a high level of youth unemployment was revealed (Rowntree and Lasker 1911). Frequent job changing was the focus of a study of 14 year olds in Birmingham, showing clearly the deteriorating prospects of chronic changers (Freeman 1914).

Subsequently a number of studies were carried out during the Great Depression of the late 1920s and early 1930s. Youth unemployment was very high at that time, with the attendant concern about demoralization and political unrest. One study of 21,000 school-leavers in Lancashire (and all done without computers!) found that employment levels of 14–15 year olds were higher than those of older age groups because industry shed labour at 16, due to the extra financial overheads incurred (Jewkes and Winterbottom 1933). Thus, there was the paradoxical situation where those with longer periods of education were least able to find employment. Another study carried out in Glasgow, Liverpool, and Cardiff produced some findings with a familiar contemporary ring to them. In these cities the young unemployed complained of getting only substandard jobs from the Employment Exchange, whereas the best jobs came through personal influence; there was a high level of dissatisfaction with pay; and young people felt they were being used as cheap labour, thus leading to frequent job changing (Cameron *et al.* 1943). The same study sets out in great detail some vivid portraits of how industrial life is laced with experiences of unemployment, with its attendant poverty and psychological hardship.

The wastage and personal disaster brought about by prolonged joblessness among the young has been described as one of the worst blots on the country's record between the two World Wars (Beveridge 1944). The same author goes on to stress how the weak position of youth in the free democracies in times of peace stood in poignant contrast to what was required of them in times of war. At that time, as Rees and Rees (1982) argue, training and employment policy for young people was based upon a definition of juvenile unemployment which emphasized 'employability' and 'demoralization'. After the Second World War there was increased effort to extend educational opportunities and create a full employment society, with the consequence that the transition from school to work was seen as relatively non-problematic. None the less, certain strengths and weaknesses of the vocational education and training system can be identified.

In the British educational system technical and vocational subjects have traditionally been regarded as inferior to academic courses. In the 1940s technical schools were expected to prepare the second quartile of the ability range for skilled work, but in reality they never took more than 4 per cent of the pupil population (Finegold and Soskice 1990). The major share of technical education, therefore, took place outside of the secondary-school system – in apprenticeships, day release, and night schools. At best the efforts to enhance technical education were marginal to the main innovations in educational policy, namely the introduction of comprehensive schools and the raising of the school-leaving age.

Thus, the further-education sector provided some technical and vocational education courses, certified by insitutions such as City and Guilds, Business and Technician Education Council, and the Royal Society of Arts. But the majority of leavers entered jobs with no formal training, or entered time-served apprenticeships. In the wake of growing numbers of school-leavers and increasing skill shortages the Industrial Training Act of 1964 set up Industrial Training Boards (ITBs) to represent the major employment sectors. The ITBs were staffed by union, employer, and government representatives, and drew their income from government grants and levies from employers. The funds were then redistributed to companies who trained young workers to approved standards.

DEVELOPMENTS OF TRAINING POLICY DURING THE 1980s

From the mid-1970s to the mid-1980s official unemployment rates in most western industrial countries increased from around 3 per cent to between 10 per cent and 15 per cent. Within each country there were, and still are, wide variations around the overall average rate, so that for some areas and some identifiable groups of the population 20 per cent to 30 per cent unemployment was not uncommon. School-leavers, those who are older, the unskilled, ethnic minorities, the disabled, and those previously employed in declining manufacturing industries, are particularly likely to be without jobs. One recent historical trend was the meteoric rise in unemployment among young people. In the half-decade alone between 1972 and 1977 unemployment among young people in Great Britain rose by 120 per cent compared with a rise of 45 per cent among the working population as a whole (Manpower Services Commission 1978).

Detailed analysis of long-term trends indicated that if the unemployment rate for all males rises by one percentage point then the unemployment rate for males under 20 years of age, excluding school-leavers, rises by about 1.7 percentage points (Makeham 1980). Changes in the unemployment rate for females under 20 were also closely related to the unemployment rate for all females; an increase of one percentage point in the former was associated with an increase of almost three percentage points in the latter. Long-term unemployment, once considered only to affect older workers, in the 1980s became a serious problem for young people also (Banks and Ullah 1988). For example, the numbers of 18–24 year olds unemployed for more than one year rose six-fold from 50,000 in 1980 to 300,000 in 1983. At that time they formed one quarter of the long-term unemployed.

Furthermore, as part of a more general picture of disadvantage, particular groups of youth are more likely to be unemployed than others. Most notably, the area in which young persons live, their educational qualifications, and their ethnic origin have been shown to be associated with risks of unemployment (for example, Jackson 1985). What at the end of the 1970s was considered only a temporary phenomenon had a permanent ring to it by the mid-1980s. One commentator summed up the position:

> In most countries, joblessness among the under 25s is more than twice (and in some countries up to five times) that of adults. In the seven major OECD countries, youth unemployment stood at 17 per cent in 1983, with Italy (32 per cent) and Britain (23 per cent) particularly high. Ethnic minorities are also at risk. Unemployment among black 16 to 19 year olds in the US has been running at more than double that for Whites, as it has for adult men of West Indian (Caribbean) and Asian (Indian and Pakistani) origin in Britain.
>
> (Thomas 1985: 224)

The above quotation draws attention to the United States, where high youth unemployment had been a dominant issue, and where, even during an era of public-spending austerity, youth programmes had fared better than most other public programmes (Adams and Mangum 1978; Osterman 1981). It has also been argued that the reasons for spending on youth programmes are easy to pin-point: unemployment rates for white youth were 10 per cent at the time, and 40 per cent for minority youth, unit costs of youth programmes were generally cheap, and helping young people was uncontroversial. Consequently, politicians were attracted to the issue and public sympathy was behind them. But despite all this there was no clear agreement as to why youth unemployment was so high, why minority youth unemployment was even higher, what were the long-term consequences of high youth unemployment, and what to do about it.

In the late 1970s in the United Kingdom, as in other European countries, rising youth unemployment rates, as just described, led to the introduction of special measures aimed at alleviating the more obvious and tractable consequences of being out of work. Thus, in 1977 there was a combination of rather small-scale measures directed at the problem of youth unemployment. These included Short Training Courses, Job Creation Schemes, the Work Experience Programme, Community Industry, and Unified Vocational Preparation. They were largely designed to offset the reductions in craft apprenticeships and technician traineeships caused by the recession.

THE HOLLAND REPORT AND THE YOUTH OPPORTUNITIES PROGRAMME

A year later the ‘Holland Report’ resulted from the Manpower Services Commission working party set up to examine the feasibility of a training and work experience programme for 16–18 year olds (Manpower Services Commission 1978). One aim was to bring the somewhat disjointed provisions together within a co-ordinated programme, that became known as the Youth Opportunities Programme (YOP). It was aimed mainly at the unqualified and least able, hoping to give them a foothold on to the employment ladder, through the experience of work, improved motivation, attitudes, and social skills. Evidence exists to show that YOP did fulfil a useful short-term function, but only so long as the ex-trainees managed to secure work after the scheme (for example, Stafford 1982; Banks *et al.* 1983). But quite clearly, the scheme was a provision for unemployed young people, without real integration with normal employment. The overall impact of YOP on the youth labour market has been well summed up by Raffe (1984) under four headings: (a) The effect on the level of youth employment was modest, since more jobs may have been lost through substitution than were gained as a result of YOP places; (b) YOP reduced the level of registered youth unemployment, by withdrawing young people from the official figures; (c) YOP had some marginal effect on redistributing unemployment away from the more disadvantaged; and (d) where YOP helped young people find employment it did so usually through its effect on employers' recruitment practices.

By 1981 criticism of YOP was becoming increasingly widespread, being based upon the poor employment prospects of ex-trainees, the low level of allowance, accusations of exploitation of young people as cheap labour, and, most importantly, the lack of quality training. As part of a broader consultative exercise (*A New Training Initiative*, Manpower Services Commission 1981), vocational preparation for young people was again seriously re-examined, resulting in the new Youth Training Scheme (YTS).

THE YOUTH TRAINING SCHEME

The Youth Training Scheme was launched in April 1983, initially as a one-year programme, and with that first year being dominated by the drive to create training places. Essentially the appeal to employers was based upon the social responsibility factor and the opportunity to take advantage of a protracted recruitment and selection system. But there is no doubt YTS was a higher quality scheme than YOP, initially lasting up to one year, offering work experience, a minimum of three months off-the-job training, and provision for induction, assessment, guidance, and counselling.

YTS got off to a difficult start, with a surplus of about 100,000 places, and with youngsters initially unwilling to take up places on offer (Finegold and Soskice 1990). A good indication of participation rates in England and Wales comes from the National Youth Cohort Study (Jones *et al.* 1987; Clough *et al.* 1987). In 1984, immediately after the fifth form, 10 per cent were unemployed. Over the following year about half of these remained unemployed, a quarter transferred to YTS, and 17 per cent found a job. There was, however, a corresponding inflow to the unemployed group during this period, so that the percentage unemployed in 1985 was also 10 per cent. And one year after reaching the minimum school-leaving age, 27 per cent were still in the educational system, 24 per cent were in a full-time job, and 23 per cent were on YTS. By January 1986 over a quarter of all 16 year olds in England were on YTS.

Main and Shelly (1988) looked at the operation of the initial one-year YTS in Scotland, and especially at its effects on individuals' future prospects and earnings. It has already been stressed how YTS is important in terms of numbers of participants, but the Main and Shelly analysis demonstrated the increased employment prospects of young people after YTS participation. In one sense this finding must be obvious, since many young people are retained by their training employer, with the one-year YTS essentially becoming the first year in their job. But even after allowing for this the effect of enhanced employment prospects was still present. However, the effect on subsequent earnings was less clear, partly because the issue is clouded by the operation of the Young Workers Scheme, which at the time acted as a natural extension to the one-year YTS. With some provisos stemming from this additional feature, it appeared that former YTS trainees were earning around 7 per cent less than equivalent employed young people who had not been on YTS. Thus, there may not have been short-term economic rewards for YTS participants, but the true economic value of their training, and continued training (for this was evident in many cases), would only be realized several years later.

From 1986 YTS was extended to a two-year scheme, catering for about 360,000 entrants in that year. Simultaneously, the Government announced the setting up of the Review of Vocational Qualifications, both developments considered to have wide-ranging implications for the overall provision of vocational training. Thus, it was the intention that YTS should not just increase the number of young people gaining existing qualifications, but that new qualifications should evolve based on occupational competences assessed at the work-place. At the same time YTS was playing an increased role in relation to craft and technician training. In June 1990 there were about 377,700 young people engaged on YTS (*Adult and Youth Training News* 1990). The objectives of the two-year scheme were to develop occupational competence to industry standards, to develop transferable skills and personal effectiveness, and to do these within a national framework of vocational qualifications.

Subsequent analyses from the National Youth Cohort Study illustrate clearly the impact of educational qualifications on post-16 activities (Courtney 1989). In general, those with A levels stayed on in education, most young people with either ABC1s or lower-grade qualifications went into full-time work by the age of 18–19 (as did most of the unqualified). However, having left school with no qualifications greatly increased the chance of becoming unemployed. The unqualified were twice as likely as the least qualified, four times as likely as those with higher grades, and almost eight times as likely as those with A levels to be out of work when they were 18–19.

The National Youth Cohort Study analyses further show that over one in three of their sample had spent some time on YTS, with one in eight spending twelve months or more on the scheme. And although by the age of 18–19 the great majority had experienced full-time work, there was also a sizeable minority with experience of unemployment. By the age of 18–19 about one in seven had been long-term unemployed – that is, out of work continuously for six months or more.

The extent to which YTS has penetrated the youth labour market varies considerably by region and by local labour-market conditions (Banks 1991). Thus, to some degree the inequalities of opportunity evidenced in earlier studies still persist, but in a somewhat different format (cf., for example, Ashton and Maguire 1986). Results from the Economic and Social Research Council (ESRC) 16–19 Initiative illustrate most clearly this effect in relation to the four selected local labour markets of Sheffield, Liverpool, Swindon, and Kirkcaldy. To exploit the advantages of longitudinal studies this Initiative has used the notion of early career typologies to understand the various routes into the labour market (Bynner 1987; Roberts 1987). Evidence suggests that it is most parsimonious to treat the age periods 16–18 and 18–20 separately (Roberts and Parsell 1990).

Thus, in the late 1980s it was possible to identify five main career routes immediately post-16, defined by the amount of time spent in the main institutional provisions for this age group. In brief, these are:

(1) the academic route through full-time education to A levels;
(2) just one year in post-compulsory education and then on to some other destination;
(3) through YTS and into the labour market;
(4) post-compulsory education plus YTS, usually but not always in that order; and
(5) the traditional transition straight into employment, involving neither post-compulsory education nor YTS.

Essentially, between 1985 and 1989, there was a decline in the numbers making the direct entry to employment from education at 16 from 29 per cent to 21 per cent of the age group. Furthermore, the proportions varied from over a third in Swindon to less than 10 per cent in Sheffield. The main growth over this period was in the group following educational routes, up from 44 per cent to 54 per cent overall, with most of this growth being on the two-year academic route, up from 30 per cent to 37 per cent. The proportion proceeding through the YTS routes remained constant at around 30 per cent, although towards the end of the 1980s participation rates were more sustained due to the extension of YTS to a two-year scheme.

Gender differences were such that females were more likely to take educational routes, and males were more likely to progress through YTS and to make the traditional transition straight into employment. At the same time there was increasing YTS participation among the least well qualified, as traditional transitions became rarer, and increased educational participation among the better qualified.

Considering that the above changes were taking place within less than a half decade, accompanied by falling unemployment and rising labour demand, during which the 'discouraged worker effect' (see Banks and Ullah 1988; Raffe and Willms 1989) would be less evident, it was surprising to see such a growth in educational participation and decline in traditional transitions. The most likely explanation contained three components:

(1) in the late 1980s most of the rise in labour demand among this age group was for skilled and qualified young people;
(2) the attitudes to work and training of this age group had probably changed, so that they were more likely to value their own investment in training and qualifications, as opposed to moving straight into employment at the earliest opportunity; and
(3) many 16–18 year old students were no more financially deprived than others of that age group, due to support typically received from families combined with considerable part-time employment (see, for further details, Banks 1991).

It is worth drawing attention to two additional features of current YTS provision. First, compared with earlier years of YTS there is evidence that the numbers gaining vocational qualifications are on the increase (Roberts and Parsell 1989); and second, approximately 20 per cent of trainees were retained as employees by the firm in which they did their training, a figure that was pretty constant over the different labour markets. The local labour market mattered considerably, however, in determining the destiny of those not retained. For example, in Kirkcaldy, Liverpool and Sheffield, 37 per cent became unemployed on leaving their scheme, compared with just 12 per cent in the buoyant labour market of Swindon.

After the considerable sifting and sorting that occurs in the 16–18 year period, the pattern after age 18 becomes more established, as YTS ends and the students complete other vocational and educational courses. The major route then is the employment one, with unemployment being highest among those coming through the YTS route. Even from the 16–18 academic route 29 per cent went into the 18–20 employment route, and only a half proceeded into higher education. The best predictors of 18–20 routes were educational achievement at 16 and area of residence. The previously observed gender differences tended to disappear post 18.

YOUTH REACTIONS TO YTS

In October 1988 there were 118,458 unfilled places on YTS, with particularly low rates of take-up in the West Midlands and the South East of England (Employment Gazette 1989). A number of factors may be held to account for this shortfall, but it is clear that the difficulties in filling places do not result from a lack of eligible clients (Banks and Davies 1990). Awareness of available schemes is less of a problem in the young than it is among the older unemployed, especially since the acceleration in national advertising campaigns in the late 1980s. However, whether this was a good use of large sums of public money is doubtful (see ibid.). Furthermore, knowledge about schemes and expressed interest in training are not necessarily reflected in take-up of places. Studies have shown that only a small proportion of people expressing an interest in training or retraining actually join schemes (for example, Daniel 1974; Banks and Ullah 1988). Of paramount importance, in young people's minds, for the credibility of YTS is the extent to which training leads to real jobs. As Upton (1985: 20) has written:

> Whatever professional trainers, educationalists, employers or trade unionists may say about the Youth Training Scheme the verdict of the young people who pass through it will depend on what they get out of it. Above all else that means 'Will I have a job afterwards?'

In a similar vein, Raffe and Smith (1987), in their study of Scottish young people's attitudes to YTS, noted that:

> . . . even the most lavishly funded training scheme is of little value to its trainees if it does not find them jobs. Many young people felt that YTS – or at least the schemes that were available to them – did not lead to jobs, or to good jobs.
>
> (259)

But the credibility of the link to jobs is not the only issue that influences the decision to enter schemes. Again, the Scottish Young People's Surveys provide insight into attitudes to YTS (ibid.). Of those who turned down an offer of a place on YTS, a third had positive reasons (such as a permanent job, or an educational course), but a half refused for negative reasons. The most commonly cited were that YTS was cheap labour and exploitative, that the pay was too low, and that it was a con or a dead end. Raffe and Smith write:

> This points to a substantial element of disaffection with YTS, based partly on a feeling that the allowance was inadequate and the scheme led nowhere, and partly on the perception of YTS as exploitative and a cheap labour scheme.
>
> (ibid.: 246–7)

Reasons for early leaving from schemes also offer insight into young people's attitudes to YTS. MSC data on non-completion of YTS indicated that in 1986, of all YTS leavers, approximately 15 per cent quit early without any work or training arranged (see Craig 1986). Some of these left out of necessity rather than choice (due to dismissal, illness, and so on), but many did not like the scheme for a variety of reasons, including the poor quality of training, the work itself being boring, and the low level of pay. Similar findings were reported from the Scottish Surveys (Raffe and Smith 1987).

Returning to the ESRC 16–19 Initiative, it was observed that the effects on individuals of YTS participation varied considerably by type of scheme. Employer-led schemes were clearly superior, as judged by subsequent job prospects, although colleges (as might be expected) and ITECs came off best in equipping trainees with additional vocational qualifications. The Training Workshops and Community Project schemes came off worst on all counts. They had poorer quality intake, who were least likely to gain further qualifications, and who were less successful in subsequently getting jobs (Banks 1991; Roberts and Parsell 1989). This latter feature, almost certainly, would be a consequence of these schemes being concentrated in high unemployment areas.

INTERNATIONAL COMPARISONS

The structures linking education, vocational training, and the labour market in different countries vary enormously (see, for example, Watts *et al.* 1986). From Britain's point of view, unfavourable comparisons have been made between countries (for example, NEDO/MSC 1984). It has been suggested that Britain has invested less than its main competitors in the training of both young people and adults, that its approach to training was outmoded, and the burden of financing training fell more heavily than elsewhere on national and local government, as opposed to employers.

In Western Europe the policy responses of different countries to rising levels of youth unemployment contain some similar themes, not surprising as each attempts to learn from other countries and as each EEC country is influenced to greater or lesser extents by EEC directives. In all countries youth unemployment rates rose considerably during the 1980s, with the effect of lengthening the transition from school to working and adult life. The guidance services in particular have had to develop a wider role to include the provision of support to young people as well as the more traditional form of help with educational and vocational decision making (Watts *et al.* 1986). In line with the development of the Youth Opportunities Programme in the UK, other EEC countries promoted a range of new transition programmes. While initially these fulfilled a waiting-room function, increasingly moves were made to improve the quality of training and to make the provisions more relevant to labour-market needs. In France, for example, the Alternance training scheme was introduced for young people aged 16–18, offering orientation programmes for those who had not decided on a choice of career or occupation. Over a period of 3–6 weeks the Alternance system offered young people a personal and career assessment, information about training courses and careers, and visits to or short stays in companies. The process might include tests and group work, with the aim of getting young people to take personal control over their career decision making.

In Germany the Dual System operates in a way not unlike the Youth Training System, or rather the reverse way around, since the German system preceded YTS and was much heralded as the model to aspire to. Trainees typically join the Dual System at 15 or 16, and are trained via a blend of experience off-the-job, on-the-job, and at vocational schools. The training is broad-based at first, achievements are judged by standards of competence, and the system includes career counselling with the aid of aptitude tests. Two-thirds of young people complete their training under the Dual System, and as a model it still exerts a strong influence on training policy in the UK (for example, CBI 1989). The strength of the Dual System lies in the high quality of training, run along market lines, although it has not been without its critics, especially in the way it tends to intensify labour-market disadvantages (Braun 1987).

And in Spain the system of Formacion Profesional fulfils a transitional training role between general education and the labour market (Piero *et al.* 1989); while in the United States vocational education has a different history, aimed directly at preventing skill shortages in the labour market and helping to reduce social and economic inequality by raising the earning capacity of disadvantaged workers (Doeringer and Vermeulen 1981).

SCHOOL-LEAVERS IN SCOTLAND

The structure of educational provision and vocational training for 16–18 year olds in Scotland contains some notable differences to that in England and Wales. The Scottish system is characterized by less institutional variety and a smaller further-education sector. Despite ongoing reform there are differences in the systems of academic and vocational qualifications. In Scotland there are more transition points for this age group, including a significant one at 17, and more students take Highers (A-level equivalent). Despite these differences, however, there are similarities in entry patterns to the labour market and in the role of YTS, and the gender and qualifications effects contained therein (Raffe 1988).

As far as Higher Education is concerned Burnhill *et al.* (1988) argue that changes in opportunity for entry to higher education have not kept pace with the flow of qualified school-leavers from the schools in Scotland. In a general sense changes in higher-education policy exert a downward pressure on opportunities and careers of all 16–19 year olds. But the effects are indirect, complex, and can only be noted within the confines of the present chapter. Of more direct concern is the role of YTS and vocational education in Scotland.

Fortunately the Centre for Educational Sociology at the University of Edinburgh, in conjunction with the Scottish Education Department, has carried out a series of surveys since 1977 that, through analysing the experiences of young people, shed light on the consequences of 16–18 educational and training policy north of the border (a good overview is given in Raffe 1988). Their initial analyses (Main and Shelly 1988) stress the important role of YTS in influencing the labour-market opportunities of young people. Clearly, in terms of sheer numbers it is important, since the majority of school-leavers now enter YTS at some stage. In doing so they enhance their chances of being in employment.

It is often pointed out by educational commentators that Scotland has led the rest of Britain in implementing a post-16 framework and therefore is better placed to exemplify how educational reforms can develop (for example, Tomes 1988). Since 1984 this framework has been guided by the Scottish Education Department's 16-plus Action Plan, at the centre of which are National Certificate modules, issued by the Scottish Vocational Education Council (Scotvec). These emphasize vocational competencies, are activity-based and criterion-referenced. A whole range of institutions has been drawn into the framework, enabling flexibility of entry and exit, but within an integrated structure.

Since students can choose modules rather than courses their opportunity for choice is much broader, in location, pace of study, and transfer of credits. One intended consequence of this is to increase participation rates in 16+ education, by building upon introductory modules, increasing motivation, and so forth. It was also intended to design a system responsive to changing skill demands, while at the same time simplifying the maze of vocational qualifications, further-education courses, and YTS. The extent to which the Action Plan succeeded has been partly assessed by Raffe (1988) with recourse to data on the first year group to be affected.

It was demonstrated that opportunity and choice was indeed extended, largely by making modules available to young people in a wide range of institutions and situations. Consequently the numbers gaining certification increased, although the longer-term effect on post-16 participation rates has yet to be assessed. In terms of how young people fared on the labour market the evidence was not promising, although employers held favourable opinions of Scotvec modules as vocational education for apprentices and other employees. All in all, however, Raffe's analysis may be subject to the many vagaries of early evaluation. The principal stakeholders in the Plan were still becoming acquainted with the organization and delivery of the modules, and consequently the later picture could be quite different.

RECENT AND CURRENT DEVELOPMENTS

By the end of the decade YTS was at something of a transition point. The responsibility for organizing and delivering YTS at the local level is in the process of being invested in the new Training and Enterprise Councils (TECs). Between 80 and 100 TECs were to be created over a three to four year period, each based in a distinct locality (Command Paper 540). TEC boards are dominated by local businessmen, with the clear intention of enabling training to be more employer-driven than in the recent past. Their development is modelled on the American PICs (Private Industry Councils). In fact, a former director of the Boston PIC, Cay Stratton, has been adviser to the Secretary of State on training matters (*Adult and Youth Training News* 1990). The TECs are designed to fulfil a number of key roles, underpinned by five principles:

(1) national training and enterprise programmes need to be tailored to the needs of local labour markets, hence TECs are to be locally based systems;
(2) TECs should be central to an employer-led partnership;
(3) the need for a targeted approach towards community revitalization where necessary and a co-ordination of policies and programmes;
(4) an emphasis on performance – attaining better value for money, greater efficiency, and a high return on investment;
(5) the creation of an enterprise culture.

Quite clearly the shift of emphasis is from the national to the local level, and TECs will be responsible for delivering training programmes for the unemployed and for supporting local training as best fits an assessment of local needs. The net move will inevitably be away from educational venues, towards a more entrepreneurial, near market style of employer-led scheme. The TECs will subcontract training to training providers, and responsibility for standards of achievement will be linked to National Council for Vocational Qualifications (NCVQ) levels. Among their aims is to help ensure that young people acquire the skills the economy needs, and to do this by youth training programmes. As well as seeing TECs as the regulators of the local training market, the CBI has recommended that from the age of 14 individuals should possess their own Careership profile, which 'records achievement and identifies development needs' (CBI 1989). And related to this, in October 1990 the idea of training credits was introduced, allowing every school-leaver the freedom to 'spend' a voucher for a given amount of training. Whether this will materially affect the labour-market opportunities of young people remains to be seen, although the principle behind training credits is highly consistent with changes aimed at privatizing and individualizing the training market, and it may be something of a test bed for similar applications in related educational areas.

Related to the setting up of TECs are the changes introduced and to be introduced by the NCVQ. Set up in 1986, the NCVQ aims to reform the system of vocational qualifications that will cover all categories of employment and be in place in 1991. Reform is long overdue. Currently there are no readily available statistics on the vocational qualifications of the work-force, on the number of qualifications awarded annually, or on the costs of the system. The new framework includes securing standards of occupational competence that are assessed and accredited by approved bodies. The NCVQ task is clearly a complex one and it is not without its critics (see, for example, Green 1986). While some degree of success at the lower levels (i.e. those achieved by YTS trainees) can be expected, it remains to be seen whether comprehensive coverage of all occupations can be achieved.

It has been stated elsewhere that it is impossible to separate educational and training policy when considering their economic implications (Senker 1990). While this may be true at a general level, specific practicalities in the present context demand that degree of separation. Thus, the implications of the Education Reform Act are dealt with by Walkling and Brannigan (Chapter 3). As far as post-16 careers are concerned, the consequences are yet to be fully identified, but it is likely that increased competition between schools, the faltering progress of City Technology Colleges, and the introduction of the National Curriculum will have significant effects on the opportunities of future cohorts of 16–19 year olds. Their exact consequences must await further research. More directly, however, the urgently needed reform of A levels, hopefully only temporarily shelved, may help to usher in an era of greater educational participation post 16, a growth that is essential to enhance the supply of highly skilled people needed by the economy.

REFERENCES

Adams, A.V. and Mangum, G.L. (1978) *The Lingering Crisis of Youth Unemployment*, Kalamazoo, MI: W.E. Upjohn Institute.

Adult and Youth Training News (1990) Parliamentary Questions, *Adult and Youth Training News* June: 31.

Aries, P. (1962) *Centuries of Childhood*, London: Jonathan Cape.

Ashton, D.N. and Maguire, M.J. (1986) *Young Adults in the Labour Market*, Department of Employment Research Paper No. 55.

Banks, M.H. (1991) 'Youth careers', in J. Bynner, M.H. Banks, I. Bates, G. Breakwell, N. Emler, L. Jamieson, and K. Roberts (eds) *Careers and Identities*, Milton Keynes: Open University Press.

Banks, M.H. and Davies, J.B. (1990) *Motivation, Unemployment and Employment Department Programmes*, Department of Employment Research Paper No. 80.

Banks, M.H., Mullings, C., and Jackson, E.J. (1983) 'A benchmark for Youth Opportunities', *Employment Gazette* 91(3): 91–5.

Banks, M.H. and Ullah, P. (1988) *Youth Unemployment in the 1980s: Its Psychological Effects*, London: Croom Helm.

Beveridge, W.H. (1909) *Unemployment: A Problem of Industry*, London: Longmans, Green and Co.

Beveridge, W.H. (1944) *Full Employment in a Free Society*, London: George Allen and Unwin.

Braun, F. (1987) 'Vocational training as a link between the schools and the labour market: the dual system in the Federal Republic of Germany', *Comparative Education* 23(2): 123–43.

Burnhill, P., Garner, D., and McPherson, A. (1988) 'Social change, school attainment and entry to higher education 1976–1986', in D. Raffe (ed.) *Education and the Youth Labour Market*, Lewes: The Falmer Press.

Bynner, J, (1987) 'Coping with transition: ESRC's new 16–19 Initiative', *Youth and Policy* 22: 25–8.

Cameron, C., Lush, A., and Meara, G. (1943) *Disinherited Youth: A Report on the 18+ Age Group*, Edinburgh: T. and A. Constable.

Clough, E., Gray, J., and Jones, B. (1987) 'Those who say "no" to YTS: findings from the National Youth Cohort Survey', *British Journal of Education and Work* 1(2): 79–89.

Command Paper 540 (1988) *Employment for the 1990s*, London: HMSO.

Confederation of British Industry (CBI) (1989) *Towards a Skills Revolution: Report of the Vocational Education and Training Task Force*, London: CBI.

Courtney, G. (1989) *The Youth Cohort Study of England and Wales: Note on Young People Aged 16–19 Prepared for The Prince's Trust*, Social and Community Planning Research.

Craig, R. (1986) *The Youth Training Scheme: A Study of Non-participants and Early Leavers*, Sheffield: Manpower Services Commission.

Daniel, W.W. (1974) *A National Survey of the Unemployed*, PEP Vol. XL Broadsheet No. 546.

Doeringer, P.B. and Vermeulen, B. (1981) *Jobs and Training in the 1980s*, Boston: Martinus Nijhoff.

Employment Gazette (1989) Questions in Parliament, *Employment Gazette* 97(2): 101.

Finegold, D. and Soskice, D. (1990) 'The failure of training in Britain', in D. Gleeson (ed.) *Training and its Alternatives*, Milton Keynes: Open University Press.

Freeman, A. (1914) *Boy Life and Labour: The Manufacture of Inefficiency*, London: P.S. King and Son.

Gillis, J.R. (1974) *Youth and History*, New York: Academic Press.

Green, S. (1986) 'A critical assessment of RVQ', *Personnel Management* July: 24–7.

Jackson, M.P. (1985) *Youth Unemployment*, London: Croom Helm.

Jewkes, J. and Winterbottom, A. (1933) *Juvenile Unemployment*, London: Allen and Unwin.

Jones, B., Gray, J., and Clough, E. (1987) 'Finding a post-16 route: The first year's experience', in R. Coles (ed.) *The Search for Jobs and the New Vocationalism*, Aldershot: Gower.

Kett, J.F. (1977) *Rites of Passage*, New York: Basic Books.

Main, B.G.M., and Shelly, M.A. (1988) 'Does it pay to go on YTS?', in D. Raffe (ed.) *Education and the Youth Labour Market*, Lewes, East Sussex: The Falmer Press.

Makeham, P. (1980) 'The anatomy of youth unemployment', *Employment Gazette* 88(3): 235–6.

Manpower Services Commission (1978) *Young People and Work*, London: Manpower Services Commission.

Manpower Services Commission (1981) *A New Training Initiative: An Agenda for Action*, London: HMSO.

National Economic Development Office and Manpower Services Commission (1984) *Competence and Competition: Training and Education in the Federal Republic of Germany, the United States and Japan*, London: National Economic Development Office.

Osterman, P. (1981) 'Interpreting youth unemployment', *New Society* 27 August: 344–6.

Piero, J.M., Hontangas, P. and Salanova, M. (1989) 'La Formacion Profesional – 1, Es una via de acceso al mercado laboral? Implicaciones para la orientacion profesional', *Papeles del Psicologo* 39/40: 21–30.

Raffe, D. (1984) 'Youth unemployment and the MSC: 1977–1983', in D. McCrone (ed.) *Scottish Government Yearbook*, Unit for the Study of Government in Scotland, University of Edinburgh.

Raffe, D. (ed.) (1988) *Education and the Youth Labour Market: Schooling and Scheming*, Lewes, East Sussex: The Falmer Press.

Raffe, D. and Smith, P. (1987) 'Young people's attitudes to YTS: the first two years', *British Educational Research Journal* 13(3): 241–60.

Raffe, D. and Willms, J.D. (1989) 'Schooling the discouraged worker: local labour market effects on educational participation', *Sociology* 23: 559–81.

Rees, G. and Rees, T.L. (1982) 'Juvenile unemployment and the state between the wars', in T.L. Rees and P. Atkinson (eds) *Youth Unemployment and State Intervention*, London: Routledge and Kegan Paul.

Roberts, K. (1987) 'ESRC – Young people in society', *Youth and Policy* 22: 15–24.

Roberts, K. and Parsell, G. (1989) *The Stratification of Youth Training*, ESRC 16–19 Initiative Occasional Paper No. 11, City University, London.

Roberts, K. and Parsell, G. (1990) *Young People's Routes into UK Labour Markets in the Late-1980s*, ESRC 16–19 Initiative Occasional Paper No. 27, City University, London.

Rowntree, B.S. and Lasker, B. (1911) *Unemployment: A Social Study*, London: Macmillan.

Rutter, M. (1979) *Changing Youth in a Changing Society*, London: The Nuffield Provincial Hospital Trust.

Senker, P. (1990) 'Some economic and ideological aspects of the reform of education and training in England and Wales in the last ten years', *Journal of Educational Policy* 5(2): 113–25.

Stafford, E.M. (1982) 'The impact of the Youth Opportunities Programme on young people's employment prospects and psychological well-being', *British Journal of Guidance and Counselling* 10(1): 12–21.

Tawney, R.H. (1909) 'Economics of boy labour', *Economic Journal* 19: 517–37.

Thomas, D. (1985) 'Taking the measure of unemployment', *New Society* 16 May: 223–5.

Tomes, N. (1988) 'Changing certification: vocationalism and the school curriculum', in D. Raffe (ed.) *Education and the Youth Labour Market*, Lewes: The Falmer Press.

Upton, R. (1985) 'What next for youth training?' *Personnel Management* April: 20–4.

Watts, A.G., Dartois, C., and Plant, P. (1986) *Educational and Vocational Guidance Services for the 14–25 Age Group in the European Community*. Report of a study carried out on behalf of the Commission of the European Communities (Directorate-General for Employment, Social Affairs and Education).

5 Sport and leisure

The not-so-hidden curriculum?

Leo Hendry

INTRODUCTION: POLICY IN THE 1960s AND 1970s

Historically the British have believed in the character-building values for young people of the 'playing fields of Eton', and the last forty years or so have seen the appearance of a number of significant reports and recommendations which have 'set the scene' for mass participation in sport, and for sports policies for youth in present-day society.

The changing social conditions of the 1950s – economic growth, rise in real wages, expansion of the consumer market, the beginning of 'affluence' – led to a growing governmental concern about the declining influence of the community and family, and the related problems of an increasingly autonomous 'youth'. This concern was expressed in a range of government-sponsored initiatives which concentrated on the role of the education and youth services. From Crowther's (1959) concern with early school-leaving and the fate of 15–18 year olds, through Albemarle's (1960) criticisms of the effectiveness of the youth services to Newsom (1963), there was a questioning that education and youth services were not catering for changing social and economic needs. Such reports were symptomatic of a feeling in society that change was restructuring family and community relations and was changing the relationships among education, work, and leisure.

The Crowther Report (1959) argued that there was a new freedom 'of unsupervised association' (p. 448) for young people, many of whom had too much time on their hands, and with a lack of purpose had too little to do in their leisure time. The Report suggested that more directed activities would be required outside school hours. The Albemarle Report (1960: 32) on the Youth Service referred to 'a new climate of crime and delinquency . . . the crime problem is very much a youth problem'. The report referred to a 'gap' in provision for physical recreation when young people left school. Not only was the leisure time of youth perceived to be a 'problem', but the nature of work itself was changing so as to reduce its potential for self-fulfilment.

It was within this context of the effects of social and economic change and the relevance of social institutions that the Central Council for Physical

Recreation established the Wolfenden Committee. Many of the issues which it addressed were concerned with the problems of organized sport: administration and finance of sport; amateurism; international sport; and the need for increased financial assistance for coaching. However, the report adopted a relatively broad remit; to

> . . . examine the factors affecting the development of games, sports and outdoor activities in the United Kingdom and to make recommendations to the Central Council for Physical Recreation as to any practical measures which should be taken by statutory and voluntary organisations in order that these activities may play their full part in promoting the general welfare of the community.
>
> (p. 10)

Within this concern for 'the general welfare of the community' the report repeated the concerns expressed by the Crowther and Albemarle Reports, and so a key constituency of Wolfenden was 'youth'. Although the report was restrained in its claims regarding the role of recreation in reducing what Albemarle had referred to as a 'new climate of crime and delinquency', it nevertheless felt able to state that: '. . . It is widely held that a considerable proportion of delinquency among young people springs from the lack of opportunity or lack of desire for suitable physical activity' (p. 30). In addition to stressing the need for leadership, training, and guidance Wolfenden pointed towards the importance of the post-school 'gap':

> . . . the manifest break between, on the one hand, the participation in recreative physical activities which is normal for boys and girls at school, and, on the other hand, their participation in similar (though not necessarily identical) activities some years later when they are adults.
>
> (Wolfenden Report 1960: 41)

In this regard the report stressed the nation-wide shortage of all types of recreational and sporting facilities.

The Advisory Sports Council was established in 1965 to advise government on matters relating to the development of amateur sport and physical recreation, to foster co-operation amongst statutory authorities and voluntary organisations and to establish priorities for expenditure. Rather than merely creating the conditions for voluntary participation, sport was to be rationally and systematically planned. Further, the political aspects of independence and accountability, and of representing the interests of the governing bodies and developing a broader social policy for sport, were highlighted by the establishment of an executive Sports Council in 1971. This move marked fundamental changes in the relationship between sport and government, the role of sport in social policy, and the role of voluntary organizations. The Central Council for Physical Recreation was designated the role of 'consultative body', grant-aided by the Sports Council and guaranteed a percentage of membership on the

Council. Thus, although the Sports Council was designated as an official institution for sport, the wider plurality of groups and bodies with an interest in sport was given official recognition. This representation was extremely wide-ranging and included local authorities, education, countryside and water recreation, the armed services, the communications media, and planning and research. At this time there were no representatives from ethnic minority groups or from youth organizations although the members of such groups were to be among the recipients of Sports Council policy.

From a different perspective, Davis (1990) has shown, by tracing historically the general public 'images' of adolescents in society, that themes of rebellion, delinquency, moodiness, energy, aggression, and excitement still have currency in the public consciousness, and, reinforced by the media, in creating stereotypical pictures of youth in Britain today. Concern with 'recreational deprivation' was not, therefore, simply a concern with the 'needs' of particular groups or individuals but also reflected a growing concern for the 'needs' of social integration in a situation of deteriorating social and economic conditions:

> By reducing boredom and urban frustration, participation in active recreation contributes to the reduction of hooliganism and delinquency among young people . . . the social stresses on many young people today are enormous . . . if we delay too long in tackling the causes of these stresses constructively, the problems which arise from them will be magnified, and the cost of dealing with their results greatly increased. The need to provide for people to make the best of their leisure must be seen in this context.
>
> (Department of the Environment 1975)

The general thrust of the White Paper was endorsed by the Sports Council, who referred to 'the threat of boredom stemming from an inability to make meaningful use of time' and the ability of sport to act as 'a sociable and socialising activity, adding an important dimension to an integrated community life. It can bridge gaps between ethnic groups and cultures . . . ameliorate social problems such as juvenile delinquency' (Sports Council *Annual Report* 1974–5).

In the 1970s against a background of growing economic decline, rising levels of unemployment, problems of inner-city decay, and community dislocation, there was a quickening of the pace of direct government intervention in other areas of sport and recreation. In 1976, for example, the Urban Programme was extended to include environmental and recreational provision; in 1977 the Department of the Environment launched the *Leisure and the Quality of Life Experiments*; and published the study, *Recreation and Deprivation in Inner Urban Areas* (Department of the Environment 1977b).

POLICY OVER THE LAST DECADE

From these policy initiatives of the 1960s and 1970s a vast array of policy documents, 'state of the art' reviews, and official recommendations have emerged about sport and leisure in Britain and many of these recommendations have been directed towards young people. In a series of collaborations between the Social Science Research Council (now the Economic and Social Research Council) and the Sports Council a series of papers was produced in the late 1970s and early 1980s examining existing research in various topic areas, and from these reviews policy implications and recommendations were presented on sport and leisure. For example, there was a focus on *Women and Leisure* (Talbot 1979), *Ethnic Groups and Leisure* (Kew 1979), and *Adolescents and Leisure* (Hendry 1981), and documents were produced about sport for the unemployed (Glyptis and Riddington 1984), sport and leisure in inner-city settings (Sports Council 1978; Rigg 1986), and promotional campaigns aimed at encouraging young people to participate in sports, such as *Ever Thought of Sport?* (for example, Barron 1985; White and Coakley 1986).

Many commentators remarked that there was a growing congruence between the policies of government and those of the Sports Council (for example, J. Hargreaves 1984; Carrington and Leaman 1982). This congruence was seen in terms of the changing definitions of the role of sport in social policy. There was a shift from demand-led strategies to increasingly instrumental uses of sport to promote social integration in situations of growing tension.

In bringing these policy developments up to the present, it is important to point out that the speed and rapidity of social and technological change have had implications for us all, but perhaps particularly for young people growing up in an ever-shifting context. Higher divorce rates and changes in family living patterns, including many more single-parent units and 're-constituted' families, have evolved. In addition there have been moves towards 'equality of opportunity' with a higher percentage of women in the labour market – though not necessarily real equality in the domestic sphere! The migration and settlement of many ethnic groups and the presence of a migrant work-force from the European Community have focused attention on the extent of cultural diversity in Britain. But the most striking change of recent years has been the high increase in youth unemployment which has placed post-16 training on the political agenda and has made the general public much more aware of disadvantage and deprivation among adolescents. There has been a greater public awareness of the illegal use of drugs and the sexual abuse of young people. There is now greater public concern about personal and community health, for example the current AIDS problem and ecological pollution. There are also increases in stress-related illnesses and smoking, drinking, and drug taking. However, running alongside these 'problem' behaviours are others which indicate a trend towards greater longevity and more active healthy life-styles being created among senior citizens, which offer a positive role for sports in society.

A EUROPEAN PERSPECTIVE

Since 1966 the member states of the Council of Europe have been formally committed to the policy of 'Sport for All'. Intensive promotion of leisure sports, especially in the last twenty-five years, has converted leisure participation into an expression of mass culture and in most European countries this development has been dominated by the notion of 'Sport for All' (European Sports Charter 1975). Thus, the British Sports Councils have adopted a more promotional and marketing role, seeking to influence the climate of opinion about the value of sport in society in order to motivate previously inactive individuals and groups to participate. In the light of social change not only are opportunities for sport and recreation seen as a right of citizenship but the 'true citizen' might also be said to be an active participating one!

THE PRESENT NETWORK OF SPORTS PROVISION

As far as the United Kingdom is concerned these policy reports and documents have provided a firm baseline for the creation of a network of sports provision that runs from schools to adult society. In 1982 the Sports Council produced a discussion paper, *Leisure Policy for the Future*, in which they set out the pattern of leisure-time use in a changing British society, and pointed towards the need for co-ordination among voluntary bodies, commercial and private organizations, local authorities, statutory agencies, central government, and the leisure industries. The paper also indicated that ordinary people themselves were involved as leisure providers since much leisure is home- and community-based in which people themselves are the prime movers. The paper emphasized the important role of schools in introducing young people to sporting and other leisure pursuits and motivating them to a continuance in active leisure across the life-span. It did, however, offer a timely warning that, for some pupils, the association of leisure pursuits with school discipline and control could alienate them from future sports participation. The emphasis on the co-ordination of various agencies in provision and the important initiating role of schools has been carried forward in such reports as *Sport and Young People* (1988), which in its recommendations indicated varying but co-ordinated roles for central government, local authorities, schools, teacher-training institutions, the physical education profession, the Sports Council and regional councils for sport and recreation, the Central Council of Physical Recreation, governing bodies of sport, local sports clubs and organizations, youth services, coaching associations, the National Children's Play and

Recreation Unit, parents, and the media. This was matched by a report of school-age sport in Scotland (Scottish Sports Council 1989) which again emphasized the co-ordinating roles of various agencies in the promotion of sport, ranging from the primary school through voluntary organizations to the private sector. The Department of Education and Science (1983) also brought out a number of proposals for young people's leisure in the 1980s. In looking towards the next century the Scottish Sports Council (1988) produced a consultative document, *Sport 2000: A Scottish Strategy*, which again stressed the need for related roles among social agencies, the need for greater degrees of co-operation and flexible arrangements among the public, voluntary and private sectors, and the development of new ways of funding sporting facilities and delivering services.

All this would suggest that various sports policies in relation to youth have created a system whereby young people are well catered for. There is an extensive network of sports provision from the primary stage of formal schooling through community provision, voluntary organizations, sports clubs, private clubs, and youth services.

Thus, based on the philosophy of the Alexander Report (1975) emphasis in more recent years has been on the provision of lifelong leisure participation of various kinds. In the wake of the Wolfenden Report (1960) and the European Charter '*Sport for All*' (1975), the social and recreational needs – and the sporting interests – of adolescents have been clearly recognized, perhaps in the hope that through leisure facilities and sporting interests, together with the resulting socializing experiences, a sense of community may be developed in young people and their integration to adult society ensured. Yet over the last twenty-five years a number of researchers (for example, West 1967; Scarlett 1975; Coleman and Hendry 1990) have all suggested that many activities provided by society are not sufficiently 'youth oriented' to attract certain adolescents. For instance, Bone (1972) provided more details on this issue by indicating that commercial venues were preferred by adolescents for their greater lavishness and unrestrictive, undemanding provision. McCusker (1985) has also shown the importance of the ways in which young people perceive the social context of sports as being important to their continued involvement in physical recreation or withdrawal to other types of leisure pursuit.

EVALUATING THE CURRENT SITUATION IN PHYSICAL EDUCATION, SPORTS, AND LEISURE

What is being suggested here is that despite the wide-ranging provision for youth sports, the policy makers have made certain assumptions in relation to initiating and integrating young people into adult society. This congruence of values offers to work for some adolescents, but for others the policy ensures their alienation from participation and involvement. One of the most obvious manifestations of adolescent 'dissonance' from adult-organized and led activities is the lack of consultation and negotiation that occurs with young people in setting the social context, organization, and 'rules' surrounding particular activities. In the face of adult 'imposition' many young people choose *not* to be involved. It is possible to propose, therefore, that a 'hidden agenda' of values operates within sports which impinges on, and influences, young people in a way that facilitates the sports involvement of some but constrains the regular participation of many. In a similar way to Hartley's (1985) argument about the present-day role of schooling in the lives of many young people, organized sports present a value system to young people in terms of structural conditions which are conducive to optimal experience, but which appear to fall short with respect to such qualities as self-expression and individuation (for example, Kleiber and Rickards 1985). Compared to other leisure activities sports do not offer the intrigue and free interchange of certain casual peer involvements, nor the personal tutorial to be found in one-to-one hobbies.

In discussing the value system in education Hartley (1985: 96) wrote:

> Hitherto, there was little need to formalise the hidden curriculum because its subliminal messages were, for the most part, effectively assimilated. In the main, pupils were adequately socialised by the hidden curriculum to fit into society. Now, however, it appears that pupils cannot be assumed to have acquiesced either in the formal goals of education or in their justification. When teachers justify schooling in vocational terms, the message is questioned by children who know full well that academic credentials are no guarantee of a job . . . the meaning of schooling must therefore undergo change.

A similar argument might well be offered in relation to sporting and leisure skills and participation. A sporting 'hidden curriculum' may exist which is as pervasive as the one Hartley (1985) presents for formal education, and one which confronts young people with the dilemma of choosing to participate in a situation which, if anything, perpetuates adult dominance in an adolescent's experience, perhaps in exchange for the training of well-regarded skills and the advantages of social status (for example, J.S. Coleman 1961) or to select some alternative form of leisure pursuit. The possibility that illegal or deviant activities may be among the more attractive alternatives for youth should serve as a challenge for the policy makers and professionals in identifying and nurturing the wealth of abilities, talents, and interests which adolescents possess.

Conformity and subordination of the self clearly define socialization within sports contexts, and sport in general is regarded as a primary means of conservative socialization (for example, Snyder and Spreitzer 1978). It is predictable, then, that most young people who participate in sports will be middle-class youths who choose to take the path to adulthood which is prescribed for them and who associate closely with the values of their parents and adult society generally.

THE 'HIDDEN CURRICULUM' IN EDUCATION

If we look at the school situation in Britain evidence is available about young people being 'shaped in the image of their teachers'. As Henry (1966: 292) wrote, 'School metamorphoses the child . . . then proceeds to minister to the self it has created'. In this process various elements of the school system can combine to differentiate pupils in terms of their attitudes toward teachers, their self-images, and their scholastic success. In this connection it may be important to note that school sports participants tend to produce better academic results than non-participants, and have higher educational aspirations (for example, Schafer and Renberg 1970; Spreitzer and Pugh 1973; Hendry *et al.* 1989). As Start (1966) has written many years ago pupils who play for school sports teams also tend to accept the academic pupil role so that sport becomes another manifestation of school culture.

The labels which teachers may use in 'getting to know' their pupils have been outlined by Hargreaves *et al.* (1975): (a) appearance; (b) conformity (or its opposite) to discipline role aspects; (c) conformity (or its opposite) to academic role aspects; (d) likeability; and (e) peer-group relations. Similarly, a number of researchers have demonstrated the effect of pupils' physical attractiveness on teachers' expectations and evaluations (for example, Clifford and Walster 1973; Dion 1972; Dusek 1975; Rich 1975), even when teachers have been made aware of teaching bias (Foster *et al.* 1975). It can be argued that conformity, attractiveness, skill, and even 'hidden' sex roles, could be major factors in the teacher's expectancies of pupils' performance, especially (but not only) in practical subjects like physical education. Physical-education teachers may use certain perceptual impressions of pupils to construct an overall evaluation of their physical ability and personal qualities, which is conveyed to pupils, setting up matching self-estimations in these pupils as part of the differential effect of a 'hidden curriculum' within school sports.

The 'hidden curriculum' has been described as the unplanned and often unrecognized values taught and learned through the process of schooling (for example, Apple 1979; Dreeben 1968; Henry 1966; Silberman 1970; Snyder 1971). Various writers (for example, Holt 1964; Hargreaves 1967; Dreeben 1968; Jackson 1968; Illich 1970) have offered somewhat different versions of the 'hidden curriculum', but all of them have indicated that it interpenetrates with, and is communicated alongside, the official curriculum in teacher – pupil interactions and can be as highly structured and organized, detailed, and complex as the formal curriculum.

Henry (1966) has pointed out that communication systems, such as telephones and radios, generate 'noise' along with the official, intended communication. In the classroom the teachers' communications to the pupils – usually communications about the official curriculum – also generate noise. This noise is the 'hidden curriculum'. Thus, it has been suggested that the 'hidden curriculum' teaches the pupil norms and values necessary for transition to, and integration into, the adult world (for example, Dreeben 1968; Haller and Thorsen 1970), and so an emphasis on socialization – order, control, compliance, and conformity – has been persistently reported (for example, Jackson 1968; Leacock 1969; Rist 1970; Adams and Biddle 1970). On the other hands, some writers have criticized these implicit qualities as stressing consensus and social orientation not in the best interests of the individual (for example Henry 1966; Silberman 1970; Apple 1979). Further, the 'hidden curriculum' has been described as a vehicle for possibly unjustified differential treatment of pupils often on the basis of race, academic ability, social class, or gender (for example, Illich 1970; Rist 1970; Apple 1979; Frazier and Sadker 1973; Hargreaves *et al.* 1975; Willis 1977). This interpenetration of curriculum – interactions between teachers and pupils, inferred from consistencies in class organization, teacher behaviours, and procedures – has been assumed to have a powerful impact on the values, norms, and behaviour of pupils.

THE 'HIDDEN CURRICULUM' IN SCHOOL SPORTS

This model of the 'hidden curriculum' can be usefully extended beyond the academic curriculum and schooling to include physical education and sports, and utilized in order to gain insight into a number of important social and psychological issues within physical education and sport for young people in British society.

Schools' attempts to promote leisure and sport activities often create attitudes and perceptions about leisure pursuits which persist into later adolescence. An emphasis in schools on organization and structure in leisure may run counter to the perceived needs of young people and may hasten the flight into alternative youth cultures.

Physical activities and sports figure prominently in most leisure education programmes in schools and can be seen as a potential route to future involvement associated with initiatives like the 'Sport for All' Campaign (European Sports Charter 1975) or the 'Ever Thought of Sport' Initiative (Barron 1985). However, discussing the possible role of physical education in young people's leisure development, Whitfield (1971: 239) wrote:

> If physical education is to contribute significantly to the synnoetic (i.e. social and interpersonal relations) realm in addition to promoting bodily health, a change of emphasis from the acquisition of particular physical skills to an understanding of others in the context of play and leisure is required.

Such social education within the physical education programme need not detract from aims concerning post-school life:

> Physical education . . . should have helped pupils both directly and indirectly in that they will have had an introduction to the kind of sports they may pursue as young adults.
>
> (Scottish Education Department 1972: 9)

Whereas, historically physical education was seen as health related, ensuring the future health of the race, today health objectives tend to be more concerned with 'encouraging and promoting an active life-style' and 'making the most of oneself' (Almond 1983). Most physical education teachers see physical education as a means of encouraging fitness to counteract the problems and excesses of nutrition, alcohol, smoking, and an increasingly sedentary life-style.

In British schools, however, pupils are offered a fairly traditional range of physical activities, though it is a broad menu – especially since it includes compulsory timetabled lessons and extra-curricular activities – with an emphasis on achievement and competition. Hence, the context of most physical education curricula is rather heavily biased towards selective competitive activities of both team and individual forms, even although potentially there may be a wide sports programme available to pupils. Physical education remains compulsory (in theory) up to school-leaving age in most authority schools. However, the move towards national examinations in the subject in both Scotland and England may create processes of selection and opting-out in the early stages of secondary schooling for pupils. In some schools this may mean no compulsory physical education for some pupils after the age of 14 years. In general, physical education is taught in single-sex groups with isolated exceptions where a particular activity is taught to mixed groups throughout a specific year. The trend is towards mixed groupings for 'options' in later years of schooling, although often this appears to be for economic and organizational convenience rather than any 'educational' justification (Scraton 1986).

All this suggests that school sports will be most liked by pupils who are highly skilled, competitive, and achievement-oriented. Thus, in the school setting, evidence indicates that it is middle-class pupils who 'do well' in school who are by and large the pupils who take part in extra-curricular activities including physical recreation and sports (Start 1966; Emmett 1971; Reid 1972; Hendry 1978; Hendry *et al.* 1989), and non-sporting clubs and pursuits like school choir or debating society (Reid 1972; Hendry 1978) and become prefects (Hargreaves 1972). These trends have evident implications for post-school sporting and leisure interests (Hendry 1983).

School sport provides a clear differential effect on pupils – for many there is a decline in interest in sports across the secondary-school years as has been noted (Ward *et al.* 1968; Hendry *et al.* 1989), and this decline becomes more marked as pupils reach the minimum leaving age (i.e. 16 years of age in Britain) (for example, Saunders 1979). The programme and the ensuing teaching processes create a lessening in pupils' involvement – especially for working-class pupils and girls – across the school years (Whitehead and Hendry 1976; Moir 1977; Hendry 1978; Hendry *et al.* 1989). It has been argued that this decline in interest in school sports is a reflection of a more general syndrome of 'school rejection' (Hendry and Thorpe 1977).

What is clear is that school influences provide important constraints and opportunities for young people's leisure. Further, the school's sporting offerings contrast somewhat with many young people's leisure interests where the emphasis can be on informal social activities, often centred on pop subcultures (Brake 1980; Hendry 1983; Coleman and Hendry 1990).

An attempt to study psychosocial (and other factors) related to school sports was carried out by Hendry (1978) with over 3,000 adolescents aged 15 to 16 years in fifteen comprehensive secondary schools. Pupils were classified on the basis of their involvement in extra-curricular (i.e. voluntary) school sport as: competitors, recreational participants, or non-participants. The data were analysed by cluster analysis.

For both boys and girls a grouping or clustering of physical and physiological components linked to physical education teachers' perceptions and pupils' own self-estimates in relation to sports were seen to be most closely associated with school-sports participation. Within a second circle of constellated variables there was a relatively 'mixed' range of items linking 'home factors' such as parental encouragement, watching sport on television; 'social aspects' like leisure-sports involvement, intentions to continue sport after leaving school; 'relational considerations' such as perceptions of and attitudes about physical education teachers; and 'personal factors', for instance, extraversion, attitudes to sport, body esteem, and so on. Social class, academic attainment, and favourable attitudes to school were also shown to be closely linked.

The evidence further suggested that the differential perceptions of teachers and perceived differences of pupils can create a hidden curriculum of school sports potentially every bit as divisive as one operating within classroom subjects (for example, Willis 1977).

Hendry's findings showed that physical education teachers held differential views of pupils, with more favourable attitudes towards sports participants. Of the three groups, competitors were seen by teachers to be most enthusiastic, friendly, popular, reliable, and of attractive appearance, and muscular physique, as well as being highly skilled physically.

In their turn, pupils who were participants in extra-curricular school sports had more favourable opinions of physical education teachers than non-participants; yet the majority of pupils, regardless of participation category, perceived physical education teachers as friendly and approachable, able to get on well with pupils and to establish good relationships with pupils. Yet at the same time, they were seen by most pupils as competitive individuals, giving differential treatment to pupils by paying more attention to the more highly skilled and by being less interested in pupils who were not especially skilled or enthusiastic about school sports.

In rather the same way as classroom teachers, certain personal characteristics may be used by physical education teachers as the basis for differential treatment of pupils. It seems that the interactions between the teacher and pupils, either in the classroom or on the games field, may be crucial in conveying a hidden curriculum of 'messages' of praise or disapproval, and attention or neglect, which subsequently influence different pupils' attitudes, interests, and performance in school activities and perhaps into post-school life.

THE 'HIDDEN CURRICULUM' AND YOUNG WOMEN

Adolescent women in particular may be influenced by the 'hidden curriculum'. Their experiences at adolescence often centre around the culture of femininity. In terms of the 'physical' the expectation is one of inactivity, passivity, neatness (reinforced through socialization, media, and schooling).

As Scraton (1985) has suggested, peer-group pressure intensifies the culture of femininity. Whereas an individual may still be interested in playing netball or swimming in a team, it is often pressure from friends which encourages her to 'drop out' or lose interest. Physical education on offer to young women may conflict with their interest and attitudes not simply because they are undergoing the biological changes of puberty but because of cultural expectations.

Physical education for girls in most secondary schools remains dominated by team games. Team games are synonymous with sport which in our society is problematic for female participants. The relationship of sport to masculinity is well documented (Young 1980; Hargreaves 1982). Young women spectate; they do not expect to participate.

Furthermore, sport in the form of team games is problematic not only in definition but also in form. Young women's cultures which emphasize the 'best friend' or small groupings do not relate easily to the collective team situation. Physical education stresses the collective through team sports, gym clubs, dance groups, athletic teams. Young women often reject these situations as incompatible with the expectations of adult femininity (Leaman 1984). In studies by Kane (1974) and Hendry (1978) 'preparation for leisure' was stated as a primary aim of physical education. This, however, is problematic for adolescent young women. Recent work on women's leisure has emphasized the problem of defining leisure for women. Women's leisure is constrained by many factors including class, race, age, and not least men, collectively and as individuals (Deem 1984). Both Deem (ibid.) and Griffin (1982) question the very existence of 'leisure' for women as it has been traditionally defined.

Anxiety around physical education for adolescent young women is also caused by showering after a lesson and indeed changing in large, group changing rooms. This relates to the fact that girls reach puberty and mature physically at different rates. While this is experienced throughout the school, the 'physical' nature of physical education intensifies the problems (Measor 1984). Physical education provides the platform where physical differences are revealed. The problem is not physical appearance as such, but the desire of young women to achieve an 'acceptable', sexually attractive physique of womanhood. The media reinforces this imagery even when dealing with women involved in sporting activities (Graydon 1983). Women athletes are presented *positively* as conforming to the desired image, or alternatively *negatively* as having overstepped the boundaries of femininity.

School physical education fails to provide 'meaningful experiences' for many young adolescent women because it appears at odds with the culture of femininity.

The physical education teacher is not immune from the 'hidden curriculum' either. The teacher has to create teaching styles and strategies commensurate with the demands and constraints of the organization of teaching situations and of the school and at the same time has to transform various societal influences and expectations into a sports curriculum and a process of physical education teaching.

In Hendry's (1978) study, pupils were aware of prestige activities and of differential treatment given to those pupils who represented the school in various forms of competitive sports and pursuits. In this way the relational potential of the subject in developing social understanding, relations, and social skills (so often cited as a crucial aim for the subject) is ignored so that pupils receive 'messages' of differential prestige and status with consequent effects on their self-esteem, particularly in relation to sports participation in both their present and future leisure.

A reputation for success in school sports may provide greater incentives for continued involvement in post-school life. A series of post-school studies has shown that despite an association between school sport and leisure sport and between past and current involvement in sport, there was a pronounced tendency to reduce the extent of participation or to stop participation in sport on leaving school (for example, Emmett 1977), but this tendency was less marked among the group who were competitors in school (see Hendry and Douglas 1975; Hendry 1976).

THE 'HIDDEN CURRICULUM' AND COMMUNITY SPORTS

The decline in sports participation after leaving school has been described as a temporary state of affairs (Wolfenden Report 1960). This has become known as the 'Wolfenden Gap'. But it may be a misconception. While some young people do return to sports participation after some years' break, the more likely pattern shows a successive lapse which creates a declining trend into adulthood (Moir 1977; Spry 1977; Hendry 1981; Hendry *et al.* 1989). Contrary to Wolfenden's claims, this drop in sports participation may begin in the last few years of compulsory schooling.

In order to test the validity of the 'Wolfenden Gap' theory Hendry and Marr (1985) sought to establish the principal ways in which a sample of former pupils of one school spent their leisure time. (These pupils had been in the fourth year some four years earlier.) Little evidence of a return to the types of activity which they had experienced at school by 19 and 20 year olds was evident. Participation in sports of any kind was limited. About 30 per cent of males and 16 per cent of females were involved fairly regularly in some form of sport. Schools often explain non-participation in terms of what they believe to be the shortcomings of the pupils rather than the deficiencies of their approaches and attitudes. Hence, non-participation may be seen as stemming from such factors as limited sporting ability, lack of identification with the school, and so on, rather than from school effects and influences.

The patterns established in relation to school sport and its divisive 'hidden curriculum' may well repeat themselves in leisure sports within the community. School-based leisure education as presently constituted may have little interest or relevance for many pupils in later life. In this connection Leigh (1971) has argued that school-based activities and sports interests bear little resemblance to the out-of-school leisure pursuits of teenagers. He suggested that the failure in school-based pursuits lay in the teaching emphasis and organizational patterns; in other words, its 'hidden curriculum'.

The reasons for the decline in participation in community sports for many adolescents are important to seek and understand. It is clear, for instance, that the solution to non-participation in adolescence does not lie simply in giving more time or attention to physical education in schools or by providing better recreational facilities. There are complex attitudinal and subcultural factors to be taken into account. This may be due, in part, to a continuance of values conveyed by a 'hidden curriculum'.

Emmett (1977) has reported in a 'follow-up' study of 2,000 19 year olds that factors of gender, social class, occupation, academic attainment, and peer-group allegiances continued to exert an influence on recreational involvement. Further, Emmett concluded that some of the reasons to which post-school sports decline can be attributed are:

(1) some participation in school sport is compulsory and competitive, and this affects attitudes to out-of-school activities;
(2) post-school years are courting years;
(3) young people at work have more money and greater freedom from parental control in choosing leisure pursuits; and
(4) at 18 years of age they are legally entitled to drink in public houses.

It is possible to suggest, therefore, that the differential effects of schooling on particular interests create attitudes and perceptions about leisure sports pursuits which persist into later adolescence. These attitudes may be directed more towards organization and structure than to the leisure activities themselves: a 'hidden curriculum' of leisure sports.

THE 'HIDDEN CURRICULUM' AND ORGANIZED LEISURE

Adults can play an important part in adolescents' sports and leisure participation. Sports clubs, hobby groups, youth clubs, uniformed organizations (for example, Scouts and Guides) all tend to be arranged for adolescents by adults, and are often closely supervised by adults. This may be significant because the degree to which adults are directly involved is likely to influence the relationships among adolescents. Adolescents' involvement in such adult-sponsored situations, though nominally voluntary, may not be genuinely self-chosen. Consequently, many adolescents will choose *not* to become involved in such settings (Hendry 1983).

In studying youth and community centres, one of the models which Eggleston (1976) found to be of major relevance was what he called the 'socialization model' in which adolescents are seen to be socialized or made ready for adult society – learning and accepting approved patterns of social behaviour, knowledge, and values.

A study by Hendry and Simpson (1977) and a replication study by Hendry *et al.* (1981) on regular users of an urban sports and community centre revealed a differing pattern in terms of leisure pursuits and life-styles. It was clear from these studies that two distinct and separate teenage groups existed with little or no contact between them: one group following sports activities, the other using the facilities as a social amenity, sitting around the community area, chatting, drinking coffee, listening to pop music.

This brings us to the important question: why did the majority of young people in the neighbourhood of the centre choose *not* to attend the sports area? Many of the community-area members complained that there were too many rules surrounding the sports area, that sports-area leaders were unable to mix well with young people and were unsympathetic. They agreed with the necessity for rules and were not advocating a sports area without rules. Instead, rather than subject themselves to the strict discipline and rules, they preferred not to attend, thus opting out of the organized atmosphere of sports for the relaxed, informal, less restrictive atmosphere of the community area: a further example of the 'hidden curriculum'.

As the adolescent grows older he or she becomes more critical, questioning, and sceptical of adult-oriented organizations, and wishes to use peers to reinforce an emergent self-image. The need to feel independent may be a vital reason why the older adolescent moves towards commercial leisure provision. Thus, Eggleston (1976) believed that many problems in youth clubs might be solved by allowing a greater measure of 'shared responsibility' between leaders and members.

For those adolescents who attend organized clubs and structured activities there is an opportunity to associate with adults (beyond the family) on a regular basis. At the same time in pursuing more casual leisure interests they can continue to align themselves with their peers. In this way they can have a foot in both camps, so to speak, have the opportunity to experience a wide range of social roles, and perhaps are given the chance to develop a greater versatility in their social relations while absorbing and accepting adult attitudes and values.

FUTURE POLICY INITIATIVES

Paradoxes, dilemmas, and young people's developing life-styles

In bringing together adolescents' sporting and leisure needs and priorities within the context of social change in the transition from childhood to adulthood, perhaps we should be trying to ensure that the ways in which young people understand and perceive themselves, their own agency and personality, and their various social situations have a powerful effect on their subsequent reactions to various life events in the transitional process from childhood to adulthood and maturity. We also need to create realistic policies which will enhance their social development.

It is here that the function of leisure, in its widest sense, may be significant in creating opportunities for self-agency and identity development, social meaning, levels of competence, and intrinsic satisfaction. This is possible because alternative forms of self-presentation and style can be tried out without too many dire consequences should they fail to impress. At the same time these individualistic aspects of behaviour are carried out within institutionally defined roles, with relatively expected and predictable behaviours and rules. Adolescents need to learn skills in thinking, planning, self-orientation, and organization in the social and sporting and leisure domains as well as in cognitive and work-related spheres in order to develop a clear-cut personal and social identity.

At present few clear policy guidelines have emerged which might assist such worthwhile experiences for adolescents. Nevertheless, Hendry *et al.* (1989) have offered a number of findings and major policy implications from the first stage of their seven-year longitudinal study of 10,000 young people aged 10–20 years:

(1) The changing focus in the social networks to which young people are linked is important to understand in relation to sports and leisure policies. Young adolescents are willingly associated with adult-led clubs and organizations – and this may be an important stage at which adults can work with young people. The transition towards more casual peer-

oriented activities (given certain gender and social-class differences), and then to smaller group leisure pursuits often within commercial leisure provision in late adolescence, suggests the need for different styles of professional association between adults and youths, and might also suggest the need for different social contexts for their encounters beyond early adolescence.

(2) In post-school life gender exerts a more powerful influence on sporting and leisure pursuits than occupational status in that both working and unemployed young people basically wish for similar elements in their developing life-styles: security, friends, money, and enjoyable leisure. But sports and leisure activities are traditionally gender-based, and were found to be so in Hendry *et al.*'s (1989) study; and the issue here is whether these gender differences should continue to be reinforced across generations or whether policies and provision should be adjusted to break down existing social stereotypes.

(3) Organized sports participation as a regular leisure pursuit was popular with just under 60 per cent of adolescents. This statistic is further complicated by the fairly obvious inclusion of age, sex, and social-class differences. Put simply, sports are more popular with younger rather than older teenagers; with young men rather than with young women; and with middle-class rather than with working-class adolescents. However, many young people are not necessarily inactive in their leisure lives. Almost all appear to experiment with various kinds of sports and physical activities in an intermittent way; and regular casual activities (for example, swimming, aerobics at home, or cycling to work) are popular. Perhaps some consideration should be given by providers to the reasons young people have for engaging in sports (mainly social), to the *context* or *setting* (less formal, peer-organized), and to the *motivations* (for enjoyment and/or self-achievement [i.e. competence] rather than for competition).

(4) Nevertheless, characteristics and attitudes of sports participants differ from non-participants. In particular, competitors seem to have a range of qualities and positive motivations which set them apart from non-participants (and even to some extent from more casual participants). A challenge for promoters and organizations, therefore, is to design ways of offering a system of sports provision which can incorporate the desire of many adolescents to engage in physical activities in a less formal way for enjoyment and social reasons with the wishes of some adolescents to develop their competitive skills to the highest levels.

(5) Schools appear to create both positive and negative effects on young people's sports participation and leisure involvement. They are more effective in generating interest and participation in pupils who are academically able, come from a middle-class background, and who have positive attitudes to school. Sport does not appear to offer an alternative 'success' syndrome for less academically able pupils. The challenge for

school sport is to provide a programme of activities, and a system of teaching and learning that is more positively motivating for young people and enables them to have greater insight and understanding of their physical-activity involvement. In this way they may feel that they have greater agency and choice and are encouraged to develop an active life-style which they can 'carry' into adult life.

(6) There appears to be little continuity between school and community leisure provision. Those who experience success within the educational system are the adolescents most likely to continue sports participation in post-school life. Perhaps better links between school and community clubs and sports organizations in terms of both information, encouragement, and opportunities would ensure more continued participation into post-school life. This might also demand a changing emphasis in the social and coaching settings of community sports clubs so that there are more effective links between school and community.

(7) Perceived mental health has been associated with a range of leisure pursuits, including sports. One general element in all these activities was the desire of young people for social settings within which to interact with peers and adults. This social dimension is a recurring theme throughout the findings and its significance should be noted by those organizations and individuals who have a responsibility and commitment for working with adolescents.

(8) Various elements of different life-styles in adolescents were identified within the project. A configuration of social factors (such as gender, social class, and age) and of individual activities and attitudes can be seen to describe components of an active healthy life-style in some adolescents. Equally, others seem to be developing less active life-styles. How can a rich variation of life-styles be maintained allowing for individual socialization and growth towards adulthood within different social ecologies, while at the same time eradicating the less healthy elements and conditions of living which many young people experience?

The general implication from this important study is the creation of a process to enable young people to develop their self-agency and social skills in linking into adult society.

The empowerment of youth?

Mundy and Odum (1979) have proposed such an 'enabling' approach which aims to develop a person's ability to think through, evaluate, and make his or her own decisions and choices regarding leisure while understanding the impact of his or her choices upon his or her own life and upon others in society. Thus, Mundy and Odum favour the learning of decision making and evaluative/social skills. But as Hargreaves (1981: 200) has stated:

> Perhaps the concept of leisure has outlived its usefulness and can be discarded; certainly the concept of work will have to be transformed and disconnected from paid employment. Perhaps it would be easier to speak of 'ways of life', or 'life-styles'.

What may be lacking for most adolescents at present is some element in their education and socialization which transmits to them the skills necessary to evaluate themselves and their needs in modern society so that they can make informal choices from among a set of leisure alternatives, according to their personal and social circumstances.

The development of empowerment in young people is relevant to sports and leisure settings since these can be 'non-serious' but dramatic and valued learning contexts for many youths.

A focal theory of leisure

It has been suggested that the leisure focus across the adolescent years shifts from adult-organized clubs and activities, through casual leisure pursuits, to commercially organized leisure: and that these transitions occur roughly at the ages at which the main relational issues postulated by Coleman (1979) – sex, peers, and parents – come into focus (Hendry 1983). Additionally, an ongoing longitudinal project of Hendry *et al.* (1989) has demonstrated the strength of peer involvement in mid-adolescence, the greater allegiance of middle-class youth to adult-led organizations and clubs, and the findings in general support the transitions of the proposed focal model.

If we look at the pre-adolescent period, we find that as children emerge from the middle years of childhood they are engaged in play patterns that are basically traditional, conformist, and possibly strongly influenced by family patterns, but that these are slowly eroded by a more adult concept of leisure and recreation. In particular, Hendry and Percy (1981) found that by the upper stages of the primary school social pressures and the influence of the media were pushing boys and girls into much more gender-specific roles in terms of their leisure activities. Socio-cultural factors would seem to predominate over physical and psychological ones at this juncture between childhood and adolescence. With these social triggers young people move towards the setting of organized adult-run activities as a context for slowly acquainting themselves with the opposite sex after a middle childhood where single-sex groupings are the norm. Such activities include clubs run at school, youth clubs, sports, church groups, and so on.

Conversely, the process which triggers the transition from organized activities towards casual activities a few years later is one where physical and physiological factors may be to the forefront. This second leisure focus concerns peer relationships in conjunction with casual pursuits. Because this focal leisure area involves not only peers and casual activities, but also occurs at about the period when the minimum school-leaving age is reached, it contains perhaps the stage of greatest diversity of pattern. In part, this conjunction of peer relations and acceptance of subcultural values with an interest in casual leisure may offer some additional insights into anti-school subcultures (Hargreaves 1967; Murdock and Phelps 1973; Willis 1977). The lure of the peer group in terms of behaviour is irresistible. Thus, while conformist youths may continue to be more attracted to organizations and adult influence, such structured clubs do not touch many adolescents, who pursue leisure life-styles which derive identification from subcultural attempts to resolve the contradictions of school and work or unemployed situations. It has been suggested that these contradictions are mediations of class differences in society (Murdock and Phelps 1973). The general feeling among many young people is that official youth clubs are too tame or over-organized to appeal to them and are too much like school. For girls in particular, the relatively rapid changes in body shape and size, and the onset of menstruation, may well explain the rapid loss of interest in physical activity and organized games at this stage. The physiological and psychological changes experienced by all adolescents, however, require them to reappraise their self-images, and at this stage it is important for these self-images to be reinforced by peers. This results in strong sex differences in leisure pursuits – many girls, for instance, may seem at first to skip this stage of casual peer-oriented activities except in sharing fashion or social strategies with one or two close friends within 'the culture of the bedroom', as Frith (1978) has described it. Furthermore, race can produce significant differences, for patriarchy is not experienced in the same way in all cultures. In British society black women and women of colour face different opportunities and restrictions in relation to school, family, work, and leisure.

In addition, women, especially young working-class women, have little access to 'space'. Social and sporting facilities are usually dominated by men and male groups with the pub, working-men's clubs, snooker halls, rugby/cricket clubs clearly male domains (Scraton 1986). Often the street corner where 'the lads' can be found is unsafe territory for young women as they regularly face harassment. Nevertheless, Cowie and Lees (1981) suggested that young working-class women can be found in groups hanging around shopping centres or street corners. They conclude that:

> Girls' appearance on the street is always constrained by their subordination. It would seem that for many young women the answer is, as McRobbie (1978) suggested, to retreat to a 'home base' where best friends can meet, chat and negotiate their existence.
>
> (Cowie and Lees 1981: 30)

However, middle-class young women may have greater opportunity for participation in social and sporting activities. Not only do they have economic support, but also parental help to transport them to the gym club, swimming pool, youth centre.

Without the influence of caring adults at this period of adolescence, and without the contact with adult-organized clubs and activities, various deviant patterns of subcultural life-style may begin to emerge in some adolescents' leisure, reflecting particular value systems and reinforced by adult society and identification with peers. These leisure pursuits can include drugs, alcohol, sexual activity, and more general adventurous excitement-seeking and delinquent behaviour, often within gangs.

At the next focal stage an interest in commercial leisure provision is linked to the peak of conflicts with parents. Adolescents in this period of their lives are closer to being perceived as adults and their leisure-time pursuits will be adult-oriented leisure interests. This fact alone will create a climate for intergenerational disagreements, even although the actual leisure patterns of adolescents may closely match their subcultural heritage.

The factors which lead to an involvement with commercial leisure are more socio-psychological than somatic in character and have to do with the growing adolescent's desire to be seen as playing an independent adult role. Pubs, clubs, discos, commercial leisure facilities, and even foreign travel all feature in the leisure activities of young people at this stage.

Clearly, participation in these sorts of activities is influenced by occupational status and subcultures, peer-group membership, and whether or not by this stage 'courting' dyads have been formed. Hence, the broad influencing factors are mainly socio-cultural values, available cash and employment opportunities, family commitments, associations with adult society, and the effects of the broad leisure interests developed in the previous stages.

THE NOT-SO-HIDDEN CURRICULUM?

In this connection Cochran and Bo (1987) stated that: '. . . Boys with good academic skills and "winning" personalities have the abilities needed to make themselves attractive to teachers, trainers and youth group leaders, and so become socially connected with such people'. Thus, adults can provide role models of life in the adult world.

In this way, social roles are developed in work and leisure, and conformist youths are socialized in the image of their adult mentors. But in its wake, this process of socialization, transition, and absorption of adult values raises questions about self-agency and adaptability in young people who face adult life in a rapidly changing society. As Mundy and Odum (1979: 117) wrote:

> Young people need to develop a cognitive, conscious awareness of their own behaviour and beliefs . . . establish criteria for leisure issues and decisions . . . and develop skills related to enriching self-determination, pro-activity and meaningful control over their own leisure lives.

Is it possible to enable young people to make the transition to adult life encouraged and guided by adults, but with a developing sense of self-agency?

The most commonly identified motives for young people in sport have been shown to be: to have fun, to improve or learn new skills, to be with friends, for excitement, to win or be successful, for physical fitness. Conversely, reasons given for dropping out of sport often include a lack of playing time, no skill improvement, no fun, overemphasis on winning, parental pressure, and dislike of the coach (Fox and Biddle 1988; Hendry *et al.* 1989).

In a study of school-leavers in England, White and Coakley (1986) reported that negative memories of physical education included boredom, lack of choice, feelings of incompetence, and negative evaluation from their peers. Girls often associated physical education with feelings of discomfort and embarrassment, and it was frequently the environment itself that was mentioned, such as rules pertaining to kit and showers.

The belief that participation in childhood sports will lead to an active life as an adult has yet to be demonstrated (Powell and Dysinger 1987), and it is likely that the quality of the experience is the crucial factor in the carry-over of activity from childhood to adulthood (Blair *et al.* 1989; Simons-Morton *et al.* 1987; Simons-Morton *et al.* 1988).

Young people are likely to be influenced in their activity patterns by school, home, and the community. These will not be particularly successful if the experience young people have is limited to competitive sport although, of course, competitive sport does contribute to physical and psychological well-being in some (Hendry *et al.* 1989). Young people need to feel competent in a range of physical activities.

Hence, we need to dismantle the divisive 'hidden curriculum' in sports which runs from schools and into society; and which offers to be 'not-so-hidden' from the young people's perspective. To be truly participatory, and to allow young people to share in their societal inheritance, adult society's future sports and leisure policies may need to involve more carefully joint planning and negotiations with young people as equal partners. Policies regarding facilities and provision are important but so too is non-directive leisure education in which 'individuals develop an understanding of self-leisure, and the relationship of leisure to their life-styles and the fabric of society' (Mundy and Odum 1979).

REFERENCES

Adams, R. and Biddle, B.J. (1970) *Realities of Teaching*, New York: Holt, Rinehart, and Winston.

Albemarle Report (1960) *The Youth Services in England and Wales*, London: HMSO.

Alexander Report (1975) *Adult Education: The Challenge of Change*, London: HMSO.

Almond, L. (1983) 'A guide to practice', *British Journal of Physical Education* 14(5): 134–5.

Apple, M. (1979) 'The hidden curriculum and the nature of conflict', *Interchange* 2: 27–43.

Barron, R. (1985) 'Observations on the Sports Council's "Ever Thought of Sport" Campaign', in *Proceedings of the Leisure Studies Association Conference*, Ilkley, Yorkshire: 3.5.1.–3.5.6.

Blair, S.N., Clark, D.G., Cureton, K.J., and Powell, K.E. (1989) 'Exercise and fitness in childhood: implications for a lifetime of health', in C.V. Gisolfi and D.R. Lamb (eds) *Perspective in Exercise Science and Sports Medicine: II. Youth, Exercise and Sport*, Indianapolis: Benchmark Press.

Bone, M. (1972) *The Youth Service and Similar Provision for Young People*, London: HMSO.

Brake, M. (1980) *The Sociology of Youth Culture and Youth Sub-Cultures*, London: Routledge & Kegan Paul.

Carrington, B. and Leaman, D. (1982) 'Work for some, and sport for all', *Youth and Policy* 1: 3.

Clifford, M.M. and Walster, E. (1973) 'The effects of physical attractiveness on teacher expectations', *Sociology of Education* 46: 248–58.

Cochran, M. and Bo, I. (1987) 'Connections between the social networks, family involvement and behaviour of adolescent males in Norway', paper presented at the Meeting of the Society for Research in Child Development, Baltimore, Maryland; quoted by L.B. Hendry (1989), 'The influence of adults and peers on adolescents' life-styles and leisure styles', in K. Hurrelsmann and U. Engel (eds) *The Social World of Adolescents*, Berlin and New York: Walter de Gruyter.

Coleman, J.C. (1979) *The School Years*, London: Routledge & Kegan Paul.

Coleman, J.C. and Hendry, L. (1990) *The Nature of Adolescence*, 2nd edn, London and New York: Routledge.

Coleman, J.S. (1961) *The Adolescent Society*, Glencoe, Ill.: Free Press.

Cowie, C. and Lees, S. (1981) 'Slags or drags', *Feminist Review* 9: 17–31.

Crowther Report (1959) 15–18, Central Advisory Council for Education, London: HMSO.

Davis, J. (1990) *Youth and the Condition of Britain: Images of Adolescent Conflict*, London: Athlone Press.

Deem, R. (1984) 'The politics of women's leisure', Proceedings of the Leisure Studies International Conference, Brighton, 4–8 July.

Department of Education and Science (1983) *Young People in the 80s: A Survey*, London: HMSO.

Department of the Environment (1975) *Sports and Recreation*, London: HMSO.

Department of the Environment (1977a) *Leisure and the Quality of Life Experiments*, London: HMSO.

Department of the Environment (1977b) *Recreation and Deprivation in Inner Urban Areas*, London: HMSO.

Dion, K. (1972) 'Physical attractiveness and evaluation of children's transgressions', *Journal of Personality and Social Psychology* 24: 207–13.

Dreeben, R. (1968) *On What is Learned in Schools*, Reading, Mass.: Addison-Wesley.

Dusek, J.B. (1975) 'Do teachers bias children's learning?', *Review of Educational Research* 45: 661–84.

Eggleston, J. (1976) *Adolescence and Community*, London: Arnold.

Emmett, I. (1971) *Youth and Leisure in an Urban Sprawl*, Manchester: University Press.

Emmett, I. (1977) Unpublished draft report to the Sports Council on 'Decline in sports participation after leaving school', London: Sports Council.

European Sports Charter (1975) *European 'Sport for All' Charter*, European Sports Ministers' Conference, Brussels, Belgium.

Foster, G.G., Ysseldyke, J.E., and Reese, J.H. (1975) 'I wouldn't have seen it if I hadn't believed it', *Exceptional Children*, April: 469–73.

Fox, K.R. and Biddle S.J.H. (1988) 'The child's perspective in physical education: II. Children's participation motives', *British Journal of Physical Education* 19(2): 79–82.

Frazier, N. and Sadker, M. (1973) *Sexism in School and Society*, New York: Harper & Row.

Frith, S. (1978) *The Sociology of Rock*, London: Constable.

Glyptis, S. and Riddington, A.C. (1984) *Sport for the Unemployed*, London: Sports Council.

Graydon, J. (1983) 'But it's more than a game – it's an institution. Feminist perspectives on sport', *Feminist Review* 13.

Griffin, C. (1982) 'Women and leisure', in J. Hargreaves (ed.) *Sport, Culture and Ideology*, London: Routledge & Kegan Paul.

Haller, E.J. and Thorsen, S.J. (1970) 'The political socialisation of children and the structure of the elementary school', *Interchange* 1: 45–55.

Hargreaves, D.H. (1967) *Social Relations in a Secondary School*, London: Routledge & Kegan Paul.

Hargreaves, D.H. (1972) *Interpersonal Relations and Education*, London: Routledge & Kegan Paul.

Hargreaves, D.H. (1981) 'Unemployment, leisure and education', *Oxford Review of Education* 7(5): 197–210.

Hargreaves, D.H. (1982) *The Challenge for the Comprehensive School*, London: Routledge & Kegan Paul.

Hargreaves, D.H., Hester, S.K., and Mellor, F.J. (1975) *Deviance in Classrooms*, London: Routledge & Kegan Paul.

Hargreaves, J. (1984) 'State intervention in sport and hegemony in Britain', Proceedings of the Leisure Studies Association International Conference 'People Planning and Politics', Brighton.

Hartley, D. (1985) 'Social education in Scotland: some sociological considerations', *Scottish Educational Review* 17(2): 92–8.

Hendry, L.B. (1976) 'Early school leavers, sport and leisure', *Scottish Educational Studies* 8(1): 48–51.

Hendry, L.B. (1978) *School, Sport and Leisure: Three Dimensions of Adolescence,* London: Lepus.

Hendry, L.B. (1981) *Adolescents and Leisure*, London: Sports Council/SSRC.

Hendry, L.B. (1983) *Growing Up and Going Out*, Aberdeen: University Press.

Hendry, L.B., Brown, L., and Hutcheon, G. (1981) 'Adolescents in community centres: some urban and rural comparisons', *Scottish Journal of Physical Education* 9: 28–40.

Hendry, L.B. and Douglas L. (1975) 'University students: attainment and sport', *British Journal of Educational Psychology* 45: 299–306.

Hendry, L.B. and Marr, D. (1985) 'Leisure education and young people's leisure', *Scottish Educational Review* 17(2): 116–27.

Hendry, L.B. and Percy, A. (1981) 'Pre-adolescents, television styles and leisure', unpublished memorandum, University of Aberdeen.

Hendry, L.B., Shucksmith, J., and Love, J.G. (1989) *Young People's Leisure and Life-styles. Report of Phase 1*, Edinburgh: Scottish Sports Council.

Hendry, L.B., and Simpson D.O. (1977) 'One centre: two subcultures', *Scottish Educational Studies* 9(2): 112–21.

Hendry, L.B. and Thorpe, E. (1977) 'Pupils' choice, extra-curricular activities:

a critique of hierarchial authority?', *International Review of Sport Sociology* 12(4): 39–50.

Henry, J. (1966) *Culture against Man*, London: Tavistock.

Holt, J. (1964) *Why Children Fail*, London: Pitman.

Illich, I. (1970) *Deschooling Society*, New York: Harper & Row.

Jackson, P.W. (1968) *Life in Classrooms*, New York: Holt, Rinehart, and Winston.

Kane, J.E. (1974) *Physical Education in Secondary Schools*, London: Macmillan.

Kew, S. (1979) *Ethnic Groups and Leisure*, London: SSRC and Sports Council.

Kleiber, D.A. and Rickards, W.H. (1985) 'Leisure and recreation in adolescence: limitation and potential', in M.G. Wade (ed.) *Constraints on Leisure*, Springfield, Ill.: Thomas.

Leacock, E.B. (1969) *Teaching and Learning in City Schools*, New York: Basic Books.

Leaman, O. (1984) *Sit on the Side Lines and Watch the Boys Play*, London: Longman.

Leigh, J. (1971) *Young People and Leisure*, London: Routledge & Kegan Paul.

McCusker, J. (1985) 'Involvement of 15–19 year olds in sport and physical activity', Proceedings of the Leisure Studies Association Conference, Ilkley, Yorkshire.

McRobbie, A. (1978) 'Working class girls and the culture of femininity', in *Women Take Issue: Aspects of Women's Subordination* (ed. by the Women's Studies Group Centre for Contemporary Cultural Studies, University of Birmingham), London: Hutchinson, pp. 96–108.

Measor, L. (1984) 'Sex education and adolescent sexuality', quoted in S. Scraton (1985).

Moir, E. (1977) *Female Participation in Physical Activities: A Scottish Study*, Edinburgh: Dunfermline College of Physical Education.

Mundy, G. and Odum, L. (1979) *Leisure*, New York: Wiley.

Murdock, G. and Phelps, F. (1973) *Mass Media and the Secondary School*, London: Macmillan.

Newsom Report (1963) *Half Our Future*, London: HMSO.

Powell, K.E. and Dysinger, W. (1987) 'Childhood participation in organised school sports and physical education as precursors of adult physical activity', *American Journal of Preventative Medicine* 3: 276–81.

Reid, M. (1972) 'Comprehensive integration outside the classroom', *Educational Research* 14(2): 128–34.

Rich, J. (1975) 'Effects of children's physical effectiveness on teachers' evaluations', *Journal of Educational Psychology* 67(5): 599–609.

Rigg, M. (1986) *Action Sport: An Evaluation*, London: Sports Council.

Rist, R.G. (1970) 'Student social class and teacher expectations: the self-fulfilling prophesy in ghetto education', *Harvard Educational Review* 40: 411–51.

Saunders, C. (1979) 'Pupils' involvement in physical activities in comprehensive schools', *Bulletin of Physical Education* 14(3): 28–37.

Scarlett, C.L. (1975) *Euroscot: The New European Generation*, Edinburgh: Scottish Standing Conference of Voluntary Youth Organizations.

Schafer, W. and Renberg, R. (1970) 'Athletic participation, college expectations and college encouragement', *Pacific Sociological Review* 13: 182–6.

Scottish Education Department (1972) *Curriculum Paper 12: Physical Education in Secondary Schools*, Edinburgh: HMSO.

Scottish Sports Council (1988) *Sport 2000: A Scottish Strategy*, Edinburgh: Scottish Sports Council.

Scottish Sports Council (1989) *Laying the Foundations* (Report on school-aged sport in Scotland), Edinburgh: Scottish Sports Council.

Scraton, S. (1985) 'Boys muscle in where angels fear to tread: the relationships between physical education and young women's sub-cultures', *Proceedings of the Leisure Studies Association Conference*, Ilkley, Yorkshire: 2.5.1–2.5.40.
Scraton, S. (1986) 'Images of femininity and the teaching of girls' physical education', in J. Evans (ed.) *Physical Education, Sport and Schooling*, London: Falmer Press.
Silberman, C.E. (1970) *Crisis in the Classroom*, New York: Vintage Books.
Simons-Morton, B.G., O'Hara, N.M., Simons-Morton, D.G., and Parcel, G.S. (1987) 'Children and fitness: a public health perspective', *Research Quarterly for Exercise and Sport* 58: 295–302.
Simons-Morton, B.G., Parcel, G.S., O'Hara, N.M., Blair, S.N., and Pate, R.R. (1988) 'Health-related physical fitness in childhood: status and recommendations', *Annual Review of Public Health* 9: 403–25.
Snyder, B.R. (1971) *The Hidden Curriculum*, New York: Knopf.
Snyder, E. and Spreitzer, E. (1978) *Social Aspects of Sports*, Englewood Cliffs, NJ: Prentice-Hall.
Sports Council (1974–5) *Annual Report*, London: Sports Council.
Sports Council (1978) *Sport and Recreation in the Inner City*, London: Sports Council Research Working Paper, 7.
Sports Council (1982) *Leisure Policy for the Future* (Chairman's Policy Group), London: Sports Council.
Sports Council (1988) *Sport and Young People* (School Sport Forum), London: Sports Council.
Spreitzer, E. and Pugh, M. (1973), 'Interscholastic athletics and educational expectations, *Sociology of Education* 46: 171–82.
Spry, R. (1977) 'Leisure and the school leaver in Stoke-on-Trent', in W.M. Fox (ed.) *Leisure and the Quality of Life*, London: HMSO.
Start, K.B. (1966) 'Substitution of games performance for academic achievement as a means of achieving status among secondary school children', *British Journal of Sociology* 17(3): 300–5.
Talbot, M. (1979) *Women and Leisure*, London: SSRC/Sports Council.
Ward, E., Hardman, K., and Almond, L. (1968) 'Investigation into pattern of participation in physical activity of 11 to 18 year old boys', *Research in Physical Education* 3: 18–25.
West, D.J. (1967) *The Young Offender*, Harmondsworth: Penguin.
White, A. and Coakley, J.J. (1986) 'Making decisions: the response of young people in the Medway towns to the "Ever Thought of Sport" Campaign', London and SE Region Sports Council.
Whitehead, N. and Hendry, L.B. (1976) *Teaching Physical Education in England: Description and Analysis*, London: Lepus.
Whitfield, R.C. (1971) *Disciplines of the Curriculum*, London: McGraw-Hill.
Willis, P. (1977) *Learning to Labour*, Farnborough: Saxon House.
Wolfenden Report (1960) *Sport and the Community*, The Report of the Wolfenden Committee on Sport, London: Central Council for Physical Recreation.
Young, I.M. (1980) 'Throwing like a girl: a phenomenology of feminine body comportment, mobility and spatiality', *Human Studies* 3: 187–90.

6 Youth work and informal education

Janet Paraskeva

In this chapter the history and development of a service designed to deal with a 'direct responsibility for youth welfare' is traced from its origins in the philanthropic ideals of wealthy individuals to its current state as a Youth Service depending increasingly on centralized policy for direction yet locally for its resources. The voluntary sector, from which the service originally emerged, continues to play an important and radical role both nationally and locally and even though the larger organizations, in coming to rely more and more on government grant, have linked themselves unequivocally with national priorities, the plethora of smaller community-based voluntary youth groups continues to change the nature of the service on the ground and give it a richness and diversity not always mirrored in the statutory service.

THE ORIGINS OF YOUTH WORK

Early voluntary youth organizations began in the mid-nineteenth century. The YMCA established its base in 1844 'in order to serve young men, not Christians only, and to meet all their needs, not only their need for religion in the narrower sense'.

Then as now within the emerging service there were those whose sense of injustice and inequality was more sharpened by their contact and work with young working-class people, or young women for example, and more recently with young Black people. And so, by the time the then Board of Education published its Circular 14/86 in November 1939, a voluntary youth sector had already established its role in offering compensatory social and educational programmes for young people and in its own way challenging some forms of oppression and prejudice. The circular, its title *The Service of Youth*, was the first explicit identification by government of the importance of informal education for young people. It urged all local authorities to take a direct responsibility for the welfare of young people and it built on the emerging work of the voluntary youth sector in combating the effects of economic depression. It expected, through this new service, to help prevent the reoccurrence of many of the social problems which had arisen for young people during the previous World War through character-building activities and programmes. Some would argue that its real purpose was to establish a state apparatus whose purpose was to 'remedy deficits in the activities of the family, church, schooling, police and wider welfare institutions', a theme which has consistently emerged in all debates about the nature and purpose of the present Youth Service.[1]

Following a second circular in 1940, legislation was soon drafted and the 1944 Education Act placed a duty on Local Education Authorities (LEAs) to secure provision for young people for social, physical, and recreation training. This clause, as amended by Section 120 of the 1988 Education Reform Act, is all that provides the legal base for youth-service provision despite numerous attempts through the 1970s to introduce more explicit legislation with clearer reference to objectives, content, and outcome.

The Youth Service, then, was founded, like many early educational services, from a perspective of welfare and patronage, but there has been a shift in the fifty years of its existence regarding increased influence by central government, and this can be charted through the progressive movements of the 1960s and the community dimension of the 1970s, to the individualism of Thatcherism and more recently moves towards more clearly defined output and performance indicators. In the 1990s, in a climate of greater accountability the Youth Service is attempting for the first time to make some move towards agreeing some commonly held aims, objectives, and outcomes. Hitherto it might be argued that the Service has hidden its light under a bushel of diversity. The question now is whether the Service can shine at a moment in the history of education typified by a reduced resource base, reorientation, and some disarray. The resource base of the Service itself is under threat, located as it is for the most part within the disintegrating power of LEAs. For some this had been thought to mean a safer, if more institutional, base in schools and colleges, while for others a redefinition of its organization as a client-based service meant it continued as a directly funded service managed by local-authority officers and elected members on an ever-decreasing budget.

THE BIRTH OF INNOVATION

Historically the Youth Service has never really been a priority for local authorities and, consequently, much of its experimental work and many of its developments have been seriously constrained by lack of resources. Even so, although the Youth Service and youth-work methods have given birth to a range of innovatory styles of work with young people that others have copied and developed, it has never really been thought of as a service equipped for action. Its inadequate resource base has not helped, nor has its unwillingness to come together as any kind of national force on behalf of young people. Its statement that the variety of provision was its strength has become a smoke-screen hiding much of the work that was and is being done. While successive reports claimed that the role for the Youth Service was to help young people develop a critical involvement in shaping their own lives, the Service itself has gained only a small foothold in an ascent to recognition which would give it credibility, status, and security. One reason for this, some might claim, could be the lack of any coherent theory of youth-work practice. While a professional ethos was established in the National College for the Training of Youth Leaders set up in the early 1960s, and indeed a major contribution made to the literature of youth work by its staff, there was none the less more emphasis on developing non-judgemental attitudes in the youth workers it trained than in grounding any developmental practice in theory which might be based on systematically extracted data. In the absence of any body of knowledge against which to measure practice, the theories of other professions have been raided – often successfully – for indications of possible developments, and because of the absence of any defined boundaries, the Youth Service pushed out the boats in a range of associated educational welfare services. But it also lost control for exactly that reason. It was the Youth Service, for example, that gave birth to detached and street-based work mirrored now by social-service departments in street welfare teams and community outreach programmes. The Youth Service had also always worked with young people at risk and in trouble and again its experience had much to contribute to the ideas on which intermediate treatment projects were founded. It was the Youth Service too that developed experiential groupwork now favoured as a mainstream method in formal education. Indeed, it was also this Service that gave birth to the phrase 'social education', now more commonly associated with aspects of Youth Training and even included within the core-skills areas proposed for post-16 education. Even some of the content of youth work, its knowledge base including the rights and responsibilities of young people – their process of enfranchisement – has been reinvented and is applied within the formal sector of education by a citizenship movement that seems to believe it invented the concept with the rebirth of the word. The contribution made by volunteers, too, is another 'born-again idea'. Volunteers have always provided the backbone of the work-force in the Youth Service, both young volunteers and older members of society. Indeed, in all, around half a million volunteers are working in the Youth Service nationally. Yet the experience of the Youth Service has almost been ignored in the contemporary and 'Royal' campaign to engage the young in particular in giving their time and energy to serve the community. The Youth Service has given birth to many innovatory ideas but most seem to have been adopted by others whose remit was arguably at least more clearly defined.

A MOVE FROM WELFARE

The Youth Service then moved from its welfare base, papering over at least some of the cracks left by the poverty and depression of the pre- and early post-war years, through a range, if loosely made, of definitions and understanding which perhaps started with Sir John Radcliffe Maud's famous description in 1951 of a service offering 'individual young people opportunity in their leisure time complementary to those opportunities at home, in formal education and at work'. The next definitive phrase of development was heralded by the Albemarle Report[2] of the early 1960s which established social education as the purpose for the Service, transforming the welfare service into one of progression and responsiveness. Already, however, even this new Youth Service role was beginning to be eroded. The raising of the school-leaving age and the increase in the numbers of young people staying on in further education brought with it the inclusion of social-education programmes within the formal curriculum. And with the gradual increase in youth unemployment and establishment of programmes specifically designed to assist in the transitions from school to work, one major Youth Service client group began to find its needs answered elsewhere. The Albemarle Report, however, had established the National College for the professional training of youth workers and this, in some senses, set the scene for the development of the Service for the next thirty years. Indeed, many of its first trainees, born in the era of non-directiveness, entered and remain in officer and training posts thirty years later. As well as training programmes for professional leaders, the Albemarle Report also brought about a massive building programme, but the design of most centres was almost outdated by the time the mortar was dry. It also placed a useful emphasis on the need for partnership between the newly emerging and so-called statutory sector and the more long-standing voluntary organizations, and nine years later the Milson Fairbairn Report paved the way for even greater developments of this sort, even though its recommendations were never implemented at government level. This next report, *Youth and Community Work in the Seventies*,[3] introduced the notion of political education as an area in which youth work should be involved, and introduced community-based youth work as an appropriate context. It also advocated the increase of school-based provision in general and in some ways perhaps jeopardized the future of a continuing, separately organized Youth Service. There was no framework within which the Youth Service could grow or against which it could measure its potential and there was still no attempt to introduce any academic or intellectual rigour into training courses beginning to emerge in colleges and polytechnics. Instead, the Service continued to train just 30 per cent of its full-time work-force to be caring, supportive individuals, person-centred and non-directive, but unconfident and lacking in a secure base when called to account for itself. Some had already begun to foresee the end of a separate Youth Service. The range of 'new work' heralded by Albemarle and Milson Fairbairn had given rise to a range of different ways of describing different forms of work. Character building and welfare care had been overtaken by person-centred youth work and community-oriented perspectives. A new language was born for work with young people. Discussions around partnership defined the voluntary sector as different to the local-authority-maintained or so-called statutory sector. Workers were classified as full- or part-time workers. Locations tended to become important as if they defined the content or quality of the work undertaken. Youth work became described as detached or building-based and buildings known as either school sites or church or community halls, even young people were labelled as uniformed or non-uniformed. One major youth-club organization prided itself on being the largest non-uniformed voluntary organization in the Youth Service. Distinctive categories of youth work were described but few embraced any clear definition or explanation of what was actually going on under that heading.

A COMMON THREAD

The publication of Butters and Newell's *Realities of Training*[4] in the late 1970s had tried to draw a thread through many of these categories. It offered instead a new way at looking at, or mapping out, just what youth work had to offer. Butters and Newell suggested that there were three main approaches taken in youth work. The first they saw as one of *character building* – the aim being to integrate young people into society and so produce 'mature citizens that emerge (and) find a way to make the institutions of the country run smoothly'.

The second they described as embracing *a social-education repertoire* – or youth work which aimed to move young people through cultural adjustment (symbolized, they argued, by Albemarle[5]) and through an involvement in decision making in the community (or the community development proposed by Milson Fairbairn[6]) to an ability to work for structural change and institutional reform.

They described their third approach as *self-emancipation* – undoubtedly to describe if not to encourage the more radical elements in service to engage young people in a struggle to overthrow dominant ideologies by, as Tony Taylor[7] argues, 'entering (its) corridors from outside, armed with revolutionary socialist theory'. Exciting stuff, but as ever, the rhetoric way far from the practice.

Overall, Butters and Newell felt that the Service needed to describe more aptly what it was about. They saw the Service to be offering a wide range of programmes and activities and a description of the Service was born of a 'heterogeneous hundred ring circus'. This analogy has indeed seemed an accurate one since the performances in many of the rings have not only been undertaken by a variety of performers but also by those whose purposes and aims have sometimes seemed to be so different or at least so unclear as to appear to work either in opposite directions or at least in rings around each other.

A SEARCH FOR CLARITY

During the 1970s, however, a number of attempts were made, not only to clarify the objectives of the Youth Service but also to specify the range of services which should be laid down in legislation in order to commit LEAs to a common purpose in providing Youth Services able to deliver political and social education for young people which might include the development of social and personal relationships and the encouragement of greater participation in the community.[8]

All attempts at legislation failed but government did respond to the increased political energy of the Youth Service by establishing a Review Group on Youth Service in England under Alan Thompson. The Review Group agreed with Butters and Newell and indeed linked what they described as 'a lack of cohesion and sense of direction in the Service, as preventing the resources available from being used to the greatest advantage'.

The Review Group, the Thompson Committee, was established to review the Youth Service and to compile a report. The result was the publication in 1982 of *Experience and Participation*,[9] which probably initiated the greatest degree of organization and policy thinking (despite inevitable reductions in resources) that the Service had known until recently. The Thompson Report was both challenging and wide-ranging but it will probably be best remembered for its impact at local-authority level in acting as a catalyst for processes of review and reassessment. Douglas Smith documented the results of these reviews, focusing his more substantial work, *Taking Shape*,[10] on a survey asking about policies and priorities in three different areas: organization and delivery, curriculum issues, and priority groups for young people. By far the greatest concerns identified in terms of organization and delivery were training, staff development, and partnership with the voluntary sector – the gap in grounded theory for the development of practice and the need to mend the split caused by the separate categorization of voluntary from statutory sectors clearly being a concern.

In terms of curriculum issues the participation of young people achieved the highest rating, with antisexist and antiracist work following closely behind. What was interesting, however, was the fact that despite the high numbers of authorities claiming these issues as a priority, only half of those making this bold declaration had developed policies, and from a reading of Her Majesty's Inspector's (HMI) reports still fewer had actually addressed the issues in practice. None the less, the importance attached to equality of opportunity and access identified in the Thompson Report appeared to have generated a response, if only in the aspirations of the policy setters.

A particular example of just how far away policy and practice can be in the Youth Service was demonstrated by Youth Clubs UK (once the National Association of Youth Clubs).

At the same time as 80 per cent of the national survey returns to the National Youth Bureau showed that girls and young women were a priority target for the work of the Service, the National Association of Youth Clubs (NAYC) was busy cutting off at a stroke the National Girls Work Unit which had grown from weekend conferences for young women to the appointment of a girls worker, the development of a specialist team, and the establishment of a regular newsletter all in the decade spanning the Thompson Review.

A PERIOD OF REVIEW

In terms of priority groups, the Service was again facing the question of whether it provided a service for all young people, or a more specialist service for those it saw to be in greatest need.

In the post-Thompson reviews that took place locally a number of trends were evident: for example, the targeting of provision for the upper-end of the age range – a reverse position of the under-14s movement of the 1970s, but brought about by the availability of money for programmes addressing the needs of the young unemployed of the early 1980s. The influence of the then Manpower Services Commission (MSC) on Youth Service provision was enormous in some areas, with Department of Employment funding temporarily underpinning major areas of development and then having a catastrophic effect when withdrawn. During this period some Youth Service authorities became managing agents of youth training programmes and youth workers got involved in a variety of aspects of pastoral care or personal-effectiveness training. Work with other priority groups too was identified as important, awareness being raised by Thompson, by the Department of Education and Science memoranda on Grants to National Voluntary Youth Organizations (NVYOs), and by consequent HMI reports on the differentiated needs of young women, gay and lesbian young people, young people in inner-city areas, and the disabled. Policies around partnership were also addressed as a result of *Experience and Participation*.[11] The report had reaffirmed the partnership principle in the Youth Service by identifying an urgent need for better collaborative co-operation at local level and recommended joint committees to which power should be delegated. But as the Coopers Lybrand Deloitte Study[12] found in 1990, there is evidence only of very weak representative structures at local level and little acknowledgement of the growing independent sector despite an estimation of it providing a similar amount of work in innovative settings and with priority groups.[13]

All the reviews taking place did so during a period in which local authorities were beginning to feel even greater pressure to be seen to be providing value for money. Cut-backs in the late 1970s and early 1980s had been made in haste in both voluntary-sector work and in LEAs, and speed had often meant little time for coherence or planned decision making.

A central problem remained for the Service. There was still a reluctance to prioritize. In the post-Thompson reviews priority areas of work were identified but ranking order was found difficult and attaching any resource allocation even more problematic. Reviews resulted in the reshaping of some services and sharpened the need for clearer definitions of youth work and what it uniquely offers to young people. Much attention was given, once again, to Youth Service buildings to encourage their greater use by young people. Some of the old post-Albemarle stock was refurbished and other forms of site adapted to meet what were seen to be the more urgent areas of need. The establishment of sites for other areas of development – the growth of high street advice and information shops for young people is a good example. The concern about empty buildings was also answered by a deliberate policy to expand detached and outreach work, particularly in areas where existing facilities were inappropriate but also in response to what appeared to be a more crisis-focused arm of the Service and development work with those deemed to have been put at risk by society. In some areas this included a major change in the pattern of Youth Service work with daytime youth work expanding to deal with the increasing demands of young people who were unemployed.

Thompson had identified a number of gaps in provision. In particular he mentioned work with young women, ethnic minorities, the handicapped, the unemployed, and the alienated. Thus labelled and specially funded, over time these groups have become marginalized and extremely vulnerable to local political change. Thompson had not succeeded in describing or encouraging a holistic approach to young people and their needs and so, except in particular and largely poorly funded projects, the experiences of unemployed Black young women, for example, were rarely addressed.

But his report had set down new patterns for the Service and its recommendations had also established a Youth Service Unit at the Department of Education and Science, the appointment of a National Advisory Council for the Youth Service (NACYS), a review of the National Youth Bureau, and the establishment of a Council for Education and Training in Youth and Community Work to undertake accreditation and endorsement of training. Even so the greatest difficulty facing the Service still remained, and despite prolific reports from working parties of NACYS including one entitled 'Directions for the Youth Service',[14] no clear unambiguous basis for the Service emerged.

TOWARDS MEASURABLE OUTCOMES

The greatest difficulty facing the local-authority and voluntary sector alike was the identification of measurable outcomes. A real reluctance was fed by a fear of centralized policy and outcome-linked resources and this led to a build-up of tension before the first Ministerial Conference on a core curriculum for the seminar in December 1989.

By the end of the 1980s, however, the position of the Youth Service had significantly changed. The climate was one of much stricter financial control and there was pressure for the Service to reduce its claims on the public purse.

The Youth Service was asked to be more accountable for the monies it received and to voice more clearly, and with one voice, its aims, objectives, and purposes, and to outline the indicators of its success.

A STATE POLICY

There was little doubt that increased direction of policy for the Youth Service by central government had been a feature of the previous ten years. If policy defines the limits within which practice can take place, then it is important to see where and why that policy is constructed. Government's direct influence on the local-authority Youth Service has been explicit in the setting of national priorities for training and through particular funding policies, as well as by implication in the reorganization of educational management. And yet the Service is still vulnerable, having no real statutory base. Consequent on the reforms of 1988, a number of local authorities had experienced severe cut-backs as a result of central government's intervention in local-authority affairs. Government had also been explicit in its policy-making role in quasi-governmental organizations and non-departmental public bodies and, indeed, though less explicitly, through its clearer definition of funding, the central role of government policy can be very clearly seen.

Mark Smith[15] argues that as a result of this and in terms of governmental objectives, Youth Service delivery looks distinctly hit or miss as compared with services for young people which are increasingly being developed with substantial legal frameworks and within which young people are compelled to undertake activities. He cites Intermediate Treatment (IT) and the Youth Training Scheme (YTS) as two examples and suggests that perhaps the Youth Service did not deliver what was promised for it – at least not that part of Albemarle's vision which had to do with the containment and control of troublesome youth. If this argument is followed through it might be argued that if the Youth Service had allowed itself to address what might be described as state-sponsored policies, then it could have had a more influential role in provision for young people – for example, in IT. Originally, IT was envisaged as being very closely linked to existing youth provision, but in reality its involvement has been patchy to say the least.[16] Its location originated in the 1969 Children and Young Persons Act[17] and its recent development has been as a fully fledged alternative to custody orders. Although some Youth Services have found it possible to work within, for example, new multi-agency juvenile justice liaison bureaux, most were wary of being drawn into non-voluntary relationships with young people labelled at risk and so be seen to ally themselves with a state policy of surveillance or control. Thompson had made it clear that the Youth Service was not about this form of policing. It is, however, a clear example of central government policy going in one direction and the lack of clearly defined policy for the Youth Service leaving it outside fairly major developments for young people. It will be interesting to see if any clearer role with young people at risk emerges for the Service following the recommendations of the Children Act 1989, for instance, where there are obvious roles for the Youth Service in, for example, work and educational supervision orders. None the less, a state policy is emerging for the Youth Service and if, as Bernard Davies[18] argues strongly, state policies are those implemented by governmental agencies local and national, or by those whose content is determined often by hidden processes involving professional advisers, then very little of the Service as we know it can stay outside. Indeed, if Bernard Davies is right then most of the Youth Service, 'statutory' or voluntary, local or national, needs to acknowledge the sanctioning role of its activities by central government and we should not, according to Bernard Davies, identify Government simply with the party in power at the time. It is this fact above all others which all sectors in the Youth Service have in common in the partnership which makes up the Service. But it is a fact which the voluntary sector has only recently really realized and begun to come to terms with. Increasingly, central government policies are linked directly to funding initiatives and in the Youth Service this has been explicit in the setting of Education Support Grants, national priorities for training for LEAs, and programme funding for the national voluntary sector. More particularly, and more recently, the single channel of funds to one national Youth Service body unequivocally declares that what central government will pay for is that policy and 'action' not only with which it can agree, but which it actually helped to set, and set according to a different set of goals than other parts of the education service.

MINISTERIAL INTERVENTION

When Alan Howarth, the Parliamentary Under Secretary of State for Education, asked the Service at his first Ministerial Conference in December 1989 to produce a statement which clarified the core of what the Youth Service is uniquely best placed to provide, he was probably unprepared either for the degree of unanimity or for the clearly stated intent of the Service to stand up and be counted as a force for equal opportunities and a challenge to oppression. Indeed, his response to strong recommendations of this nature at his second conference in 1990 showed how clearly oppression was not a notion he was prepared to acknowledge.

So where had this radical policy come from? The Service had moved from a position where a list of special-needs groups was identified to a commonly agreed position on equal opportunities addressing and encompassing everyone, but particularly benefiting those most disadvantaged by institutional oppression. Butters and Newell had indicated this possibility though in some ways posed it as threatening and as radical and revolutionary. The Thompson Report had issued a challenge to both central and local government to reassess the existing forms and structures of the Youth Service, and against a backdrop of concern about the worsening position and future of young people, the majority of local authorities reviewed their services during the space of the next five or so years, prioritizing antisexist and antiracist work. Content and comment in HMI reports also considerably influenced policy directions in both the voluntary and statutory sector's work, as did selected examples of radical practice published in their booklets 'Effective youth work'[19] and 'Responsive youth work'.[20]

But Thompson had said that a consistent understanding of youth works' purpose as social and political education was not easy to achieve. He had exemplified a major dilemma: 'While to some young people', he said 'the Service may appear simply as a means of pleasurably extending their experience, to others it may be a real rescue service.' He challenged the Service to examine its client groups and implicitly accused it of 'confused and reactionary attitudes' to some young people, and this debate continued throughout consultations for both Ministerial Conferences.

The purpose of the first of these Conferences was to build on the work of the National Advisory Council for the Youth Service and to provide a forum to identify common ground in terms of purpose and action with the Youth Service.

In the consultation period that followed, despite some general concern about the time-scale of the process and the language of the documentation, the responses called overwhelmingly for a statement of purpose for the Service which addressed equality of opportunity for young people offering opportunities which are educative, participative, and empowering, and which challenge oppression. The policy which was emerging from a tightening of the reins seemed to be more radical and dynamic than had ever existed in what had previously been described as the strength of the Service – its variety and so-called freedom. Could a consequence of an emerging core curriculum for the Youth Service mean, even in times of great financial stringency, that the best might yet be saved?

As part of the consultative process a definition of youth work had also emerged as 'informal opportunities offered to young people through the transition of childhood to adulthood to encourage and support their personal and social development and progression'. The Youth Service was described and defined as the collection of institutional arrangements for the delivery of youth work in voluntary, statutory, and independent sectors, those being part of it being those engaged in youth work.

THE SERVICE RECOMMENDS

The second Ministerial Conference on the Core Curriculum in November 1990 agreed that national outcomes should be set, but only after two days of heated and awkward debate largely to do with the terminology proposed in an amended Statement of Purpose drafted as a result of national consultations.

Suddenly frightened by monitoring and evaluating how the Youth Service could redress all forms of inequality, the Service 'wobbled'. The Statement of Purpose recommended stated that

> The purpose of youth work is to redress all forms of inequality, to ensure equality of opportunity for all young people to fulfil their potential as empowered individuals and members of groups and communities; and to support young people during the transition to adulthood.

The Minister too found the language difficult and in his response to the five recommendations agreed by the Conference suggested that not everyone (would) be at ease with some of the language, particularly some of the more politically charged terms. He said that the relationship of the Youth Service to politics needed the most careful consideration. But he went on, 'This does not mean to say that you the workers should not fight, on behalf of young people, for what they believe to be right.'

The Minister had signalled in his first conference that he was not interested in finding a universal service. He had asked whether the Service should concentrate on 'those who are failed by other services and systems, who are prevented in some way from benefiting from them or who simply can't afford them', and the Service in large part agreed. The Service recommended that its main purpose be to redress the balance and to promote equality of opportunity through the challenging of oppressions such as racism and sexism.

Perhaps that was not quite what he meant but the emerging documentation gave even those authorities or organizations sceptical of all things national something to hang on to and use in their own arguments to try to save the resource base of the Service as local-state control continued to collapse with the diminution of the number of functions managed by local authorities and a reduction in resources as a result of the switch from rate to revenue support. Whether this will be strong enough in the light of current government policy remains to be seen, particularly following the Minister's obvious disagreement with the field. Discussions about the future control of education could, of course, mean that a centralized grant-giving structure with costed programmes submitted to local or regional co-ordinating bodies is not too far away. But to whose

Statement of Purpose and to which target groups and outcomes would any performance indicators be linked? What role the newly established National Youth Agency will be allowed to play remains to be seen. The Agency has been established on the basis of the work currently undertaken by the four National Youth Service bodies and its role and function clearly laid down by its main funder, the DES, as working within government policy and areas of development. What is clear is that although the Youth Service and, indeed, the educational world are somewhat different from the times when the first circular announced its service to youth, the time is surely ripe for it to hold itself accountable for its own main title and purpose – and at least try to withstand the competition with other providers in the market-place of social education. As an integrated service it could, as some have argued, disappear. But perhaps it has never been integrated anyway – and at least more functional definitions of the work it represents will have a chance to continue.

It is interesting to compare a European view of youth work described by Stephan Betsky in a paper for the European Communities[21] as a field of social education, its primary objective the cultivation and improvement of the desire and capacity for cultural, social, and political participation in democratic life.

Certainly philosophies across Europe are similar and any different expression probably reflects the different Youth Service structures in other member states where youth organizations and associations are primarily voluntary bodies based on the self-determination of members between the ages of 15 and 26. The voluntary youth movement in the UK, on the other hand, tends to involve children and young people from a much lower age range and have less of a political context, a feature which emerged in the continuing consultations on the core curriculum for the Service in England and, indeed, during debate at the second conference in November 1990. A particular difficulty was in achieving an agreement on age range, not only because the memberships of voluntary organizations and associations are predominantly under 15, but also because local-authority funding both for its own youth services and as grant aid to the voluntary sector rarely funds work with those under 14. In many senses, then, it is perhaps the local-authority sector of the Youth Service in the UK which aligns itself more closely with voluntary youth organizations in other member states, at least in terms of local delivery. Most EC countries, however, have important national superstructures with clear roles and relationships with their governments. Many of these include a representative role acting as a lobby and a political pressure group on behalf of young people.

In the UK, however, the amalgamation of the National Youth Service bodies in one high-profile agency, the National Youth Agency, has left out the young people's pressure group and lobby element – the British Youth Council, and separated this role and the representation of young people internationally from the main services identified as needed by a national body.

In terms of future policy, at least in England, the NYA is charged with many functions, including carrying out such government policy as is appropriate. This is perhaps the nearest the UK will get to the Youth Service bodies being regarded as partners on youth-related matters, although interestingly some particular programmes of youth information and the development of European youth cards in the UK are beginning to bring government departments together around their common interest in youth.

What is more important is the continuity of youth work and effective youth-work practice. Of course it will be possible as the Minister suggests to interpret even a radical statement of purpose agreed by the second conference in many ways. And for the voluntary sector that flexibility will be particularly important. It might also be the key to the influence of youth-work practice in other areas of education and welfare services. And what of leisure services? Centrally the establishment of the Ministry for Sport in the Department of Education and Science will open up fresh thinking on the role of sport in youth work and youth work in sport. And what are the implications of a joint ministerial portfolio for the Youth Service and sport? Will Robert Atkins's appointment herald a closer operational relationship between leisure departments and informal education provision and perhaps jeopardize, if not reverse, the clear advance made by his predecessor, Alan Howarth, to see the Youth Service as primarily educational?

It will be interesting to take part in the struggle ahead and to develop what we know to be good and unique about youth work. But against all these changes it will likely need some of that early energy pragmatism and voluntary effort that gave birth to the Service in the first place.

It must be timely to capitalize on the development of a core curriculum for the Service and even the possibility of a core curriculum for training. A unified structure could lead to possible degree status with a variety of access points, modular organization, and credit accumulation, all in the context of educational reform, and it may be more appropriate in the future to look at the development of youth work in terms of services to young people contracted by local authorities in a variety of ways including provision by voluntary bodies. Resource allocation is now more likely than ever to include the possibility of formula funding applied to individual youth clubs or youth projects as ideas of local management take hold and are encouraged. Formula funding might, however, be applied at area level or, indeed, a contract for whole service delivery as a direct service organization or an independent Youth Service plc established.

Some resource and management delegation to geographical areas within the Youth Service is already not uncommon and devolved and targeted funding is already well developed in some areas. Some schools and colleges have always made provision for youth work and recently the Government has encouraged the role of youth work working with disruptive pupils and students or adding to developments in personal, social, and health education.

The Education Reform Act has, however, created uncertainty for separately funded school-based provision where, as a rentable resource with local management, the premises might become too expensive for the local youth group. Given the growing need for youth-work support in schools and in the post-16 sector, it is likely that under local management of schools individual schools could begin to budget for youth work and become significant employers of youth workers. Some FE colleges are also entering this area with youth workers assisting with the delivery of student services, the pastoral curriculum and with personal and social educational aspects of the identifiable core skills. The impact of the recent White Paper,[22] however, and the removal of funding control for FE from the local authorities might diminish this area of work. Given the lack of any statutory base, monies for the Youth Service are now more vulnerable than ever. Evidence of late 1990 budgeting is already indicating disastrous effects in some particular areas. It is likely that the Youth Service of the future will have to compete for funds with other employers of youth workers – schools, FE colleges, welfare organizations in the voluntary sector, even employers organizing youth training.

Everywhere quality assurance is being sought, no less in education where the role of monitoring and evaluation is particularly being felt in school and college sectors. Output indicators have become more important than input indicators as measures of quality and through the consultations on the core curriculum the Youth Service is struggling with this particular change perhaps more than any other. The Youth Service has always found it difficult to demonstrate its achievements in a way that those outside the Service can understand. The fear of central control and appraisal needs to be addressed and the field needs, once again, to be reassured of its own control over delivery locally and the need, therefore, for evaluation to be rigorous but none the less locally based. Performance indicators need to be seen as supportive tools in evaluating work for those involved in the delivery, providing information about the work to those involved and to those who may become involved. Most particularly in this contract culture Youth Service needs to be able to describe and demonstrate its effectiveness to those, frequently with little or no Youth Service background, who might be deciding which tenders to accept for the delivery of informal social education opportunities for young people within whatever new local authority boundaries are drawn. The question remains to be asked – who, locally, will decide which Youth Service provision will be funded, and will the Youth Service manage to hold on to its radicalism on behalf of young people? Of course, it is likely that even seemingly radical statements about the purpose of youth work can be twisted to fit government policy whatever its colour. But it was ever thus.

NOTES

1 T. Taylor, in T. Jeffs and M. Smith (eds) *Youth Work* (Macmillan, 1987).
2 *The Youth Service in England and Wales* (London: HMSO, 1960).
3 Milson Fairbairn, *Youth and Community Work in the Seventies: proposals by the Youth Service Development Council* (London: HMSO, 1969).
4 S. Butters and S. Newell, *Realities of Training. A Review of the Training of Adults Who Volunteered to Work with Young People in the Youth and Community Service* (National Youth Bureau, 1978).
5 Albemarle, op. cit. (note 2).
6 Fairbairn, op. cit. (note 3).
7 Op. cit. (note 1).
8 Youth and Community Bill, Trevor Skeet MP 1979/80, Clause 2(2) a.
9 *Experience and Participation: Report of the Review Group on the Youth Service in England* (London: HMSO, 1982).
10 *Taking Shape: Developments in Youth Service Policy and Provision* (National Youth Bureau, 1989).
11 *Report of the Review Group on the Youth Service in England* (London: HMSO, 1982).
12 Coopers Lybrand Deloitte, *Management of the Youth Service in the 1990s* (May 1991).
13 *A Thousand Links: Youth Activity in Croydon*, Report of an action research project (Croydon Guild of Voluntary Organizations, 1986).
14 'Directions for the Youth Service: a position paper' (1989).
15 Mark Smith, Developing Youth Work: Informal Education, Mutual Aid and Popular Practice (Milton Keynes: Open University, 1988).
16 Alison Skinner, *Intermediate Treatment and the Youth Service* (National Youth Bureau, July 1989).
17 The Children and Young Persons Act (London: HMSO, 1969).
18 Bernard Davies, *Restructuring Youth Policies in Britain: The State We're in* (National Youth Bureau, 1981).
19 London: HMSO, 1988.
20 London: HMSO, 1990.
21 Stephan Betsky, 1990 paper to DG5 Commission of the European Communities.
22 *Education and Training for the 21st Century* (London: HMSO, May 1991).

7 Health matters

Sylvia Tilford

INTRODUCTION

Over the last fifteen years a number of documents (DHSS 1976; WHO 1977, 1989) have posed the view that adolescents have health needs sufficiently different from children and adults to warrant special consideration for health-care provision. Such provision is said to be made only rarely in most countries. One concern of this chapter will be the policy of the health-care sector in the UK as it relates to young people. Health matters, however, are not only a concern of the health-care system. Most policy sectors have the potential to contribute, directly or indirectly, to the health of youth – education, employment, housing, and leisure being specific examples. This potential may be further enhanced if we adopt conceptions of health that define it as multidimensional – mental, physical, and social – and as a state of positive well-being, rather than merely the absence of disease. The determinants of health are multiple and can be categorized as in Figure 7.1. The relative impact of the specific factors varies according to time and place, is difficult to assess and is open to debate. A popular view, for example, tends to equate health with the consumption of health services but McKeown (1976) and others have demonstrated persuasively that the major declines in mortality which occurred from the latter part of the nineteenth century in industrialized countries owed little to the medical services and much to improvements in the nutritional status of the population and to public-health measures. By contrast, in the mid-1970s, individual health-related behaviours came to be heavily targeted in the effort to reduce the contemporary causes of ill-health. 'Health'-related policies may be oriented separately, or in combination with the various determinants of health: to services which prevent ill-health and treat sickness, to specific health-related behaviours of individuals, or to various features of the environment which have a bearing on health. For example, in response to mortality and morbidity associated with road accidents, we may have national laws on the wearing of seat-belts, health education directed towards the wearing of seat-belts and safe driving, and hospital services to treat accident patients and promote rehabilitation.

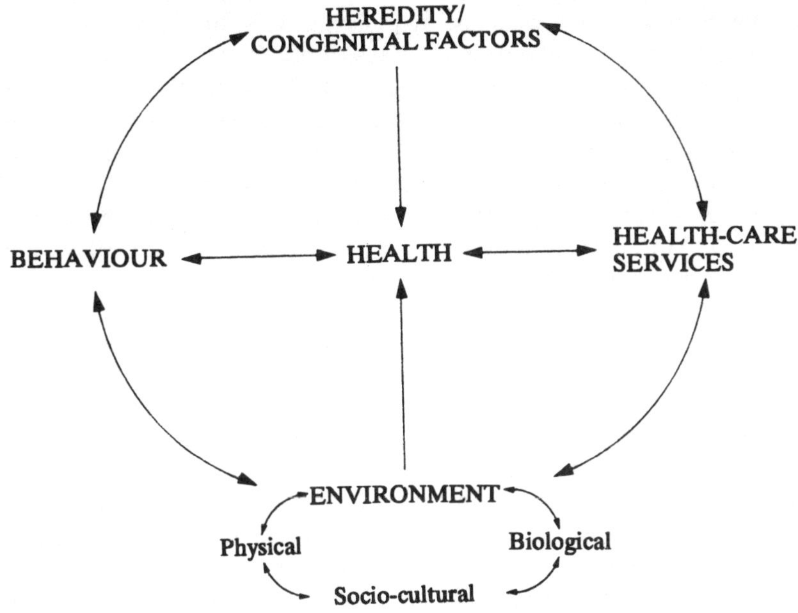

Figure 7.1 Determinants of health

The 1980s have seen the development of the health-promotion movement, characterized by renewed attention to the contribution of public-policy measures to community health and a call for a new public-health initiative paralleling that of the nineteenth century. Advocates of health promotion have considered the contribution of individual policy sectors to health but also emphasized the need for intersectoral collaboration if strategies were to be successful. Despite the rhetoric and some progress in health promotion WHO (1989: 60) has recently commented:

> policies and legislation in the many different sectors that have an impact on young people's health – education, employment, social services, youth, culture and sport – as well as health care are rarely coordinated in such a way as to provide a systematic approach to young people's health.

Space precludes a detailed discussion of all policy sectors that have a bearing on youth health and this chapter will therefore concentrate mainly on the health-care and education sectors.

Epidemiology of youth health

One stimulus to policy development is a specification of need, and the special health needs of youth were referred to above. Such needs may be defined by health professionals, by policy makers, or by the people to whom future policy is to be directed. Health needs can be derived from knowledge of mortality, morbidity, use of health services, and positive health indicators. Both objective and subjective measures may be drawn upon. Common practice is to use routinely collected health statistics and survey data augmented by a variety of other available data. There are shortcomings in providing complete pictures of the health of defined populations. Morbidity, for example, is incompletely documented, and measures of negative health are more common than positive ones. When we come to assess the health of a segment of the population it is possible that not all routine sources employ it as a regular category in data collection. Where youth is concerned countries differ in the age range to be attached to this term and variously collect data related to it. The World Health Organization (WHO) (1989), for example, defines adolescence as 10 to 19 and youth as 15 to 24, while the Health Promotion Authority for Wales (1990) lists 19 as the cut-off point for its youth programme. In some UK data sources youth is not a separate category and data on health is contained within the child and/or adult categories. Drawing on routine statistics a brief summary of youth health can be offered. Demographically, youth forms a significant and increasing percentage of the world's population. Between 1960 and 1980 total world population increased by 46 per cent, that of young people between 15 and 24 by 60 per cent (WHO 1989). Four out of five of these young people live in developing countries. In health terms, if overall mortality alone is examined, youth is a relatively healthy stage in the life-span – the lowest all-causes age-specific rates in the UK being in the 15 to 24 year age group. In countries where infectious diseases still constitute a major problem these are significant causes of death for young people. Elsewhere the major causes of death are commonly accidents (largely associated with the use of motor vehicles), suicide, and neoplasms. Figures for leading causes of death for the UK, and differences between young men and women, are shown in Table 7.1. It should be noted that accident rates for young men are the highest in any age group under 85. Suicide rates, while clearly a matter for concern world-wide and believed to be rising in this age group, are lower in the UK than in many other European countries. However, comparisons do have to be made with care because of variations in practice in categorization of a death as suicide. World-wide there is concern with deaths associated with pregnancy and childbirth – elevated risk levels between 20 and 200 per cent are recorded, with the 15 to 17 year olds at especial risk (Friedman 1989).

While preventable mortality has to be one concern of policy makers, it is morbidity, in ill-health terms, which is the commoner event in young people. Figures from a recent survey illustrate the common picture of morbidity in youth (Table 7.2). It can be seen from the table that symptoms

Table 7.1 Leading causes of death, 15–24 years, England and Wales (OPCS 1989)

	Death rates per million population			
	Males		*Females*	
	15–24	*All ages, E & W*	*15–24*	*All ages, E & W*
Motor Accidents	303	149	76	59
Suicide	87	116	20	48
Neoplasms	70	2,926	50	2,560
Diseases of the Nervous System	42	210	18	210
Circulatory	31	5,332	21	5,194

relate equally to physical and mental health. Young people are regular users of general practitioner (GP) services. World-wide there are estimated to be 500 million people with defined disabilities, of whom about half are under 25. It is further estimated that 70 per cent of all disabled people do not receive the care that they need (Paxman and Zuckerman 1987).

In the 1980s two issues pertinent to youth health were widely debated in the UK – unemployment and social inequalities. In 1980 a well-designed study (Stafford *et al.*) clearly demonstrated in a cohort of school-leavers the negative consequences of unemployment for mental health, and its impact on other aspects of health has also been demonstrated. It is ten years since the Black Report (Townsend and Davison 1982) reawakened public interest in health inequalities. It has been generally assumed that such inequalities apply to all stages of the life-span although it has been difficult to comment on youth from a class perspective because of the paucity of information in

Table 7.2 Percentage reporting symptoms/illness in past 12 months, by sex

	Age 15 years		
	M	*F*	
Colds/flu/throat infections	75.8	84.5	
Headaches/migraine	41.1	54.4	
Sickness/diarrhoea	28.0	34.6	
Allergies	25.5	23.2	
Skin conditions	24.9	23.0	
Weight conditions	7.1	17.9	
Nerves/depression	7.1	14.9	
Sleep problems	10.0	11.3	
Faints	10.6	10.6	
Asthma	8.9	5.7	
Dysmenorrhoea	–	45.6	
Mean Symptoms	2.6	3.4	N = 1,009

Source: West *et al.* 1990

the published data generally used in making comparisons. From a recent analysis of data collected for the Occupational Decennial Supplement and the General Household Survey, West (1988) has concluded that youth is characterized more by the absence than the presence of class variations in mortality and morbidity terms. The re-emergence of differences in young adults can be linked to the delayed impact of health-damaging behaviours for which there is strong evidence of class (and gender) differences in youth. In this same decade issues associated with disabilities received greater recognition if not appropriate responses.

When health concerns of youth are being discussed the emphasis is frequently on behaviours which are believed to have either immediate or long-term consequences for health. Typically identified are smoking, alcohol use, illegal drug use, sexual behaviours, eating behaviours, and road use. The levels of concern and associated policy responses are not necessarily closely correlated with the measurable health risks. Society's wishes to control those behaviours of young people which are defined as threatening can be more influential than the actual morbidity and mortality evidence in defining policy actions. The power of vested interests to influence the nature and levels of responses to behaviours with health consequences is also important. Reactions to sexual behaviours and illicit drug use are examples where social control has clearly been an important consideration; alcohol behaviours a case where policy responses have been relatively modest.

If health is defined as positive well-being measures of positive rather than negative health are of interest. Ongoing large surveys such as that provided by the Exeter Health Behaviour Questionnaire provide some useful information on positive features of young people's health. The strategy documents of the health education and promotion authorities in England and Wales (1989, 1990) also include a number of positive indicators by which the health of youth can be monitored. Finally, this chapter will argue that the participation of young people ought to be an element of the policy-making activities relating to their health. It should be noted that young people's own views of their health concerns do not entirely equate with those of adults (Balding 1987; Friedman 1989).

The following sections will consider the ways in which the health of youth has been a consideration for policy in education, health care, and related sectors, beginning with the period from the late nineteenth century.

HISTORICAL BACKGROUND

A pre-condition for youth-focused policy is a recognition of youth as a category and one which merits specific responses. As adolescence and/or youth emerged as a defined stage in the life-span, this development was not equally matched by policy-related responses. In some instances special health needs may have been recognized but any response was subsumed within either child or adult policy – in other instances, special needs have been unrecognized. Policies which have developed have built on varying mixes of prevailing conceptions of adolescence and youth. Within the health-care service, policy may be directed both to the prevention and to the cure of ill-health. In the UK health-care services developed along tripartite lines – hospitals, GP and local community services (including health services to schools). In the period leading up to the National Health Service Act in 1946 (since the 1911 National Insurance Act had not extended cover for GP services to the dependants of the insured), it was local-authority services which provided non-hospital care for the greater proportion of young people of school age. Within the education sector the school health services might be complemented by health education in the curriculum and by other features of the school such as school milk and meals. From the mid-nineteenth century onwards regulations concerning age and conditions of employment also had implications for the health of youth. The developments in the education and health-care sectors up to the late 1970s will be discussed separately.

Education system

By the end of the nineteenth century a mix of activities directed towards young people's health had started to develop. These included health inspections, school meals, treatment of minor ailments in clinics, and direct attention to health in the curriculum, mainly around the concept of hygiene. The development was characterized by local variation. At the turn of the century general concern over the health of recruits to the Boer War stimulated a number of interdepartmental committees, one consequence of which was the 1907 Education (Administration) Act. The Act affirmed the duty of all local authorities to inspect the health of schoolchildren and gave them the authority to attend to the health of all children in elementary schools (extended to secondary schools in 1918). A fuller range of school health services slowly emerged. To the extent that such activities made effective contributions to health they would have reached a proportion of young people. In 1921, for example, 90 per cent of 13–14 year olds, 30 per cent of 14–15, and 10 per cent of those between 15 and 16 were in full-time education (Report of the Committee on Child Services 1976).

The point at which youth, under the term 'adolescence', clearly formed the topic of an educational document was in 1927 with the publication of the Hadow Report. This report described the separate and distinct needs of education for children and education for adolescents. It was strongly imbued with child-centred progressive philosophy speaking as it did of placing youth 'in the hour of its growth in the fair meadow of a congenial and improving environment' (p. xxiii). However, it also had a clear eye towards education's role in fulfilling societal expectations when emphasizing the adequate training of youth for full and worthy citizenship. In emphasizing the importance of facilitating the all-round development of young people, the report had, in a general sense, a positive health orientation. It considered health more directly in discussing the subjects within the curriculum – science, housecraft (for girls), and physical education being singled out. There was a strong emphasis on hygiene and also on the particular health responsibilities of girls. Courses should be arranged, it said, to make girls realize that an ordered knowledge of health would increase the general well-being of themselves and every member of the household and they should also be shown that on the efficient care and management of the household depended the health, happiness, and prosperity of the nation. The report makes no reference to the constraints under which so many would have to carry out such responsibilities – graphically described in the book *Maternity: Lives of Working Women* (Llewellyn Davies 1915/1978).

In the same year as the Hadow Report the Central Council for Health Education was set up. Maintained by both the Ministry of Health and local authorities, it worked in co-operation with the Board of Education. This body, and its 1962 replacement, the Health Education Council (HEC), developed policy and gave active support to health education in schools. Beginning in 1928 the Board of Education (later the Ministry of Education, and then the Department of Education and Science) issued a series of guidelines for teachers on health education in the curriculum (Board of Education 1928: 34, 39; Ministry of Education 1956; Department of Education and Science 1968: 77). A strong moral thread ran through the earlier of these documents with their emphasis on the inculcation of health as an ideal and the development of individual responsibility. The 1934 edition devoted particular attention to adolescent pupils in response to the expansion of senior schools. While the documents pointed out that they were not offering prescriptive courses they did include discussion of key topics – both individual health and public health themes. In discussion of infant care, for example, the girls' responsibilities were again stressed:

> the object of educating children is to equip them for the duties and responsibilities of life and if a girl leaves school ignorant of one of the most important duties which may subsequently devolve upon her our system of education can hardly be said to have fulfilled its aim.
>
> (1934: 80)

The discussion of infant care in these early handbooks was not prefaced by any on sex education although the reasons for the omission are not discussed. The Board of Education did publish its 'Simple hints for youth group leaders' in 1928, which included a short section on sex and venereal disease. In 1923 a Commission on Youth and Race (Greaves 1965) urged Boards of Education to provide facilities in teacher training so that teachers would be adequately prepared to impart suitable sex education – although they did not specify such content. It was not until 1943 that the Board of Education provided the first official recognition that sex education was within the province of the teaching profession. Quite clearly official policy statements are only one source of information on possible practice in schools – where schools are relatively free to innovate, practice may have been ahead of policy. Since, however, many barriers to full sex education are still not overcome fifty years later, it is unlikely that schools in general were much ahead of either official thinking or much popular sentiment in this particular aspect of health education. In the later handbooks there was a reduced emphasis on hygiene and associated public-health measures but a new emphasis on emergent problems such as smoking and fuller discussion of the organization of health education in the curriculum. In the absence of detailed evaluations in the earlier period it is not easy to say how far the exhortations of policy makers translated into health education within the curriculum.

The National Child Development Study in 1974 (Fogelman 1976) provided some feedback on the sex-education element of health education. In the 12,010 sample 76 per cent recalled lessons on how babies are conceived, 74 per cent on how babies are born, 57 per cent on causes of VD, 32 per cent on the care of babies and 40 per cent on the practical problems of family life. Significant percentages wanted to know more about these areas. From the published report it is not clear whether these young people were asked about work on the emotional and personal aspects of sexual relationships – arguably a more immediate concern than the care of babies. As a subject, health education can be organized in various ways within the curriculum and may be relatively hidden where it is provided contextually within other subjects. The other features of the total school curriculum can also make contributions to health, sometimes complementary, at other times contradictory to health education in the formal curriculum (Figure 7.2). While some of the potentially health-promoting features of schools received attention in this early period many did not. From the 1960s there was major curriculum development activity in schools. Health education became the subject of such activities from the mid-1970s with the support of both the HEC and the Schools Council. This latter period, and the philosophical approaches which have informed school health education, will be discussed in a later section.

Health care

In the 1930s the number of school dentists and clinics increased and the school medical service enhanced both its treatment and preventive services. By 1935, for example, the provision of child-guidance clinics had been accepted as a legitimate addition to the services. Within the hospital sector while specialist child provision increased and the welfare of young children in hospital was addressed (Platt Committee 1959), there

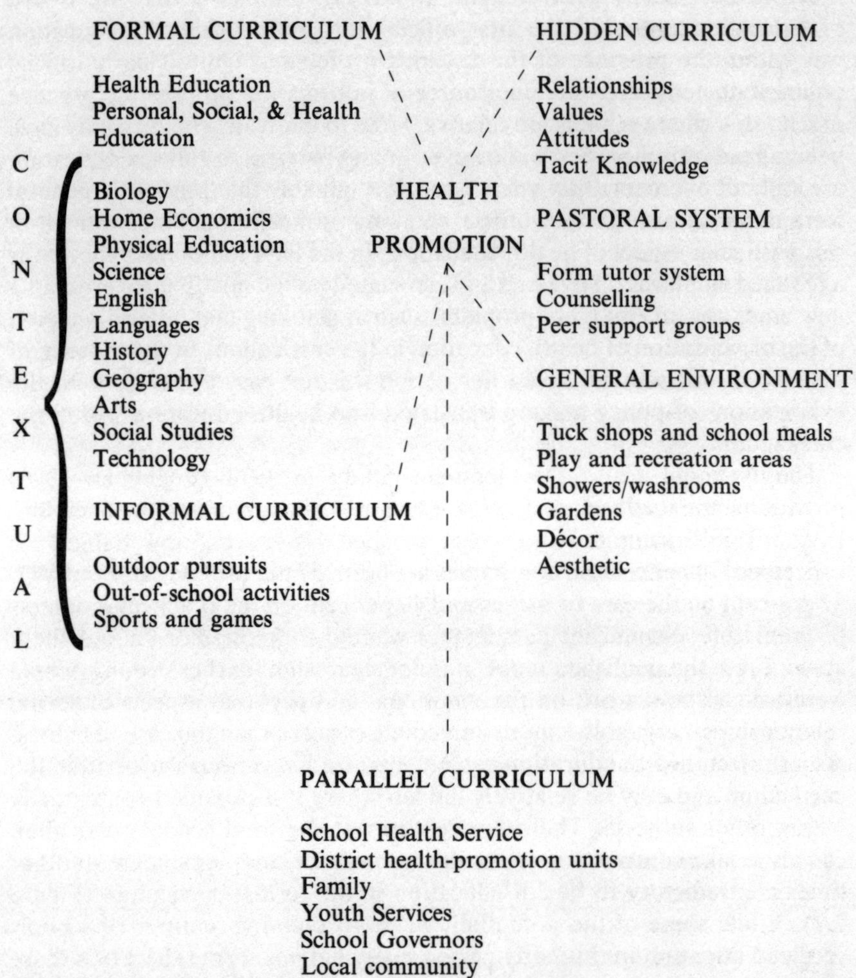

Figure 7.2 Health promotion in the school

was limited attention to adolescent needs outside psychiatry and a small number of specific conditions. The major policy documents of the 1940s – the NHS Act of 1946 and the National Education Act of 1944 – were both important for the health of youth. The latter said that local authorities were obliged to provide comprehensive facilities for free medical treatment for pupils in maintained schools, and parents were obliged to submit children for medical inspection. Local authorities were to provide school meals and milk, and clinics were to provide a range of free medical services. The main aim of the later NHS Act was to provide for free health services for all at time of use. Young people, especially those leaving school at 15, had, for the first time, universal free access to GP services.

In the period before 1980 the major policy document in the UK for the subject of youth health was *Fit for the Future*, commonly known as the Court Report (Report of the Committee on Child Services 1976). This provided a review of current child health services and offered comprehensive proposals for their future direction. It gave special consideration to the health concerns of 'adolescents'. A welcome element in the evidence drawn on by the committee was the results of a small-scale survey of 5th- and 6th-formers in nine secondary schools. This survey reported the view of young people that medical personnel did not communicate effectively and did not have time to discuss health and personal problems in the required depth. A large proportion of the sample favoured doctors holding clinics to which they could go for personal health advice and counselling and there was a general call for information on health-care services. The report argued that at both primary and supporting care levels, adolescents had needs unique to themselves for which improved services should be provided. It recommended the integration of child health services, based on primary care, and linked to supportive consultant and hospital care and the creation of specialist practitioners. At the hospital level it called for better facilities for adolescents in acute hospitals. In considering community services the need for independent access by all young people was recognized – in particular it looked at the needs for counselling provision and the requirements it should meet:

> the main need is for counselling services which take account of the adolescent's desire to do his own thing and which are based in a variety of settings which he will find acceptable and be prepared to use. If they are to be successful they will need to recognise that for some young people sex is an activity undertaken in its own right, and not in the context of family life or parenthood.
>
> (p. 168)

The contribution of voluntary groups, such as Grapevine, in this context was acknowledged. The Report also emphasized that handicapped young people should be able and encouraged to seek help and guidance on their own initiative and should themselves have direct access to the professionals involved in their treatment. In the event of psychiatric disorders, collaboration should be between child/adolescent psychiatrists and 'adult' colleagues. Finally, the report provided consideration of education for health in schools, referring to the potential role of health professionals and health education in the curriculum. It showed itself as sensitive both to the complexities of health education in the classroom and to the needs for collaboration: 'there was a need for doctors and nurses training to give greater understanding of the aims of education and the experience of teachers and of the role of social workers and to pay more attention to interprofessional collaboration' (p. 160). It should be noted that the direct role of health workers in classroom health-education activities has been much debated and the consensus view is that their most appropriate role is as a support to the professional teacher.

Conclusion

By the mid-1970s, therefore, the notion of specialist health needs of youth had been clearly enunciated in a major health-sector policy document, although, as might be expected in a health-service-oriented document, there was an emphasis on 'problems' as defined by adults and experts. None the less, the document had also acknowledged an emerging right to some autonomy in using services and some young people's views had been sought although the brief survey had nothing to offer on ethnic responses to health services. The report as a whole was generally silent on ethnicity and the health service, and as the quotation below shows, prone to sexist use of language. Within the education sector the handbooks on health education in the curriculum, other educational reports, and curriculum development activities had led to a gradual development of health education in secondary schools. The nature and extent of this provision varied between schools within any one authority and also between authorities. However, in general, it remained a low-status subject and both girls and lower-ability pupils were more likely to experience it than boys and higher-ability pupils. The school health service had made a contribution to the monitoring of health and provided some forms of treatment. These services were transferred to the area health authorities after the NHS reorganization of 1974. The Court Report assessed current problems with the school health services, noting in particular that 'the services have attempted to serve the interests of the adolescent indirectly through advice to parents and teachers but rarely to meet his needs as he himself experiences them'.

THE LAST TEN YEARS

Dominated as it was by the ideology of Thatcherism, this period had major significance for all policy sectors – not least those in the welfare area. Efforts to cut welfare expenditure affected some areas more strongly than others – education and housing being particularly badly affected. Among the many issues which stand out in the decade some had particular significance for the health of young people, including: unemployment; housing shortages in major cities and the associated homelessness; and HIV/AIDS. The decade began with the publication of the Black Report, reminding people, not for the first time, that inequalities in health, related particularly to class but also to gender and race, characterized the UK. A recent ten-year follow-up report (Smith *et al.* 1990) affirms that class-based inequalities are continuing to widen. It has, however, also been the decade in which the health-promotion movement has developed. Within some interpretations this could be seen as embracing the emergent consumerist approach to health and health care, but in the widely influential conceptualizations of the WHO, it offers a challenge to government thinking. The decade closed with major changes in both the health care and education sectors in the early stages of implementation.

This section will continue to focus predominantly on health care and education sectors. It is probably helpful to go back to the period around 1976 as a starting point for examining the 1980s. The year 1976 saw, at a time of growing questioning of educational expenditure, Prime Minister James Callaghan's call for a great debate on education in order to reach a new consensus. This debate in the latter period of the last Labour Government can be seen to have prepared the way for the succeeding Conservative one. Meanwhile, in the health sector the 1976 document *Prevention and Health: Everybody's Business* was the first of a series of publications which examined the role of prevention in influencing community health. These documents recognized that while much contemporary disease could be alleviated by modern medicine it could not be cured. At the same time the escalating costs of health care and a worsening economic climate stimulated review of health-care spending. Recognition of the role of life-style factors in the aetiology of major causes of mortality and morbidity led to a new emphasis on prevention of disease achieved by changing individual behaviours – life-style factors such as smoking, eating, alcohol use, and so on and use of preventive health-care services. The underlying environmental determinants, while not denied, were not targeted in the same way; the overriding emphasis was on individual responsibility for health (Figure 7.1). Health education was seen as a necessary prerequisite for achieving prevention – within the conceptual framework of the medical model education attempted to change health-related behaviours using a variety of techniques. Health educators did not, however, all conform to this preventive model of health education. Various categorizations of approaches to health education have been discussed (Caplan and Holland 1990; Tones *et al.* 1990; French and Adams 1986).

Advocates of a social-change or radical model criticized the preventive approach as victim blaming and as overlooking the environmental determinants of ill-health. Health education should, they said, address all causes of ill-health and generate campaigns for social and environmental change, i.e. campaigns against tobacco advertising rather than persuading individuals to stop smoking, or action against poverty rather than exhortations to adopt behaviours which incomes could not support. As with the preventive approach educators could still be vulnerable to the critique that they also adopt persuasive techniques. A third approach – an educational or empowerment model – aims to develop health decision-making skills.

It also acknowledges the barriers to making and implementing health choices and aims to empower individuals and communities so that they can counteract the barriers. This requires the development of such personal attributes as self-esteem, assertiveness, social skills, and group skills such as advocacy and campaigning. Within the confines of what is seen to be socially responsible behaviour, the right of individuals and groups to make their own health decisions is respected. These decisions could include the modification (or not) of personal health behaviours, campaigning for health services or a variety of environmental and social measures that directly lead to health or enable people to make healthy choices. The measures of success will vary between the models. Health educators may commonly use a mix of approaches depending on context, age of client group, aspect of health in question, and so on. Schools, for example may be expected to give strong support to educational models, while, within health-care contexts, the dominance of the medical model would lend support to the preventive approach. Much of the thinking of supporters of the radical and empowerment approaches has come to be incorporated into the health-promotion movement. This term has come to embrace the combination of health education, health-care services, and the range of policy and environmental changes which facilitate health (Figure 7.3).

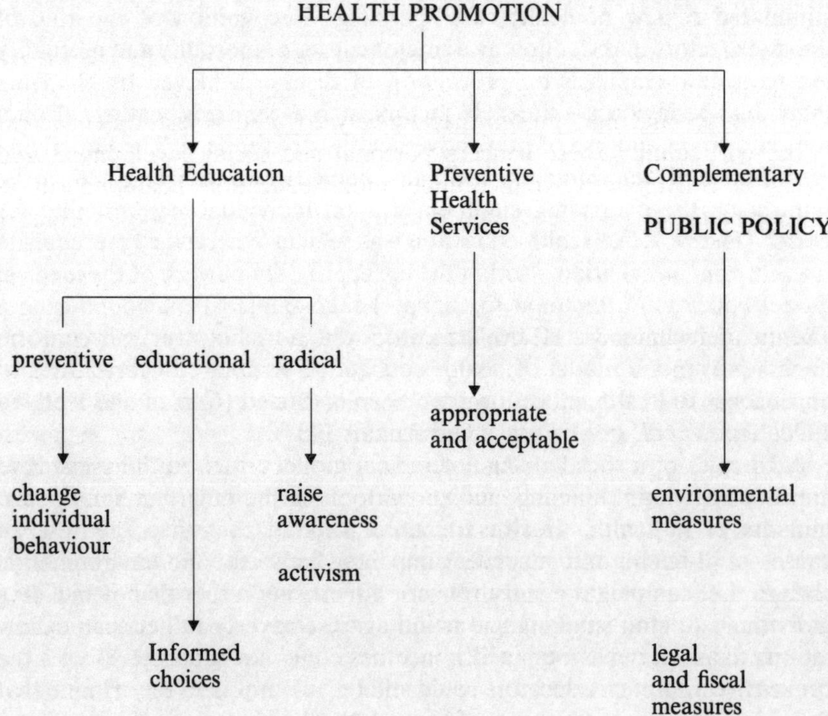

Figure 7.3 The elements of health promotion

Education sector

From 1976 onwards a range of policy documents debated the purposes of education in the latter part of the twentieth century and in particular discussed the nature of the formal curriculum – both the case for a common core curriculum and the aims and objectives of curriculum subjects. It is probably fair to say that the earlier discussions of a common core curriculum were characterized by motivation to provide a better educational experience for all young people as individuals as well as future workers. As the 1980s progressed there was especial emphasis on making schools more efficient at preparing young people for work and on the project of shifting the balance between central and local control of education. The culmination was the Education Act of 1988 which set out the requirements for a National Curriculum in state schools.

The general place of health education in the curriculum was commented on in the general educational reports and it was also the subject of two reports from the Inspectorate (Department of Education and Science 1977b, 1985). The general recommendation was that health education should take place in all schools, be provided through cross-curricular approaches, and associated with other topics as a constituent of a broad strand of personal and social education:

> there are some essential constituents of the school curriculum which are often identified as subjects but which are as likely to feature in a variety of courses and may be more effectively covered if distributed across the curriculum. These concern personal and social development and can be conveniently grouped under moral education, health education (including sex education) and preparation for parenthood and family life.
>
> (DES 1981: 7)

The link between moral and health education was made clearer in the same document: 'moral education is most effectively achieved – in particular but not exclusively – in the context of literature, of religious and health education'. Further, the 1985 Curriculum Matters document on health education also viewed health education as necessary for physical and moral well-being. Both this and the earlier HMI publication outlined a broad set of aims and objectives for school health education, addressing not only knowledge but also attitudes and values such as self-esteem and skills such as decision making, together with discussion on specific health topics and organizational issues. Some bland discussion of health education in a multiracial society was included in the 1985 document but there was little comment on gender issues. The most detailed subject-specific comment was on sex education – one element of health education which came in for direct government attention in the 1980s.

Sex education

Curriculum Matters 5–16 (DES 1985) gave strong support for sex education in saying that 'the importance of sexual relationships is such that sex education is a crucial part of preparing children for their lives now and in the future as adults and parents' (p. 17). It proposed a broad sex-education curriculum and saw the need for schools to deal 'sensitively and appropriately' with such issues as contraception, sexually transmitted diseases, homosexuality, and abortion. Its discussion was open to criticism – for example, for the impression created that homosexuality is a 'phase' which 'persists' into adult life for some young people. There is evidence that both young gays and lesbians have found school sex education failing to meet their needs (Aggleton *et al.* 1988). Despite the moral tone of the documents, sex education became the target for legal intervention. Both the Education Acts of 1980 and 1986 and Clause 28 of the Local Authority Reorganization Act had repercussions for sex education. The 1980 Act required local authorities or school governors to inform parents of the manner and context in which education about sexual matters was to be given in schools. Schools had moved towards broad-based programmes although variations existed between the percentage of young people who had considered particular issues and the extent to which sex education either formed a part of a broad curriculum on personal relationships or was more narrowly topic-focused. Surveys generally indicated full parental support for sex education in schools (Allen 1987). The Education Act (No. 2) of 1986 (DES 1986) went further than the 1980 one and gave governing bodies specific powers in relation to sex education and asserted that it should be given in such a manner as to encourage those pupils to have due regard to moral considerations and the value of family life. Governors had the duty to consider whether sex education should form part of the secular curriculum, and to make and keep up to date a written statement of their policy. In carrying out their duties they should do so in consultation with head teachers and have regard to representations made to them. While it would be wrong to assume that governing bodies would automatically take a reactionary stance on this aspect of the curriculum, this ruling did give new powers to restrict classroom activities. The Health Education Authority (HEA) responded pragmatically with the School Governors Project designed to support governing bodies in their health-education policy role and setting sex education in a broad personal, social, and health-education context (forthcoming). As the HIV/AIDS problem developed, dilemmas emerged. If governing bodies did not permit sex education in their schools, the perceived necessity to target young people in the Government's HIV/AIDS campaign would not be adequately supported. Where sex education did happen, the consideration of sexuality became problematic following Clause 28 of the Local Government Act which stated that homosexuality should not be promoted in schools. This generated confusion about what was possible in sex education in schools. In 1988 the Education Unit of the Family Planning Association (1988: 4) made the following comment: 'young people have the right to be informed about homosexuality, as well as other issues they will need to understand as part of sex education. Including discussion about homosexuality does not, and cannot "teach" people to be homosexual.' In 1988 the Department of the Environment stated that Clause 28 did not apply to the teaching of sex education in schools as this was now the responsibility of school governors. Finally, as it became necessary to acknowledge that HIV/AIDS in the UK could not be labelled as largely associated with gay life-styles and drug abuse, schools could no longer pretend to set sex solely in a context of family life if all young people were to be helped to adopt safe sex practices.

An ongoing debate in school health education has centred on whether courses should address what are seen to be the currently relevant health topics or whether they should develop a set of transferable skills and personal competencies such as self-esteem and decision-making skills drawing on specific health areas as exemplars. Where health education has formed part of a broad personal, social, and health-education curriculum, the tendency has been towards the latter, and certain projects, Lifeskills Teaching and Healthskills, particularly support this approach (Hopson and Scally 1981; Anderson 1988). Irrespective of preferred approach, schools in the 1980s almost invariably addressed drugs education (including smoking and alcohol as well as illegal drugs), a second element of health education selected for government concern. In the mid-1980s financial support was offered to local authorities to fund drugs co-ordinators for three years as one part of its overall response to the perceived increases in drug abuse among young people – especially involving heroin. The co-ordinators were intended to provide training for the range of professionals working with young people. This initiative was criticized for separating out one element of the health-education curriculum and for appearing to focus more on illegal drug use than the arguably more serious problem (in population health terms) of smoking and alcohol. In retrospect it appears that drugs co-ordinators have complemented other curriculum development work in local authorities and in many cases supported generalist health education (Turner *et al.* 1989).

By the end of the decade when there had been support for general health education in schools as well as particular attention to elements of this curriculum there was surprise when it was omitted as either a core or foundation subject in the Consultation document in the national curriculum. It later emerged that it was expected to continue as a cross-curricular element much as advised in *Curriculum Matters 5–16*, but this omission has done little to raise the status of health education.

Youth services

It was in the 1980s that the potential of the youth services to contribute to health education was properly recognized, both in local-authority and voluntary youth organizations and the youth-training schemes (Chaplin 1987). In 1985 the Young People's programme in the HEC extended beyond its previous emphasis on schools to include these contexts. The 1988 summary of this programme listed the concepts which it thought should underlie all work with young people – grouped together as personal concepts: self-esteem; decision making; growth and change; fitness; and social concepts – social class, gender, ethnicity, environmental conditions, relationships, and group support. The concepts addressed and the particular health topics discussed could, it said, be negotiated with young people themselves. Specific projects for use with youth services have been developed with HEA support.

In common with other population groups young people in the 1980s have initiated self-help health-care activities. In some cases local-authority support has been available. Support in areas of sexuality, pregnancy, and abortion can be singled out.

The health sector

Throughout the 1980s the Government, as part of its general commitment to reduce welfare expenditure, to demonstrate cost-effectiveness, and to develop consumerism, instituted changes in the NHS. A reorganization had taken place in 1974 and this was followed up by a further one in 1982 and, following the Griffiths Report, by the introduction of general management in 1984. At the end of the decade a review of the NHS took place and three key papers issued: *Community Care: Agenda for Action* (Griffiths 1988); *Promoting Better Health* and *Working for Patients* (Secretaries of State for Health, Wales, Northern Ireland and Scotland 1987, 1989). Despite the declared intention to cut spending on welfare there has been argument over whether any overall real cut in health spending did take place. There is also a view that because of changing definitions it became increasingly difficult to draw comparisons in this area. It would be generally agreed that expenditure did not rise in line with changing needs and demands and that, therefore, prioritizing took place and cuts to parts of the service did occur. Efforts made to redistribute resources within the services following RAWP (Resource Allocation Working Party) were difficult to achieve. An area of growth, as might be expected from the prevention documents, has been in resources for health education and health promotion. In 1980 health authorities employed approximately 200 health education officers; by 1990 there were 1,000 (including short-term funded posts) (Whitehead 1989). In addition, 'Promoting Better Health', the White Paper (Secretaries of State for Health, Wales, Northern Ireland

and Scotland 1987) which addressed general practice, set new requirements for preventive work within primary care, and in response there has been a growth of Primary Health Care Facilitator posts. Assessing the impact of changing health-sector policy on the health of youth is quite difficult. The main proposals of the Court Report were not implemented although some impact on services has been noted. An updating report on child health was jointly commissioned by the HEC and the National Children's Bureau (1987). According to this report considerable disparity existed between districts in the amount given to child health. The quality of the school health service had declined and school meals were no longer required to meet certain specified nutritional criteria. This report recommended that at least one paediatrician with special interest in community child care should be appointed in each health district. While there has been no systematic growth of medical care services targeted towards youth needs, there has been innovation, for example pregnancy clinics for teenagers. Documenting the nature and extent of such specialist provision requires further investigation.

It can be argued that overall, the most consistent youth-oriented policy has been in health education where young people have been clearly targeted in the work of the health-authority health-education units – either in community activities or through support of schools, colleges, and other youth organizations. Demonstrable successes have been noted for some health-topic-related work with this group (Tones *et al.* 1990).

Local authorities and voluntary bodies

In the latter part of the 1980s some local authorities have responded to the tenets of the health-promotion movement and have initiated their own health promotion activities. Some have set up health promotion units in parallel and not always in co-operation with those in the health authorities. A growing number of cities have set up Healthy Cities projects. Although young people could be influenced by the general strategies of healthy-cities initiatives there is not much evidence to date that their needs have been central concerns. A whole spectrum of voluntary bodies continued to contribute in the 1980s to health work in general and to youth health in particular. Organizations such as the Brook Advisory Centres, the Family Planning Association, and New Grapevine provided important and balanced contributions to sex education as a counter, in particular, to some of the narrowly focused HIV/AIDS education in the media. Bodies such as the Teachers Advisory Council for Alcohol and Drug Education (TACADE) have continued to provide curriculum-development projects to support health education with young people, initially predominantly with reference to schools but latterly also to informal and formal youth contexts and with ethnic minorities' needs taken into account.

INTERNATIONAL DIMENSION

The year 1985 was designated by the United Nations as International Year of Youth and World Health Day and had as its motto: 'Healthy Youth – Our Best Resource'. In his introduction to the day the Director General of the World Health Organization emphasised three facts that he saw as fundamentally significant for public measures to promote young people's health:

(1) adolescence is an important period for the development of health behaviour;
(2) adolescence has a great influence on later morbidity and mortality and the health condition of the next generation;
(3) health promotion of young people requires an interdisciplinary approach, a far-reaching delegation of responsibility, and the involvement of youth.

World-wide there is a growing awareness of the importance of fostering health in youth. The United Nations organization has said that the youth situation in many countries is characterized by: unemployment, deficiency in education and training possibilities, insufficient opportunities to take part in the development of society, poor health care, and by malnutrition. At a conference addressing youth health in 1985, Schmidt (1985: 20) said that special importance in achieving health promotion in youth should be attached to: 'securing of peace, democratic involvement of people in the activities and decision making process of society, the right to work, education and health care, environmental protection, comprehensive protection and relevant legislative measures.'

Quite clearly there are great variations in the importance which is attached to each of the above from country to country, in the current progress to achieving them, and in barriers to further progress. Education, for example is recognized by all countries as important in achieving social goals although there remain wide variations between countries in educational provision. More specifically, there is a clear association between the mean years of education and health indicators within countries. One of the global indicators in the Health for All 2000 Programme is the number of countries in which the literacy rates of both men and women exceed 70 per cent. Generally speaking more importance has been attached to the education of boys than of girls. There is clearly documented evidence (International Union of Health Education (IUHE) 1987) of an inverse correlation between years spent in education by girls and maternal mortality rates. It has been proposed (Paxman and Zuckerman 1987: 10) that world-wide, young women have the largest burden of disadvantage and that 'consideration needs to be given to women's perception so that they can achieve their educational, economic and social aspiration, and enhance their partnership in society with young men'.

Of the world-wide barriers to achieving Health for All and of youth in particular, especial mention should be made of poverty which is linked with health in so many ways and remains the prevailing condition for a very significant proportion of the world's youth. There are clearly marked differences between 'developed' and 'developing' countries or, using the less loaded and preferred terminology, between the 'North' and the 'South', although within the 'North' poverty also continues to be significant for disadvantaged sections of communities. Examples of two further barriers to health promotion which are unevenly distributed are: the existence of, or threat of, armed conflict leading in some cases to large groups becoming refugees, and rapid urbanization. According to the WHO (1989) children and young people account for over 70 per cent of the total rural–urban migration in the less-developed countries. It says:

> the switch from what is often a traditional and relatively stable rural society to urban conglomerations that often lack an infrastructure for family support or health care is one of the major barriers to the healthy development of young people today.
>
> (ibid.: 7)

The World Health Organization exists to monitor world health and to develop policy. It has focused on general health-promotion policies and also addressed specific health areas and the health of particular groups, including young people. The activities of the WHO are an influence, more or less pervasive, on thinking and practice related to the promotion of health throughout the world. The development of WHO health-promotion strategy is discussed in detail by Davies (1987). In brief, the 1977 World Health Assembly originated the slogan 'Health for All by the Year 2000', and subsequently a set of global indicators were developed for monitoring progress. In 1978 the Alma Ata Conference on Primary Health Care examined strategies for health development with particular emphasis on developing countries. There was a desire to address inequities in health both between and within countries by addressing the socio-determinants of ill-health and to develop accessible and acceptable health services. The concept of primary health care which emerged was defined as essential health care, scientifically sound, universally accessible, participative, and at a cost countries could afford at every stage of development. Primary health care would include not only illness treatment, but also preventive and health-promotive activities. Health education was proposed as the first of eight essential components of a primary-care strategy. The philosophy of Alma Ata had its greatest impact on countries who had yet to develop any comprehensive health-care structures. It has been variously implemented with differential impact on the health of communities as a whole, and young people in particular. Within the European region constituent concepts of the Alma Ata document have been central to the growing health-promotion movement. In 1980 the thirty-three member states agreed to a European strategy and thirty-eight targets were set. A number of documents have clarified thinking on health promotion and the Ottawa Charter of 1986 specified five essential categories of action for achieving it: building sound public policies; creating supportive environments; strengthening community action; developing personal skills; and reorienting health services. These categories will be drawn on in the last section when looking to future policy for health promotion and young people.

More specifically, WHO has issued a series of documents which have addressed the health of youth and adolescents (1965, 1975, 1977, 1979, 1986b, 1989). These documents have generally reviewed definitions of adolescence and youth, described current health and identified problems, and discussed solutions with reference to health services, education, and so on. The most recent of the documents has strongly reflected health-promotion thinking, examining policies and legislation, intersectoral action, and youth participation in health promotion. A reflection of the growing interest in adolescent health was the call by member nations of the WHO for a new programme to address it and designed to stimulate research, training, intervention, and advocacy world-wide with culture-specific activity at country level. A programme was inaugurated in 1986.

All countries have a network of policies which have a bearing on the health of young people. These may be directed towards health in a general sense: for example, policies on provision of school health services, or the legal age for consent to health services; or towards specific aspects of health – policies on smoking, drugs, access to contraceptive services, and so on. The extent and variation of general and specific policies world-wide has recently been reviewed (Paxman and Zuckerman 1987). Policy related to the universal problem of accidental death in young people can be taken as an example. As mentioned earlier the majority of accidents are road-traffic ones, associated with cars and motor cycles. Between a third and a half of all fatal road accidents in industrialized countries are caused by drivers under the influence of alcohol and drugs. Policy responses have included a number of elements – legal age for driving; medical examinations in addition to vision and hearing; mandatory seat-belt use; drink-drive legislation; and associated health education. The extent to which legislation is enforced and the penalties for infringement also vary. There is evidence that education alone on seat-belt use is ineffective if not backed up by legislation. Mandatory seat-belt use developed first in industrialized countries but is spreading world-wide. Where alcohol use and driving is concerned the general response has been to set limits – which vary from country to country – rather than to prohibit use although the East European countries have generally adopted the prohibition route. World-wide trends in accident prevention, conclude Paxman and Zuckerman (as far as young people are concerned) are towards raising the age for drinking (not easily enforceable), lowering the legally tolerated limits of blood alcohol content, and stiffening penalties for violation.

Whenever laws and regulations are specified as a response to any particular health problem, education is normally necessary to support the legislation and to complement it. While there have been active efforts to promote health education in educational contexts this has been more likely to reach young people in those countries where education continues beyond early adolescence. The role of schools in contributing to primary health care was set out in the Alma Ata proposals. An important stimulus to looking more energetically at school health education has been the recognition of the HIV/AIDS problem, which is already having a major impact on young people in many countries. This poses difficult problems in those countries where the barriers to sex education in schools are considerable and where traditional community education is not meeting the changing needs of young people. Strategies will need to address schools and community educational activities. Most countries are developing national policies on health education for schools although the gap between policy and practice can be considerable. One indicator of general effectiveness is the extent to which schools meet the criteria for a 'health-promoting school'. Within the European region Williams (1990) notes that while there is considerable sympathy and support for the concept of the health-promoting school, it remains a distant goal for most countries. There are, however, some interesting initiatives, some linked with Healthy Cities projects. Finally, there are aspects of health which are seen urgently to require active processes of integrated policy development; strategies on youth employment and on disability and handicap are two particular examples which are frequently cited.

THE PRESENT POSITION

The youth of the majority of countries form a relatively healthy section of their populations, if mortality is used as the criterion. None the less, there are some causes of mortality, where rates are significant in relation to other stages of the life-span. Accidents are the key example, especially in young men, although suicides should not be overlooked. In the case of morbidity young people experience symptoms at much the same rate as the adult population although the percentage of their symptoms which falls within a minor category is probably higher than in adults. Despite the relatively healthy status of the young, world-wide there are, as noted earlier, a large number with some form of disability. Health-focused policy may be directed towards the promotion of positive health, or to the prevention or treatment of ill-health, and may be present- or future-oriented. Countries differ in their general health-oriented policies and in the policies directed towards specific health concerns. In some cases, Paxman and Zuckerman concluded, from their comprehensive review, law and policy serve only a symbolic purpose; in others they provide a general supportive framework for health services; in yet others they offer specific solutions to pressing social and health problems. It may be policies in sectors not immediately recognized as related to health in which policy development may be most necessary. Paxman and Zuckerman, for example, suggest that perhaps the single most important condition for the healthy development of young people leaving school is employment. The Health for All 2000 initiative has provided a context within which to consider the development of the health of populations in general as well as youth. A growing acknowledgement has been given to youth in the work of the WHO.

Within the UK any assessment of the current position has to recognize the two overlapping but largely distinct perspectives on health policies. While on one side the Government promotes individual responsibility for health, cost-effectiveness and a narrow consumerist approach to health care and appears to set low priority on reducing health inequalities, health promoters adopting a WHO-influenced philosophy are advocating the consideration of health criteria in all sectors of policy making, intersectoral collaboration, empowerment of individuals and communities to enable them actively to participate in health decision making and the reduction of health inequalities. Both sides would see themselves as supporting prevention and promoting health but the former is influenced more by cost containment, the latter by creating a better society. While the Healthy Cities initiatives are attempts to put health promotion into practice, it is too early to say whether they can be effective against the countervailing pressures of current government policy on health care.

As earlier sections have shown, there has been a gradual development of youth-focused policy and practice. There have been, and continue to be, gaps between policy and practice. It is probably true to say that youth policy is likely to be more fully implemented where youth forms the major client group – in educational contexts or youth organizations rather than in the health service where they are one group among others and not necessarily viewed as a priority. At the present time the education sector is implementing the National Curriculum and the NHS is also implementing change. In both cases there are likely to be repercussions for youth. As discussed earlier, by 1990 secondary schools had generally moved to incorporating health education in their curricula, reflecting a diversity of approaches and variably effective. There has been a growing tendency to incorporate it as part of a personal, social, and health education curriculum. In the mid-1970s few secondary schools had co-ordinators for this part of the curriculum but 50 per cent of schools had them by 1983 (Williams and Roberts 1985), and unconfirmed estimates would put the figures higher by 1990. There has been some move for schools to address their status as health-promoting institutions, considering the way the various elements in Figure 7.2 both separately and together promote health. Earlier sections have alluded to contradictions in policy in school health education and these have recently been discussed by Whitehead (1989). Examples of such contradictions include:

(1) policies encouraging broadly based health education incorporating positive conceptions of mental, physical, and social health *BUT* direct government pressure from 1985 for 'crisis' education in schools on separate health problems;
(2) DES and other policies encouraging development of health education and personal and social education as essential parts of the curriculum *BUT* no place for these as core or foundation subjects in the National Curriculum;
(3) a broadening of the concept of sex education and its incorporation into wider health and personal education programmes *BUT* school governors given responsibility to decide if it should be included, and if so what and how;
(4) HMI encouragement of greater exploration of sensitive issues of homosexuality, contraception, and abortion *BUT* teachers advised not to give contraceptive advice to girls under 16 and restrictions imposed on discussions of homosexuality;
(5) schools increase health education in the formal curriculum *BUT* generally fail to develop and implement health-promotion policies for the school as a whole. Messages conveyed by the school environment and the school ethos contradict messages from the formal curriculum.

While there is growing evidence of the effectiveness of school health education in relation to specific health topic areas there is less evidence of success in achieving broader goals. For example, school education has been criticized for failing properly to provide for the differential needs of boys and girls, for young people of ethnic minorities, and those whose sexual orientation does not conform to the heterosexist norm (Aggleton *et al.* 1988; Tones *et al.* 1990). To these groups may be added young people with disabilities. It is also not possible to demonstrate that schools have developed health-education policies which have strongly and clearly addressed inequalities in health. Finally, as stated earlier health education has been a low-status subject. While more recently it has been given strong support as a cross-curriculum area, the fact that it was not designated as a core or foundation subject of the National Curriculum suggests that it may well suffer as schools focus on meeting the requirements for assessment. It may also become increasingly difficult to ensure that additional subjects are appropriately resourced if core and foundation subjects are short of books and other materials.

Comments on the significance for youth health of the NHS White Papers and the recent NHS Reorganization Act can only be speculative at this stage. *Working for Patients* (Secretaries of State for Health 1989) emphasized the need to bring up the general level of services to that of the best, to address the country-wide variations in costs for acute treatment, waiting times, drug prescriptions, and GP referrals. It noted the rising demand for services and the increased range of treatments, but did not see money, by itself, as the answer – this lay in the organization of services. Two key objectives were stated: to give patients better health care and greater choice of services available, and to provide greater rewards for those working in the service who successfully respond to local needs and preferences. It is in the statements about patients becoming active consumers instead of passive recipients that implications for young people may be sought. Patients are going to be able to change their GPs more easily and it could be thought that those practices that make a real effort to provide services in line with young people's needs are more likely to recruit them. In practice much of the population only has convenient access to a small number of practices – in rural areas probably only one. Even where choice is available the information on which to make choice may be restricted. Decision-making education in schools will have an important role in enabling young people to exercise this choice. School activities could usefully be complemented by Community Health Councils (CHCs), some of which produce youth-oriented materials. As access to hospital care will still be via the GP, any choices available will depend on constraints which will govern hospital access in future – practice budgets, district health authority contracts to buy care from other authorities, and so on. The White Paper said that hospitals should provide services for patients as people and referred to, among other features, child and counselling facilities, information, and clear and sensitive explanations of practical and clinical matters and complaints procedures. It is not clear whether criteria for these will be set against which the consumer can assess the service. The document strongly emphasizes the individual consumer but the future role of the CHC as a body which responds on behalf of patients collectively is also not clear. In principle young people should be able to respond as consumers to the health-care services and the services should respond to their expressed needs. In practice this may be very difficult to achieve.

FUTURE POLICY DIRECTIONS

In this final section it is in order to make comment on future directions not only in the light of current positions and apparent trends but also with reference to desirable, and possibly Utopian, goals. The Health for All strategy and the constituent activities for promoting health specified in the Ottawa Charter (WHO 1986b) provide a framework for making comment. To recap, the overlapping actions identified in the Charter are: building healthy public policies which support health; creating supportive environments; strengthening community action; developing personal skills; and reorienting health services. In short we are looking for policies and practice which together promote the health of all, and in the context of this discussion, of young people. This framework has previously been used in a round-table discussion on youth health in the journal *World Health Forum* (Levin 1989).

Healthy public policies

Although we may debate the balance between attention to illness and the promotion of positive health in the health-care sector, it is by definition concerned with health. The education sector also has a long history of giving attention to the health of young people although the priorities attached, and the activities carried out to promote health, have varied. Other policy areas have taken health considerations into account to varying extents but frequently as a subsidiary rather than a central consideration. As we have seen, the health-promotion movement is concerned to see the development, in all sectors, of policies which address health. At the same time intersectoral collaboration will be needed if such activities are to complement each other. We would, therefore, expect all appropriate policy areas to address the health needs of youth (and likewise the needs of any other sections of the population who have or feel that they have common interests) in policy formulation and implementation. At the international level the World Health Organization has clearly come to recognize the distinct needs of young people and begun to develop appropriate policy responses. Other international agencies continue to hide young people within child or adult categories. For example, the 'Convention on the Rights of the Child' includes all young people up to the age of 18. While a justification for using the single category of child for the full age range is provided, it can be argued that the potential to direct attention to any rights issues specific to youth may be diminished (Vittachi 1989). At the national level we have previously referred to the Young People's Programme in the Health Education Authority in England. The Health Promotion Authority for Wales has also acknowledged young people as a category. Its policy for the period 1990–3 provides for the delivery of its health action areas under three broad corporate identities: Heartbeat Wales, Good Health Wales, and Youth Life Wales. This latter programme, while addressing all young people under the age of 18 years, does include a number of targets which are specifically directed towards youth. If we accept that youth as a category extends to 24 (WHO 1989), the upper part of the age range is hidden in the Wales document within the adult category. There is one exception where a target in the area of sexuality is defined to cover the age range 16 to 24. In the future we would wish all health-related policy areas to address the need for specifically identified youth-related action and respond accordingly.

Beyond the rhetoric on health promotion there are some difficult questions to be addressed and practical strategies to be teased out. For example, to what extent and in what ways can the value of health influence policy making? There is clear evidence that unemployment damages health and also that work within areas of employment also damages health. Health-related unemployment policy has to take both these facts into account. Moreover, if health considerations govern employment policies, could this be to the detriment of overall economic policies? The promotion of health-using public policy may require an extension of state intervention into a range of aspects of life. At a time when the espoused government policy, within the UK, has been to reduce state intervention in the pursuit of welfare, health promotion appears to demand a reversal of this objective. It is not clear that a change of government would immediately lead to major reversals in policy and practice in line with achieving the goals of health promotion. With the change of Prime Minister there is even talk of a new consensus (*Guardian* 1990). Perhaps the time has come to review, and possibly to rethink, some cherished ideas on state welfare policy and to ask if Health for All might more successfully be achieved through a variety of combinations of public and private provision rather than through a full commitment to state welfare. Notwithstanding, health promotion demands intersectoral collaboration, the success of which requires detailed understanding of policy making, organizational structures, and strategies for achieving change. Such understanding is being slowly developed – in particular from evaluations of Healthy Cities projects. Intersectoral collaboration in the furtherance of youth health will demand further refinements of the strategies which are developed. At a number of points during the chapter, mention has been made of the involvement of young people themselves in policy development. This has been given particular emphasis in the most recent WHO document on the health of youth (1989) and is discussed by Levin (1989): 'It is essential, therefore, that policy formulation be fundamentally a public process with continuous inputs from young people as well as those who claim to represent them.' Levin argues that youth should organize itself so that its views are effectively expressed locally and networked nationally. Such involvement would require facilitation of access of young people to policy-making structures at local, regional, and national levels. Most importantly this requires acceptance of the view that young people are sufficiently responsible to participate, and acceptance of their right to participation. At the international level, the World Assembly of Youth offers one model for examination. As an organization it advocates youth participation at all levels, has presented youth statements at a range of health-related international meetings, and has consultative status with a range of UN agencies.

Creating supportive environments

If young people are to achieve health the environments in which they live, study, or play should be enabling. As with any other sector of the population these needs will require more careful specification, in dialogue with young people themselves, and giving due recognition to differential needs related to gender, ethnicity, disability, sexual orientation, and so on.

In addition, there needs to be a positive attitude towards meeting those identified environmental needs. One barrier to this may be the pervasive influence of media portrayals of young people which tend to emphasize the negative rather than the positive. In so far as specific elements of the environment are concerned, a significant percentage of young people are involved in formal education. The need for schools to address their health-promoting status has already been discussed and some progress has been made in reducing the potential contradictions between formal health-education activities within the classroom and other features of the school environment. Comparable analyses are required of work-places as health-promoting environments for young people. Elsewhere in the community a range of initiatives may be called for if the environment is to become supportive. For example, if we return to thinking about an important health problem of youth – accidents – good public transport, not least in rural areas and late at night, and networks of cycle routes could contribute to accident reduction. More generally, some redress of the tremendous imbalance between funds spent on health education with young people and those on advertising health-damaging products would also be most welcome. Most importantly, there needs to be a greater readiness to listen to young people's views on their environments, and to allow them space and resources to meet their own needs in their own ways with the obvious proviso that this should not be at the expense of others. Finally, young people could be encouraged to participate fully in community initiatives designed to improve the environment. One simple question which might be asked, in conclusion to this section: 'How many Healthy Cities or Health for All programmes in the UK have youth representation on their organizing committees?'

Strengthening community action

Health promotion works through effective community action. Young people may be involved in whole-community initiatives or youth-focused ones. Most particularly, the development of youth-initiated self-help health groups requires more support in future. Health professionals would need to be readier to listen to those groups, to acknowledge expertise, and work with them. A good example of this process took place in the 1990 European Conference on Health Education which had 'Youth' as its theme. Presentations by a team of young people from seven countries illustrated the process of youth-initiated education and counselling support in the area of HIV/AIDS.

Developing personal skills

Facilitating the development of the range of skills needed by young people if they are to make their own health choices and play a role in health promotion is a central concern of the education system and youth services. As discussed earlier, the importance of health education in the school curriculum is widely acknowledged and there has been some progress towards effectiveness. In England and Wales, if we accept that the National Curriculum is here to stay for the foreseeable future, the hope is that those areas, such as health education, which have been identified as cross-curriculum themes, rather than core or foundation subjects, will continue to develop. It will be necessary to argue for adequate initial and continuing training for teachers and funding for teaching resources if progress is to be maintained. In particular, a strong preference would be for support for health education within a broad programme of personal, social, and health education (PSHE) rather than for crisis-oriented health-topic interventions. Future policies and activities should be designed to ensure that the differential health education needs of young people are better met – whether related to gender, ethnic grouping, disability, and so on. A very specific need will be for health education directed towards enabling young people to understand and use the modified health services.

Reorientation of health services

Health promotion talks about people as fully active participants in health-care services. Although the NHS White Paper *Promoting Better Health* (Secretaries of State for Health 1987) refers to participation, the impression is of a more narrowly consumerist approach than that conceived in WHO documents. Participation requires: full dialogue; elicitation of community needs as well as professionally defined ones in defining and delivering services; adequate representation on district and regional health authorities; opportunities for CHCs to play an effective role in the modified service; and a comprehensive educational component, where needed, in all health care. These elements need to be achieved for the population in general, as well as for defined groups such as young people. One relatively simple objective would be the fuller collection of health-related data for the age group conforming to the category of youth and the development of responses to the questions raised by the WHO (1986b). Much fuller consideration also needs to be given to research on the form, location, and delivery of health care services for youth. The WHO (1986b) proposes the idea of promoting health through community-developed and community-based youth centres employing a holistic approach with participation of young people in planning and providing services. They write:

> The young users of multiservice centres usually see themselves as members of a club where services are available, rather than as traditional clinic patients. In the centres the sensitisation of health workers to the special needs of young people is particularly important. Their ability to listen to and respect the feelings of the young, to involve them in

decision making, to share information, and to transfer skills is essential to this approach to health care.

(ibid.: 99)

Clearly there are implications for the training of health professionals if they are to work in participatory ways with young people. Training is also required if the educational component of health care is to be enhanced for all clients, including young people. These needs are already partially recognized in nurse training as part of the Project 2000 but much still needs to be addressed in the training of doctors and other health workers. A range of examples of community-based health projects involving youth participation has been reported from a number of countries. These include the Women's Centre Project for Adolescent Mothers in Jamaica, the Grapevine Project in England, and the Regina Multiservice Centre for Youth in Canada (WHO 1986b). In the future further developments of this kind will be looked for and their activities fully evaluated. Along the lines of the recommendations of the Court Report we will also look for expansion, where needed, of youth-oriented medical care in traditional settings. The need for specialist teenage facilities in the case of cancer care has been identified and the first of a number of teenage units opened in the Middlesex Hospital in London (*Independent on Sunday* 1990).

In conclusion the aspiration is that in future, policies will be responsive to the health needs of young people, and that young people will be allowed and enabled to play a fully participative role in health-related policy making, locally, regionally, nationally, and internationally.

REFERENCES

Aggleton, P., Homans, H., and Warwick, I. (1988) 'Young people, sexuality and AIDS', *Youth and Policy* 23.

Allen, I. (1987) *Education in Sex and Personal Relationships*, Policy Studies Institute Research Report No. 665.

Anderson, J. (1988) *HEA Healthskills Project: Training Manual*, Leeds: Counselling and Careers Development Unit, University of Leeds.

Balding, J. (1987) *Young People in 1986*, Exeter: HEA Schools Health Education Unit, University of Exeter.

Banks, M.H. and Jackson, P.R. (1982) 'Unemployment and risk of minor psychiatric disorder in young people: cross sectional and longitudinal evidence', *Psychological Medicine* 12: 789–98.

Beattie, A. (1980) 'Models of health education', unpublished mimeo.

Board of Education (1926) *The Education of the Adolescent: Report of the Consultative Committee,* London: HMSO.

Board of Education (1928) *Handbook of Suggestions on Health Education*, London: HMSO.

Board of Education (1934) *Handbook of Suggestions on Health Education,* London: HMSO.

Board of Education (1939) *Suggestions on Health Education*, London: HMSO.

Board of Education (1943) *Sex Education in Schools and Youth Organisations*, London: HMSO.

Caplan, R. and Holland, R. (1990) 'Rethinking health education theory', *Health Education Journal* 49(1): 10–13.

Chaplin, B. (1987) 'Health education in youth clubs/organisations', unpublished M.Sc. dissertation, Leeds Polytechnic.

Davies, J.K. (1987) 'A review of major international developments concerning health education in Europe', in World Health Organization *Education for Health in Europe*, Copenhagen: WHO.

Department of Education and Science (1968) *A Handbook of Health Education*, London: HMSO.

Department of Education and Science (1975) *The School Health Service 1908–74*, London: HMSO.

Department of Education and Science (1977a) *Health Education in Schools*, London: HMSO.

Department of Education and Science (1977b) *Curriculum 11–16*, London: HMSO.

Department of Education and Science (1980) *A Framework for the School Curriculum*, London: HMSO.

Department of Education and Science/Welsh Office (1981) *The School Curriculum*, London: HMSO.

Department of Education and Science (1985) *The Curriculum from 5 to 16. Curriculum Matters 2 An HMI Series*, London: HMSO.

Department of Education and Science (1986) *Education (No. 2) Act 1986*, London: HMSO.

Department of Education and Science (1987a) *The National Curriculum. A Consultative Document*, London: HMSO.

Department of Education and Science (1987b) *Sex Education at School*, Circular No. 11/87.

Department of Education and Science (1988) *Education Reform Act*, London: HMSO.

Department of Health and Social Security (1976) *Prevention and Health: Everybody's Business*, London: HMSO.

Department of Health and Social Security (1977) *Prevention and Health*, London: HMSO.

Family Planning Association (1988) Press release.

Fogelman, K. (ed.) (1976) *Britain's Sixteen Year Olds*, London: National Children's Bureau.

French, J. and Adams, L. (1986) 'From analysis to synthesis: theories of health education', *Health Education Journal* 45: 71–4.

Friedman, H. (1989) 'The health of adolescents: beliefs and behaviour', *Social Science and Medicine* 29(3): 309–15.

Friedman, H.L. and Edstrom, K.G. (1983) *Adolescent Reproductive Health. An Approach to Planning and Research*, Geneva: WHO.

Greaves, J.N. (1965) 'Sex education in colleges and departments of education', *Health Education Journal* 24(4).

Griffiths, A. (1988) *Community Care: Agenda for Action*, London: HMSO.

Guardian (1990) 'Parties deny shift towards consensus', 10 December.

Health Education Authority (1990) *Strategic Plan 1990–95*, London: HEA.

Health Promotion Authority for Wales (1990) *Health for All in Wales: Strategic Directions for the Health Promotion Authority*, Wales: HPA.

Hodgkinson, R. (1973) *Science and Public Health. Science and the Rise of Technology since 1800*, Block 5, Unit 10, Milton Keynes: Open University Press.

Hopson, M. and Scally, B. (1981) *Lifeskills Teaching*, London: McGraw-Hill.

Independent on Sunday (1990) 'The families that take on cancer', 18 November.

IUHE (1987) 'Policy statement on health education for the school aged child', *HYGIE* 6(3): 5–6.

Levin, L.L. (1989) 'Health for today's youth: hope for tomorrow's world', *World Health Forum* 10(2).

Llewellyn Davies, M. (1978) *Maternity: Lives of Working Women* (orig. published 1915), London: Virago Press.

McKeown, T. (1976) *The Role of Medicine: Dream, Mirage or Nemesis?* London: Nuffield Provincial Hospitals Trust.

Ministry of Education (1956) *Health Education. A Handbook of Suggestions for the Consideration of Teachers and Others Concerned in the Health and Education of Children and Young People*, Ministry of Education Pamphlet No. 31, London: HMSO.

Ministry of Health, the Central Health Services Council, the Scottish Health Services Council (1964) *Health Education. Report of a Committee of the Central and Scottish Health Services Councils*, London: HMSO.

National Children's Bureau (1987) *Investing in the Future Child: 10 Years after the Court Report*, A Report of the Policy and Practice Review Group, London: National Children's Bureau.

Office of Population, Censuses and Surveys (OPCS) (1989) *Mortality Statistics: Cause, England and Wales*, Series DH2, London: HMSO.

Paxman, J. and Zuckerman, R.J. (1987) *Laws and Policies Affecting Adolescent Health*, Geneva: WHO.

Platt Committee (1959) *Report of the Committee on the Welfare of Children in Hospital*, London: HMSO.

Report of the Committee on Child Services (1976) *Fit for the Future: The Court Report*, Cmnd 6684, London: HMSO.

Report of a Working Group (1978) *Problems of Children of School Age (14–18 years)*, Copenhagen: Regional Office for Europe, WHO.

Schmidt, W. (1985) 'On young people's health promotion in European countries', in Institute for Health Education of the German Hygiene Museum in the GDR *Healthy Lifestyles of Young People*, Dresden: WHO Collaborating Centre for Health Education.

School Governor's Project (1989) *Governing a Healthy School*, London: Health Education Authority.

Secretaries of State for Health, Wales, Northern Ireland, and Scotland (1987) *Promoting Better Health*, Cmnd 249, London: HMSO.

Secretaries of State for Health, Wales, Northern Ireland, and Scotland (1989) *Working for Patients*, Cmnd 555, London: HMSO.

Smith, D.S., Bartley, M., and Blane, D. (1990) 'Black Report on socioeconomic inequalities and health: 10 years on', *British Medical Journal* 301 (August): 373–6.

Stafford, E., Jackson, P., and Banks, G. (1980), 'Employment, work involvement in less qualified young people', *Journal of Occupational Psychology* 53: 291–304.

Tones, B.K., Tilford, S., and Robinson, Y. (1990) *Health Education, Effectiveness and Efficiency*, London: Chapman and Hall.

Townsend, P. and Davison, N. (1982) *Inequalities in Health*, Harmondsworth: Penguin.

Turner, G., Murphy, R., and Williams, T. (1989) *Education and the Misuse of Drugs: A National Evaluation of the Drug Education Coordinator Initiative*, London: Department of Education and Science.

Vittachi, A. (1989) *Stolen Children*, Cambridge: Polity Press.

West, P. (1988) 'Inequalities? Class differentials in health in British youth', *Social Science and Medicine* 27(4): 291–6.

West, P., MacIntyre, S., Annandale, E., and Hunt, K. (1990), 'Social class and health in youth: findings from the West of Scotland Twenty 07 Study', *Social Science and Medicine* 30(6): 665–73.

Whitehead, M. (1989) *Swimming Upstream: Trends and Prospects in Education for Health*, London: King's Fund Institute.

Williams, T. (1990) 'Education for a healthy life – an overview of progress in Europe', conference paper, IUHE International Conference on Health Education, 'Communicating with Young People', Warsaw.

Williams, T. and Roberts, J. (1985) *Health Education in Schools and Teacher Education Institutions: Survey Reports*, Southampton: Health Education Unit, Southampton University.

World Health Organization (1965) *Health Problems of Adolescents*, Report of a WHO Expert Committee, Technical Report Series 308, Geneva: WHO.

World Health Organization (1975) *Pregnancy and Abortion in Adolescence*, Geneva: WHO.

World Health Organization (1977) *The Health Needs of Adolescents*, Geneva: WHO.

World Health Organization (1979) *The Child and the Adolescent in Society*, Report on a WHO Conference, Copenhagen: WHO Regional Office for Europe.

World Health Organization (1985) *Targets for Health for All*, Copenhagen: World Health Organization Regional Office for Europe.

World Health Organization (1986a) *Ottawa Charter for Health Promotion, An International Conference on Health Promotion, November 17–21, 1986*, Copenhagen: WHO Regional Office for Europe.

World Health Organization (1986b) *Young People's Health: A Challenge for Society. Report of a WHO Study Group on Young People and 'Health for All by the Year 2000'*, Technical Report Series 731, Geneva: WHO.

World Health Organization (1989) *The Health of Youth: Background Document Technical Discussions*, Geneva: WHO.

8 Mental health services for adolescents

Richard Williams and Ian Skeldon

INTRODUCTION

The provision of separate and clearly identified mental health services for adolescents is a matter of recent development. In the early 1990s they are still far from widespread and their distribution across the UK is uneven.

In 1976 the Court Report on Child Health Services (Court 1976) stated that 'adolescents have needs and problems sufficiently distinguishable from those on the one hand of children and on the other of adults to warrant consideration as a distinct group for health care provision'. Despite this recommendation and major deficiencies in existing services, the last decade has witnessed a noticeable deceleration in the development of services and erosion of pre-existing resources in a growing number of areas. This is in stark contrast to a period of enthusiasm and innovation in the 1960s and 1970s when the National Health Service, social services departments, education authorities, and the voluntary sector were working co-operatively to plan and provide treatment for troubled adolescents. This growth was based upon a growing body of theoretical knowledge, practical expertise, and professional development in the fields of psychiatry, psychology, nursing, and social work.

The history of mental health services for adolescents is linked to the development of both adult and child psychiatric services and to advances in the understanding of childhood development and disorder. As a consequence services have tended to be organized in ways which cut uneasily across the teenage years with many local and regional variations. In many parts of the UK child and adolescent mental health and psychiatry services take responsibility for young people up to the age of approximately 16 with the adult services taking over at this, or some later, age. In those areas where specialist adolescent psychiatric services are absent, 16–18 year olds get a raw deal, with many disordered young people experiencing admission to adult psychiatric wards, others being placed in social services or education provision, and perhaps the largest number receiving no adequate treatment at all. Others may drift into the criminal justice system.

This chapter traces the history and development of this scenario and offers an overview of the professional development and training of the staff who work in adolescent mental health services. A description of the changes in service experienced in one health region in England during the last ten years forms the background to a summary of the major influences on past policies for adolescent mental health services in the UK. A review of recent legislation leads into discussion of policy initiatives required to secure and promote these services in the future. The authors begin with a discussion of the nature and extent of adolescent psychiatric disorder and its significance.

THE NATURE OF ADOLESCENT PSYCHIATRIC DISORDER

Adolescence is essentially the period of growth which starts with puberty and ends with adulthood. During this rapid and important period of development young people experience changes in all aspects of their lives, some more visible than others. The changes include those in biological maturation, social expectations, relationships, and the roles of young people in their families and society (Coleman and Hendry 1990). Major anatomical and physiological changes are accompanied by developments in the psychology of thinking and attitudes to the self, others, and relationships. The achievement of sufficient autonomy to handle greater emotional separation from parents is an important task for both young people and their families. Some young people may become overwhelmed by these challenges and develop poorly adapted responses or disorder. The majority of adolescents cope well with the demands upon them. Much adolescent psychiatric disorder has its origin in earlier childhood experiences and long-standing family disturbance. The presentation of disturbance in the teenage years may reflect disturbed relationships in infancy, chaotic parenting, earlier school difficulties, or psychiatric disorder in a parent. In these circumstances the developmental processes of adolescence contribute their particular colour to the problems and symptoms presented by young people. Frequently, then, the development of psychiatric disorder is the result of the interaction of a variety of risk factors.

There still exists a traditional view that adolescence is a time of inevitable emotional turmoil and 'by its nature an interruption of peaceful growth' (Freud 1958). This can therefore be held to be the characteristic and normal state and the term 'adolescence' thereby comes to have a pathological implication. However, general population studies show little evidence of such widespread emotional turmoil or rebelliousness which would be indicative of adolescence as necessarily a period of storm and stress (Douvan and Adelson 1966; Offer and Offer 1975). This is not to deny the considerable potential for stress and that a significant proportion of teenagers will react with emotional symptoms. Up to half of all adolescents at any one time will have had recent experience of private emotional distress which is usually neither evident to others nor prolonged or handicapping (Rutter *et al*. 1976).

In contrast, serious psychiatric disorder in adolescence is clearly distinguishable from such experiences. Psychiatric disorder is generally held to be present when there is an abnormality of behaviour, emotions, or relationships which is sufficiently marked and sufficiently prolonged to cause handicap to the adolescent and distress or disturbance in the family or community. Of course such a definition is based upon the statistical clustering of symptoms and problems into syndromes and descriptions of abnormal mental states. Unlike traditional 'medical models' of illness this process will only rarely rely upon the definition of the underlying aetiology and organ pathology. This inevitably leads to the issue of value and moral judgement in the definition of cases. How severe should disturbance be to define a 'case' and at what point does treatment become indicated? In practice most adolescent psychiatrists take a pragmatic view and are guided by the concepts of chronicity, suffering, and handicap in deciding upon the appropriateness of treatment. In a National Health Service subtly shifting from its initial objectives of providing a fully comprehensive service to one providing services that are 'appropriate and reasonable' (Health Services Act 1974), these considerations take on increasing relevance in arguing for the continuity of provision for psychiatrically disordered young people.

Population studies indicate that the rate of psychiatric disorder, so defined, is around 15–20 per cent in adolescence – a rate not significantly different from that for psychiatric disorder among adults (Leslie 1974; Rutter *et al.* 1976; Graham and Rutter 1985; M. J. Gay, personal communication). Within the age range 12 to 18 years, often used to describe adolescence, boys are likely to be affected more than girls in early adolescence, with a reversal of this trend in late adolescence. Social disadvantage is associated with a higher prevalence of disorder. In early adolescence there is a strong continuity with childhood disorders of conduct, emotion, and development and with increasing age the pattern of symptoms increasingly resembles that of adult psychiatric disorder. Anxiety states, hysteria, hypochondriasis, and obsessional disorder appear and depression increases markedly. Deliberate self-harm rates also increase dramatically along with rates for completed suicide. Anorexia nervosa, schizophrenia, and manic-depressive psychosis are increasingly recognized throughout the teens. Serious psychiatric disorder in adolescence needs to be taken as seriously as adult disorder. There is no evidence that serious disturbance is transitory or self-limiting or that it is associated with less suffering or handicapping consequences. Clinical experience supports this view and although properly controlled research is thin, evidence clearly suggests that non-transient symptoms do not remit with the passage of further time alone (Masterson 1967, 1968; Pichel 1974; Ford *et al.* 1978). Effective mental health services for young people are therefore a vital part of comprehensive health services.

THE HISTORY OF SERVICE DEVELOPMENT IN THE UNITED KINGDOM

The psychiatric disorders of children and adolescents do not feature prominently in the early history of psychiatry. In the late nineteenth century, however, serious medical interest began to be shown in the emotional and intellectual problems of young people and in the importance of a developmental perspective in understanding disorder. Increasingly attention was paid to differences in intellectual ability which allowed psychiatrically disordered young people to be distinguished from those with mental handicap.

Developments in the USA and later in England were strongly influenced by the teaching of Adolf Meyer (1866–1950), whose concern with the uniqueness of the individual rather than clinical descriptions of mental disorder was enthusiastically taken up by those struggling to understand troubled young people. His psychobiological approach embracing physical, psychological, and environmental influences enabled a multifactorial clinical and social-developmental perspective to be taken. This theoretical base helped to fuse the contributions of psychiatrists, psychologists, and social workers, and in the 1920s clinics were set up in England following this model. Developments spread rapidly and by 1939 there were forty-six out-patient clinics in Great Britain based on the 'Child Guidance' model of multidisciplinary work with contributions from psychiatry, psychology, social work, and child psychotherapy. Initially there was no training for staff specific to childhood and adolescence and the staffing of many services began on the basis of those who had trained to work with adults deciding to spend sessions of their time in clinics working with children and their families.

After the Second World War, the number of clinics continued to grow until the 1970s, when a point was reached when most towns, boroughs, and counties had at least out-patient services. Services often developed in response to the needs of schools and increasingly to provide services to the courts, which valued, and continue to value, advice from experts in making difficult decisions about the needs and welfare of children. In most instances the child guidance clinics were administered and funded by the local authorities with their Medical Officers of Health providing the medical staff input and other departments of the local authorities providing social workers and psychologists. A pattern of leadership developed in many services in which one of the medical staff was designated to be the medical director.

At much the same time separate and parallel developments of NHS teaching hospital based services for children and adolescents were taking place. Once again many of the staff developed interests in working with children from a base in adult psychiatry. These services were frequently associated with existing mental hospitals or with large paediatric hospitals and offered out-patient services and later in-patient units for children and adolescents.

The result of these essentially uncoordinated parallel streams of development was that by the 1970s a situation had been reached in which many towns had two services – one offered by the NHS, which was often hospital-based, and the other offered by the local authority which was often based in the community. In some instances there was overlapping of staff but in many a formal mechanism for co-ordination between the two did not exist. This situation is an example of the circumstances of the 1960s and early 1970s wherein both hospital management committees and local authorities employed social workers and doctors. In 1974 local government and the Health Service were reorganized simultaneously. Local management of the NHS passed from the administration of hospitals and groups of hospitals to being based on that of Area Health Authorities (AHAs), each charged with providing services to a defined population within boundaries often coterminous with those of local authorities. The new AHAs took over responsibility for public health and community medicine from the local authorities with the intention of providing more comprehensive services through more rational planning. School medical services passed to the new health authorities, as did most of the medical staff who worked in the child-guidance clinics. The employment of all social workers passed to the social services departments. The Department of Health and Social Security (DHSS) required attention to be given to the development of co-ordinated mental health services for children and young people in each area.

Although these intentions were admirable, resulting in improved services in many places, the new arrangements also sowed the seeds of great difficulties for child and adolescent mental health services. Major problems have sprung from the struggle to produce effective services in circumstances in which staff were employed by, and the capital and revenue found by, at least two different authorities. Each had its own responsibilities, priorities, and planning machinery – one responsible to local government and the other direct to central government. These inherent structural weaknesses were containable throughout the 1970s, but in the 1980s they contributed powerfully to the reductions in service and the consequent forced movement away from the multidisciplinary model of services when financial pressures on public services began to bite hard.

An account has been given of child guidance and child psychiatry services because in many towns and counties separate out-patient services for adolescents have not existed. The histories of adolescent services and child psychiatry out-patient services have been indivisible. In some other places adolescent services have developed from, and in closer association with, adult psychiatry services. In many instances, where separate out-patient and community facilities for adolescents have developed, this occurred alongside expanding in-patient services.

In-patient units specifically for children and adolescents began to appear in the nineteenth century, to care for the severely mentally retarded. In the United States units were set up in the 1920s primarily for young people suffering the after-effects of encephalitis. The growing experience of the positive effects of such therapeutic environments on disturbed young people began to be reported and excited interest in the UK.

In the UK the first in-patient adolescent units were opened in the late 1940s at St Ebba's, Epsom, and Bethlem Hospitals. The number of units grew slowly until the mid-1960s. Concern over the plight of adolescents admitted to adult psychiatric wards was raised in the House of Commons and spurred the then Ministry of Health to issue Memorandum HM 64(4) (Ministry of Health 1964), which gave guidance to health regions on the numbers of beds required specifically for adolescents. This speeded up the previously slow development of adolescent units across the country with a crescendo of new services being established in the decade to 1974. Although largely provided by health authorities, major contributions of staff were made to the units by local authority, education, and social services departments. The literature indicates variations in structure, function, and therapeutic model (Evans and Acton 1972; Bruggen *et al.* 1973; Wells *et al.* 1978; Steinberg *et al.* 1981; Ainsworth 1984; Place *et al.* 1985a, b; Perinpanayagam 1987). A good general account of staff roles in, and the functioning of, UK adolescent units is offered in a text entitled *The Adolescent Unit* (Steinberg 1986). Many units developed as modified therapeutic communities and, in addition to in- and day-patient treatment facilities, have provided specialist out-patient services. Many adolescent units have come to act as resource centres offering multidisciplinary training and consultation to other professionals. Their staff have provoked rapid developments in knowledge, technique, and professional development including the specialism of child and adolescent psychiatric nursing.

The Association for the Psychiatric Study of Adolescents was founded as a multidisciplinary organization in 1969 largely to support the staff of adolescent units in their pioneering work. Since then the Association has broadened to cater for all professional staff who work with troubled young people.

RECENT HISTORY

Some sixty years after the inception of community child guidance clinics such tripartite organizations continue to exist but the idealism and optimism of the early days have faded, to be replaced by competition for control by health, education, and social services departments and wholesale withdrawal of staff by local authorities in a growing number of areas. Consideration of the history shows that the provision of psychiatric services for adolescents has owed less to policies carefully created and purposefully enacted and rather more to the enthusiasm and determination of individuals who had in common a vision of what should be done. Similarly, their demise owes less to policy change than to piecemeal fragmentation in a climate of increasing pressure on resources and increasing demands on local and health authorities.

Increased emphasis on child protection and child abuse investigation is claimed as an important factor by progressively stretched social services departments, while educational psychologists are moving into greater commitments to indirect therapeutic work with schools and face growing administrative tasks related to changes brought about by the Education Act 1981 and the introduction of the National Curriculum. Changes wrought by the introduction of local management of schools are likely to increase these demands and may even challenge the survival of school psychological services.

The natural and positive tendency for individual professions to concentrate on developing their own skills, autonomy, and differentiated identities has improved expertise. At the same time this has undoubtedly contributed to the process of separation – an intriguing and ironic parallel with the process of normal adolescent development.

Increasingly, adolescents are being treated in Health Service clinics linked to general, psychiatric, or paediatric hospitals and staffed by consultant psychiatrists, and other NHS personnel including clinical psychologists, child psychotherapists, psychiatric nurses, and child and family therapists. It seems likely that the traditional jointly provided child guidance clinic will disappear in the 1990s, along with social workers from Health Service teams. The authors predict that services for adolescents with psychiatric disorder are likely to become the sole responsibility of health authorities, with the possibility of some contribution from the voluntary and private sectors.

The growth of in-patient units took place in an unplanned and chaotic way with services developing around charismatic leaders who were able to open units in the face of the low priorities given to disturbed adolescents in mental health budgets. This led to serious problems in the geographical distribution of in-patient services and a number of major centres of population remain without facilities. The very nature of this unplanned growth, at its maximum in the 1960s and 1970s, has left the units extremely vulnerable to changes in leadership, political climate, finance, and management in the Health Service. Throughout the 1980s adolescent units have faced growing pressure with an increasing number of closures or threats of closure by district health authorities. Indeed, the recent history of services for disordered adolescents chronicles a failure to capitalize on earlier developments and reduction and fragmentation of services. In 1980 around 700 beds were available. The 5th edition of the Register of Adolescent Units published by the Association for the Psychiatric Study of Adolescents in 1990 (APSA 1990) contains sixty-eight entries for the UK. By comparison with the previous edition of 1983 (APSA 1983) it is clear that a number of services have closed and many others have been significantly reduced in size.

The failure of professional advice to influence national policy on the development of services for disturbed adolescents is clearly illustrated by the lack of impact of a recent report based on a national investigation by the Health Advisory Service (HAS) (NHS Health Advisory Service 1986). This was conducted between 1984 and 1986 in response to widespread concern about the provision of adolescent mental health resources.

The HAS team found patchy and uncoordinated services during their extensive visits, with youngsters often falling through the net. There was an absence of separate planning mechanisms for adolescents and a tendency for 'buck passing' between health, education, social services, and voluntary organizations. Their report, *Bridges over Troubled Waters*, recommended the establishment of comprehensive and integrated services for disturbed young people based on joint interagency philosophies and strategies. Clear principles were outlined on which good services should be based, and strong emphasis given to the need for those with special responsibility for the management of adolescents to interrelate and co-ordinate their activities, share expertise, and recognize each other's special skills. An increase in research into the nature of adolescent disorder and the outcome of therapeutic interventions and models of service delivery was recommended.

The report outlined an integrated model of services with local resource centres (in parallel or in combination with existing out-patient services) as the point of first contact, offering advice, counselling, and support. Each health district was recommended to support these local services with small residential facilities offering day care, assessment, and treatment, close to the young person's home. In each health region a small number of specialized, eclectic in-patient units should cater for the more seriously disturbed and difficult cases as well as acting as foci for training and outreach support to district services. The report recognized a continuing need, at national level, for the specialist care of very seriously disturbed adolescents, for instance at the Youth Treatment Centres, special hospitals and other specialized facilities, but hoped that the creation of more locally based services would diminish this requirement. The authors' evolution of this model is presented later.

Clear advice was also given to central government, particularly on the need for an Interdepartmental Standing Committee (including the Health, Social Security, and Social Services Inspectorate arms of the DHSS, the Department of Education and Science, the Home Office, and the Welsh Office) to improve national policy development for young people. Too often, policies were developed by individual government departments without consultation during development.

This detailed report, with its analysis of existing problems and extensive recommendations, was generally well received by professionals in the field. It did, though, fuel a prominent debate during the 1980s, both within and without adolescent mental health services, about the focus and primary functions of adolescent units (Wells 1986). The arguments have been highlighted by the growing financial pressures upon adolescent services. In essence the HAS Report recommended that adolescent units should offer general services and argued for a reduction in their selectivity of referrals accepted. This position has found support from those who see the main focus of adolescent units as being to provide services for those young people with the most severe psychiatric disorders and from planners in parts of the country where finance available for such services is most limited. On the other hand the concept of the 'general purpose' adolescent unit has been criticized by those who argue the difficulties of admitting, and effectively treating, those with a wide range of disorders in the same environment and within the same therapeutic ethos. The literature reflects this debate. The need for planned specialization within a wider geographical area has also been presented by those who argue that the primary focus of many adolescent unit treatment regimes should be directed towards the statistically most numerate adolescent psychiatric disorders (the conduct and emotional disorders) as opposed to the most severe disorders. They urge the allocation of additional resources to adolescent mental health services to allow specialization rather than an either/or approach.

The *Bridges over Troubled Waters* report optimistically held out a blueprint for creative change and development of better and more integrated services for the future. A view of the development and nature of adolescent mental health services and a glimpse at the lack of impact of the *Bridges* report upon Health Service planning is offered by the circumstances of one English health region.

This region serves a population of around 3.3 million people. The history of the development of its mental health services for adolescents is similar to that of many other areas of the country. Both the child guidance movement and the development of hospital-based child and adolescent psychiatry can be traced in the region with these services coming together in 1974. The bulk of out-patient psychiatric services for adolescents was provided in services which covered the whole of childhood and the first half of adolescence. A number of specialist in-patient services developed in the region around charismatic personalities but no coherent regional plan existed until 1990. A review of child and adolescent mental health services in the region was completed in 1985. It identified the resources and staff provided by the health service in a detailed way and showed that there were five units providing in-patient facilities for young people and, therefore, a degree of specialization in the mental health needs of adolescents with serious disorders. Three units offered five-days-a-week provision and two were able to provide continuing care on a seven-days-a-week basis. Only three units admitted adolescents above the age of 14. In all, eighty-five beds were available and, in addition, there were twenty-five day places for children and adolescents within the region. Even at that stage the number of places and their distribution was seen as unsatisfactory and strong recommendations were made for the development of additional resources in two densely populated cities. Less than half of the districts in the region had a separately identified specialist adolescent mental health service providing a reasonable spread of service. A pattern had developed of districts with only out-patient services referring individuals and families for more specialized treatments to the better resourced districts. Often this required adolescents and families to travel considerable distances, perhaps eighty miles or more, and this undoubtedly had an impact on referral practice and uptake of services by families.

In 1988, a follow-up survey showed that one district had closed all its twenty beds for adolescents. While a small day-service was left in its wake this was clearly only effectively available to the local population. Thereafter, severely disordered adolescents from that district and its neighbours have had to be referred to other services in the region at a greater distance, resulting in increased pressure on the remaining services. This paradoxical move away from local community-oriented services occurred at a time when pressure to provide these was rapidly increasing. In the same survey a loss of eight beds at another unit was also reported, meaning that in all a third of the total number of in-patient places available in the region had been lost in a period of around eighteen months. Despite a small, planned development of resources in one city in the region, this process has continued since, and by 1990 the accumulated loss of in-patient resource was estimated as approximately 45 per cent of the 1985 total.

Why were these changes made? Was the closure of these in-patient services planned? Could developments of this kind be seen as a good thing for young people representing a move from institutional to community forms of care?

The authors' contention is that several different, but related, processes were acting synergistically. There is hardly need to draw attention to the progressive tightening in public finance in the 1980s, and despite mental health services receiving a government designation of Priority Services, the overall growth in spending on them, in real terms, in the past decade has been small. Pressure on already patchy and incomplete adolescent mental health services increased. A second process at work was the rapid move towards increasing dissemination of services into the community which began to take effect in the 1970s and 1980s and 1990s. Child and adolescent mental health services had always been highly oriented towards community styles of practice but none the less this evolution in service and professional style demanded changes in embryonic services just as they were establishing themselves. A third factor has been the series of changes in Health Service management and administration in the 1980s and 1990s. Area health authorities were removed in 1982 and their constituent districts gained autonomy. Although the aims of this change and the introduction of general management, which were to bring planning and control of services closer to the patient, were laudable, they appear to have had a perverse impact on adolescent mental health services as many districts have found themselves, realistically, too small to support a fully comprehensive service of their own. Finally, this decade coincided with a time when a number of the original innovators were nearing retirement.

The two districts which closed beds have been able to build local services with greater community components but at the expense of reducing the services that had previously been offered to the populations of neighbouring districts. Superficial examination suggests that important benefits to patient care in the two districts have accrued but these gains have occurred at very high cost. First, there has been the loss of all the in-patient facilities in one district and their progressive reduction in the other. Second, what happened resulted from plans made on the basis of local financial interests and perceived necessities rather than being based on professional advice which considered the needs of the population of the region as a whole. It is certainly true that specialist services for young people are expensive relative to those for adults, though in relationship to 'high-tech' health services the overall costs are modest. The authors' contention is that districts which have found themselves providing services to the populations of their neighbours have determined that the service needs of their own districts take priority and consequently have reduced resources. However, the authors are very concerned that changes in style of, and investment in mental health services for young people in this century have resulted, in part from the growing insularity of health districts. The inherent problems which mental health services face in demonstrating, first, need within the population and, second, efficacy of intervention have also contributed to the difficulties for their professional staff in making appeals for increased investment and arguing for the continuing existence of resources. It is believed that a combination of these processes, amplified to national level, has contributed to further deterioration of that pre-existing uncertain and patchy picture described in the *Bridges* report. The authors contend that this seriously reduced morale in many adolescent mental health services in the UK in the late 1980s.

PROFESSIONAL TRAINING AND ACADEMIC DEVELOPMENTS

In parallel with the development and changing nature of services the professions involved in work with disturbed adolescents have undergone their own development.

Child and Adolescent Psychiatry was recognized as a Specialist Section of the Royal Medico-Psychological Association (RMPA) in 1946 and remained so when the RMPA became the Royal College of Psychiatrists in 1971. Membership of the Section is restricted to psychiatrists working in the specialty in order that this body should represent the views of practising child and adolescent psychiatrists. The advice of the Section is sought by the College whenever relevant issues arise. It acts as a focus for meetings of child and adolescent psychiatrists, discussion of current concerns, practice and problems, and the promotion of postgraduate training.

In 1976 research undertaken by the Brunel Institute of Organization and Social Studies (BIOSS 1976) identified serious confusion and uncertainty about professional relationships in multidisciplinary teams in child guidance clinics, which had led in some cases to problems in the delivery of care. In response, the Child and Adolescent Psychiatry Specialist Section of the Royal College of Psychiatrists convened a working party in 1977 to define the role, responsibilities, and work of child and adolescent psychiatrists. Its report (Royal College of Psychiatrists 1978) addressed the delicate issues of autonomy and hierarchy in different disciplines, 'primacy' in the work of multidisciplinary clinics, and how a consultant's time might be apportioned. This represented the first step in clarifying the particular role and responsibilities of the child and adolescent psychiatrist.

In 1983 the Royal College of Psychiatrists (RCPsych) gave clear recommendations for a minimum number of child and adolescent psychiatrists for a District Service (RCPsych 1983). The College document, 'The roles, responsibilities and work of a child and adolescent psychiatrist' of 1986 (RCPsych 1986) incorporated this advice. It focused on the core functions, training, and responsibilities of consultant psychiatrists employed by health authorities and their relationships with the other professionals involved in the network of those working with disturbed young people. The importance of teaching, continuing education, and research were emphasized. Compared to the report of 1978 this policy document placed much less emphasis on the intricacies of work in multidisciplinary teams and appeared to acknowledge that other disciplines had also moved on in the interval and were working more autonomously. In the subsequent College document, 'The role of the child and adolescent psychiatrist' of 1990 (RCPsych 1990), this trend towards increasing delineation of role is clearly visible. These College papers, when viewed retrospectively, provide a commentary on an interdisciplinary process, which appears set to continue, with psychiatrists and the other disciplines increasingly moving away from the multidisciplinary ethic of the 1960s and establishing their own specific contribution to mental health services, albeit alongside and in communication with each other.

The College contributes to the appointment of all consultants in the Health Service through its nomination of an approved assessor as a full member of every Advisory Appointments Committee. Through this mechanism the College endeavours to ensure the adequacy of training and clinical experience of appointees. This is recommended to be four years of higher training in a recognized post in the specialty subsequent to general psychiatric training and the attainment of Membership of the College.

The Joint Committee on Higher Psychiatric Training (JCHPT) is a body formed jointly by the Royal College of Psychiatrists and the Association of University Teachers in Psychiatry (AUTP) with responsibilities to the Department of Health for setting the standards for higher specialist training in all psychiatric specialties. It is responsible for the approval, monitoring, and review of training schemes. JCHPT requirements have become increasingly stringent, insisting upon a specified range of clinical experience, the provision of an academic programme, and the opportunity to conduct research for trainees in all schemes. The organization of training in this way has now been in existence for fifteen years and has been successful in ensuring a high, and rising, quality of training for child and adolescent psychiatrists.

The last two decades have seen a debate within psychiatry as to whether a separate specialism of 'Adolescent Psychiatry' should exist (Parry-Jones 1984). In 1976 the College published a policy statement on adolescent psychiatric services (RCPsych 1976). Although 'Child and Adolescent Psychiatry' is set to remain a combined specialty as we enter the 1990s, the authors support Parry-Jones's (1990) view that theoretical training and clinical experience in the adolescent component need to be strengthened.

From 1970 onwards there has been a slow but steady expansion in academic child and adolescent psychiatry based mainly on the academic departments of teaching hospitals. There are now twelve Chairs in the country. A rapid increase in research promises greater understanding of psychiatric disorder and its treatment. More effective and better validated approaches are likely to become increasingly available.

Despite greater professional separation, multidisciplinary clinical work, teaching, research, and organization remain hallmarks of adolescent psychiatry in the UK and this is reflected in the development of many professional organizations in the field. Two such are the Association for Child Psychology and Psychiatry and Allied Disciplines, founded in 1956, and the Association for the Psychiatric Study of Adolescents (APSA), founded in 1969. Both are multidisciplinary organizations which publish learned international research journals which receive contributions from many professions. These two organizations and the Royal College of Psychiatrists have made important contributions to developments in the field and have therefore advanced policy development in adolescent mental health services. In addition, the College and APSA endeavour to advocate for the needs of troubled adolescents for appropriate services at all levels at which policy is determined.

The development of nursing has mirrored that of psychiatry with an increasing emphasis on specialist training and a clearer understanding of the specific role and responsibility of the nurse. Psychiatric nurses have worked as centrally important members of the staff teams of in-patient psychiatric units for adolescents throughout their history and a small number of well-established advanced training courses have been set up in this area. Despite questions asked by some about the specific relevance of nurses in these teams, as opposed to that of residential care workers, nurses have continued to carry the main responsibility for care in adolescent mental health services (Hudson 1978). The last two decades have seen a rapid expansion of community psychiatric nursing services for adult patients involving specifically trained Registered Mental Nurses working in community settings, as members of community mental health teams or alongside general practitioners. In more recent years there has also been a small but definite increase in specialist community psychiatric nurses in adolescent psychiatric teams, and specialist advanced training courses accredited by the Joint Board of Clinical Nursing Studies have been developed. The general move away from institutional-based provision for adult psychiatric patients towards a model of community care is likely to see increasing numbers of community psychiatric nurses, with the possibility of closer links being established with district adolescent mental health services.

Psychologists work with adolescents both within health and education systems. The work and changing role of educational psychologists has already been touched upon with an account of their decreased involvement in interdisciplinary work and their greater involvement in schools. In 1981 around 300 of the then 1,100 clinical psychologists in England, Scotland, and Wales were working for at least part of their time with young people, although a much smaller number worked specifically with adolescents. Most clinical psychologists are employed by health authorities. After graduation they receive training as applied psychologists for a range of client groups. Psychologists are trained in the skills and science of objective assessment of a wide range of human behaviours, attitudes, and mental capacities and in the planning, conduct, supervision, and teaching of behaviour therapies. Many are trained in other styles of psychotherapy including individual, marital, sexual, family, and group therapy (British Psychological Society 1983). The Division of Clinical Psychology of the British Psychological Society, formed in the 1960s, has increasingly recognized the potential role of clinical psychology in the treatment of disordered children and adolescents and promoted its development in the Health Service. Their current distribution is uneven. Clinical psychologists work in a variety of settings with adolescents – as members of integrated child mental health teams, in in-patient units and, increasingly, as autonomous practitioners in their own departments of child psychology. The future development of this growing profession is hard to predict but the indications are towards autonomy and away from joint ventures with other mental health disciplines.

SUMMARY OF THE HISTORY OF ADOLESCENT MENTAL HEALTH SERVICE POLICY

The historical picture of policies concerning Adolescent Mental Health Services in the UK which emerges from this presentation can be divided into three significant periods. These are:

(1) Service and Professional Development prior to 1964;

(2) Service and Professional Development in the period from 1964 to 1974;
(3) Professional Development and Service Changes in the period 1974 to 1991.

In essence the first phase was one in which all psychiatric and mental health services for children and young people were thinly provided and were developing on an *ad hoc* basis. The recognition of the need for such services had been born and the responsibility for their provision was slowly being taken up both by the local authorities and also by hospital services. However, there were few separate services for adolescents. In the early 1960s political interest in services specifically for young people ushered in a period of very rapid development at a time of growing economic prosperity. This was halted by the major change in the economic climate in the mid-1970s. It is difficult to conceive how matters might have developed had not a world economic recession, in response to the Middle East Oil Crisis, resulted in a reduction of new monies available to all statutory services. At that time the new adolescent mental health services, just a decade away from the parliamentary intervention which had provoked their rapid development, were at a sensitive stage in their development. They were inevitably patchy in their distribution. In the following seventeen years the accumulated impact of changes such as the tightening of public finance, the subtle but important changes brought by a reorganization of local government and the Health Service in 1974, and changes in social policies on a broader base have put embryonic adolescent mental health services under great pressure. Since the mid-1970s they have received little increase in finance in real terms. Concern about them led to the *Bridges over Troubled Waters* report of 1986 which clearly indicates how the standstill in development has persisted. The Health Advisory Service report called for the development of rationally based regional and district policies, strategies, and objectives. In many regions little or no progress has been made in achieving these goals. The fact that, paradoxically, professional development has continued rapidly throughout this period strikes a more positive note.

What of the future for mental health services for adolescents, given this background? The Children Act 1989, the NHS and Community Care Act 1990 and the two Government White Papers (UK Government 1989a, b) which gave birth to the latter provide the context for the future. The Children Act 1989 clearly indicates the change in the social position of young people, particularly in the post-war period. The NHS and Community Care Act 1990 marks important shifts in what is expected of health and social services in the future. Both of these measures are explored in order to forecast the way forward.

THE FUTURE OF ADOLESCENT MENTAL HEALTH SERVICES

The Children Act 1989 (White *et al.* 1990) arguably presents the most far-reaching reform of the law relating to children and families in the last fifty years. Its preparation and the measures which it contains, most of which were implemented in October 1991, give evidence to the rising status of children in western society. As the survival of children in western nations has increased, particularly in the past two centuries, and life-threatening illnesses have become more easily treated, the focus in childhood disorder has moved from acute disease to injury, abuse, developmental, behavioural, and welfare problems. Concentration on preventive interventions and the continuing care of the chronically ill young person is increasing.

Parliamentary concern about the law relating to children and their families resulted in the White Paper *The Law Relating to Child Care and Family Services* of 1987 (UK Government 1987), while concerns in the legal profession led to the Law Commission publishing recommendations on the reform of private law relating to children in 1988. A series of enquiries into the circumstances surrounding the deaths of a number of children in the 1980s and the events in Cleveland in the summer of 1987 brought sexual and physical abuse to a climax of public concern (UK Government 1988). These and other influences led to the Children Act.

The law relating to children and their families has been spread across a wide number of measures in public and private law and one of the main aims of this new Act is to bring together the law relating to children in one framework. Other aims are identification of the rights of children and the achievement of a better balance between the duties of adults to protect children and the need to allow parents to challenge the intervention of the state in the upbringing of their children both quickly and fairly. The Act encourages greater partnership between the state and parents and promotes the use of voluntary arrangements. As this chapter is written the Department of Health is publishing its guidance and Regulations to the Act. General themes are emerging from those documents already published. These include the application of increasing knowledge of child development to the design of the guidance and Regulations, the determination to increase the speed of legal intervention, and the promotion of greater co-operation between health and local authorities. It is ironic that the importance of multidisciplinary co-operation in the provision of services for young people is stressed at a time when this principle is under substantial pressure in the services which are presently being provided.

Few will fault the general principles of this Act. At first sight, it appears mainly oriented towards the provision of social services for young people but it clearly makes many assumptions about the style and extent of health services too. By implication the Children Act sets a policy agenda, particularly for those children and young people who suffer the most demanding problems. The Act recognizes the professional developments of recent years but its proper implementation will demand major increases in finance, and therein lies its vulnerability.

Simultaneously, the NHS and Community Care Act 1990 gives clear indications of the style of state provision envisaged in the future. Much has been argued about the expectations of the National Health Service. The Service, introduced in 1948, was originally intended to be comprehensive and free at the point of delivery. More recent restrictions in public finance, paralleled by the rapid development in the capacity of health services, have resulted in an increasing gulf between potential and reality and a major challenge to the original intentions of the Service. The original principles have gradually been eroded. The Health Service Act of 1974 charges the Secretary of State for Health with provision of services which are appropriate and reasonable rather than comprehensive. This subtle but important change in the scope of the Health Service passed largely unnoticed by the public and those who work in it. The 1989 White Paper *Working for Patients*, which led to the proposals for the reorganization of the Health Service, clearly encapsulated this change in emphasis and took it several stages further. The intended philosophy of the Health Service will change from health authorities determining the scope of health care by the services they supply to that of services being based on 'external' evaluation of the needs of communities. At the same time the assumptions running through the changes are that services will be more limited by finance than by the abilities of practitioners to offer them and a belief that adoption of a market economy will bring competition between potential providers of services and thus better value for money. District health authorities are now responsible solely for the determination of 'need' as the 'Purchasers' of services while individual hospitals have become 'Providers' of services. Contracts for particular services and the money to pay for them now form the link between these two newly separated systems. The rapid increase in clinical audit and the requirements for 'information technology' to measure the performance of services follow from these principles. Without this information the new philosophies of the Health Service will barely be supportable.

These new arrangements were introduced in April 1991 and apply equally to mental health services provided for young people. It is clear that mental health services in general, and in particular those for children and young people, will face substantial problems in gaining and justifying the allocation of resources within these assumptions. The kind of work done does not lend itself to brief description, easy understanding, and simple measurement. It deals with the complexities of feeling and emotion of human experience and with personal processes which are usually less than visible and more difficult to measure than those of more acute physical maladies. There is great concern within many professional organizations that mental health services for the young, which have already been caught at a sensitive point in their development by the frost of greater economic austerity in the mid-1970s, will be increasingly vulnerable in a Health Service built upon the principles of the industrial/financial market-place.

An additional problem is that, in the authors' opinion, mechanisms for the rational planning of services could easily be casualties in the new system. The process of attrition of services described earlier has been made possible by a combination of an increasing accent on the responsibilities of district health authorities to local populations and in some instances the absence of effective regional strategies to guide districts in collaborative ventures. In the authors' opinion the new structure is likely to increase concentration upon services provided by individual hospitals and NHS Trusts, and threatens to accelerate the existing process. The answer to this problem lies in regional health authorities effectively using their powers to review the contracts let between Purchasers and Providers within each region. If regional health authorities were to set standards for contracts which specify the requirements for specialist adolescent mental health services and applied these, then it might prove possible to avert further attrition of resources and indeed promote rationally designed services. In the authors' view both adolescent and adult mental health services are good examples of those which require the market to be a managed one.

In summary the Health Service stands at a major point of change as it moves into the final decade of the twentieth century. There is a real risk that the Children Act will represent one side of a widening gulf between increasing public concern about the status and welfare of children in society and the actual provision of resources on the other. The development of services has been more influenced by the economy of the western world than by its policies and principles. In the view of the authors this paradox threatens to stifle the laudable aims of the Children Act.

This chapter has indicated that the contribution of deliberate, nationally agreed and implemented policy to the development of adolescent mental health services has been thin. The need for clear national and regional policies is even more critical now than in the past. Parry-Jones has reviewed current issues affecting the development of adolescent psychiatric services in a contemporary paper (Parry-Jones 1990). He advances cogent reasons for giving special attention to adolescents within mental health services. These include recognition of the maturational change and stress in adolescence, the influence of cultural and social factors, the inappropriateness of both child and adult psychiatric services for young people in this transitional phase of life, the high prevalence of psychiatric disorder which is found in up to 20 per cent of adolescents (by contrast physical disorder is relatively rare), and the nature of the disorders which present in adolescence. Practical issues such as the need for the development of specialization in the staff and the importance of group activities to adolescents in the process of growing up are further arguments for the grouping together of young people and the staff who work with them.

Cockett *et al.* (1990) have advanced a blueprint for the future provision of Adolescent Mental Health Services which develops those general principles advanced in the HAS's *Bridges over Troubled Waters* report. They emphasize the need to provide services for young people up to the age of 19 which minimize the effects of disorder on their continuing development and which promote as rapid a return to normal development as possible. They propose a pyramidal model of services with local primary care services at the base, more specialized secondary treatment facilities at district and supra-district levels, and very specialized tertiary services at regional level.

The base of the pyramid would be a network of neighbourhood health, educational, and social services, with staff and facilities provided on an integrated basis. Such services would be accessible to adolescents and their families and well linked in with a wide range of other school and youth resources. At the next level of the pyramid would lie the more central and specialized facilities of the District Adolescent Mental Health Services. These should provide out-patient and consultative services which could continue to be based within the existing child psychiatry and child and adolescent mental health services but would need to be resourced in a style appropriate to older adolescents. Specialized out-patient clinics and day attendance programmes, well integrated with other hospital-based health services, and the specialist services of the local authority and the voluntary sector, must be included. Each purchasing health authority should have access to a five-day-week adolescent psychiatric day and in-patient services for those adolescents who require more intensive therapy than can be provided on an out-patient basis alone. Preferably this should be within twenty miles of each adolescent's home. In some instances the health authorities and NHS trusts providing services will be large enough to support such a facility themselves but more usually it is envisaged that this kind of service would be provided on a supra-district basis, striking an acceptable balance between economy and ease of access. Each unit would function as a resource centre. The staff would be able to provide expertise and back-up to more local out-patient services through consultation and training. These outreach contacts are one of the most important components of supra-district services. At the top of the pyramid in each region there needs to be an in-patient unit able to offer investigation and treatment of those presenting the most intractable and demanding psychiatric problems. In practice this means the provision of highly specialized treatment programmes on a seven-day-a-week and often longer-stay basis. The staff need to have a high level of expertise.

Clearly the number of adolescents involved falls rapidly as one passes from the base to the top of the pyramid. However, the essential aim of an integrated overall regional service is that of offering treatment at the level at which it is possible to make optimal impact with both adolescent and family. The bias is clearly towards treating adolescents as close to home as possible but the requirements for specialized in-patient services for a small number must still be stressed.

In many instances regional strategies for adolescent mental health services are well overdue. In addition to providing a rational basis for planning, such strategies would provide effective advice to the new purchasing health authorities as well as offering a framework within which Providers would be able to be more effective in developing their services.

SOME SPECIFIC POLICY ISSUES FOR THE FUTURE

So far this chapter has considered adolescent mental health service policy generally. It finishes by highlighting several major issues which are likely to present particular policy challenges in the next decade.

This review indicates that most services have been reactive. Knowledge about normal adolescent processes has advanced rapidly and already many of those who work in services for young people spend significant amounts of their time teaching others and offering policy advice to the educational, health, and youth services. In addition, therapeutic techniques such as family therapy often have preventive benefits for family members other than the referred person. The skills of mental health professionals in preventive techniques have developed rapidly in recent decades. Explorations have demonstrated the continuity between untreated child and adolescent psychiatric disorder and psychiatric disorder in adulthood. The ability to offer preventive services exists but, so far, little direct investment has been made in this enormous potential. This is a very important issue which must be a major agenda item in youth policy for the future.

A major dilemma facing all child-care agencies is what should be done with that small but extremely difficult group of adolescents who are unmanageable in ordinary community settings. Locking up young people, always an emotive issue, continues to provoke strong reactions and a range of public policies. Public opinion has ranged from the view that a 'short sharp shock' is what is needed to reform recalcitrant youngsters to the more liberal views enshrined in the 1969 Children and Young Persons Act with its emphasis on welfare perspectives. This conflict remains unresolved in the 1990s and tension continues to exist between these positions.

A wide variety of young people may find themselves in security. Many of them are repeated absconders who fail to settle in open settings. Some have committed very serious offences, such as murder and arson, and are detained under Section 53 of the Children and Young Persons Act of 1933. Others, in local-authority care, have been extremely disruptive or aggressive to staff or offer a threat to the public because of malicious damage. A few are seen as in need of protection from themselves, such as the suicidal, the promiscuous (a particularly difficult group in the era of HIV infection and AIDS), and the drug addict.

Since the late 1960s there has been a steady growth in demand for secure accommodation. Inquiries and reports had repeatedly emphasized this need for a small minority of disruptive adolescents and during the mid-1960s around eighty places were created from within the approved schools system. In 1975 five young people were detained under Section 53 regulations, with that figure rising to more than 180 in 1986. Initially the units were envisaged as largely custodial and punitive but quickly their staff rejected this stance and have moved towards educational and treatment goals.

In 1969 local authorities took over responsibility for these units. A review of their functioning, undertaken by the Home Office, recorded criticism of inadequate admission criteria, their continuing 'dustbin' function, and magistrates' ignorance of the treatment potential of the units, as well as the high rate of reconviction of the boys on discharge. Secure Units took over the responsibility for Section 53 cases in 1969. Staff complaints that they were ill-equipped to offer long-term treatment for the seriously psychologically disordered and dangerous young person led to the provision of the Youth Treatment Centres (St Charles in Essex and Glenthorne in Birmingham) by the Department of Health, which assumed overall responsibility for them in 1971. These units are very highly staffed with a core of nurses, have highly selective admission policies, and place strong emphasis on therapy and rehabilitation.

The Dartington Social Research Unit has published two major reports (Millham *et al.* 1978; Bullock *et al.* 1990) in which careful scrutiny of long-stay secure units (in 1978) and of the Youth Treatment Centres (in 1988–9) poses fundamental questions about society's response to these very challenging young people. It is clear that the problem remains with us in the 1990s and its importance to policy makers is perhaps evidenced by the Regulations governing the use of secure accommodation being published as the first Children Act consultation document. In the future much greater emphasis on prevention and early intervention in the lives of young people at risk will be needed. The deep-seated serious dilemmas of the young people concerned will not be met by the efforts of a single agency.

Another extremely important challenge to young people and health-prevention policy makers is that of the possible spread of the Human Immunodeficiency Virus (HIV) and the Acquired Immune Deficiency Syndrome (AIDS). At the end of 1987 the US House of Representatives (1988) used the phrase 'a generation in jeopardy' to describe the impact of HIV on adolescents and in the autumn of 1989 an article appeared in the *Daily Telegraph* referring to the publication of 'alarming figures on the spread of the AIDS virus among heterosexual American teenagers', by the US federal government's Centres for Disease Control (Ball 1989). While the spread of the virus in the UK has been very much less, so far, the public health and personal preventive problems presented by HIV are extremely serious ones.

Adolescents face the important task of incorporating their emerging sexual potency into satisfying yet satisfactory and responsible patterns of behaviour. This involves adapting to new information and changes in body image as well as developments in attitudes and relationships. Fear and risk of pregnancy, while less problematic with improved contraception, remain significant factors affecting adolescent behaviour. In addition, adolescent psychological mechanisms for handling anxiety need to be widely understood by policy makers and health educators. The advent of the risk of AIDS increases these demands on young people, their parents, and health educators. Although the overall risks to mental health are unknown, there is some evidence that worry about AIDS has caused serious emotional problems for a few young people (DHSS 1987; Lewin and Williams 1988). Some adolescents put themselves at greater risk of a variety of sexual and other problems through experimentation, risk-taking, and oppositional behaviour as ways of handling the tasks before them. The potential cross-overs between drug usage as a response to adolescent problems and risk of HIV infection are extremely important.

Should young people be encouraged to use contraception, should they be encouraged to alter sexual and other behaviours, or should they be given information about the risks and then left to decide for themselves? These questions raise important overlaps between moral dilemmas, professional knowledge of adolescent psychology, and social policy. Research into the complex interaction between knowledge, attitude, and belief about HIV and AIDS has begun (Clift *et al.* 1989). There is evidence that adolescents have absorbed information at least moderately well but that this is not necessarily reflected in reduction of risk-taking behaviour. Professional interest in how adolescents might be helped to reduce behaviours risky to health is also developing (Hurrelmann 1990). Therefore professionals already have much to offer to social and health policy makers.

These are just two subjects in a wide range of mental-health-related youth-policy matters which face us now. Others include the continuing rise in drug and alcohol use by young people and the provision of effective services for those suffering long-term handicapping conditions. What all these issues and the overall provision of adolescent mental health services have in common is the importance of adequate financial resources, continued professional development, and the need for service agencies and professionals to co-ordinate their activities and share their expertise. No one profession can claim mastery. Professional knowledge and experience are growing and future services for young people would surely be improved if there were more collaboration between professionals and youth policy makers.

REFERENCES

Ainsworth, P. (1984) 'The first 100 admissions to a regional general purpose adolescent unit', *Journal of Adolescence* 7: 337–48.

Association for The Psychiatric Study of Adolescents (1983) *The Register of Adolescent Units*, 4th edn.

Association for The Psychiatric Study of Adolescents (1990) *The Register of Adolescent Units*, 5th edn.

Ball, I. (1989) 'Devastating spread of AIDS among US teenagers', *Daily Telegraph* Monday 9 October: 3.

British Psychological Society (1983) 'Psychological services for children. A statement of policy', *Bulletin of the British Psychological Society* 36: 288–90.

Bruggen, P., Byng-Hall, J., and Pitt-Aikens, T. (1973) 'The reason for admission as a focus of work for an adolescent unit', *British Journal of Psychiatry* 122: 319–29.

Brunel Institute of Organization and Social Studies (1976) 'Future organization in child guidance and allied work', Working Paper HS1, London: Brunel University.

Bullock, R., Hosie, K., Little, M., and Millham, S. (1990) 'Secure accommodation for very difficult adolescents: some recent research findings', *Journal of Adolescence* 13: 205–16.

Clift, S., Stears, D., Legg, S., Memon, A., and Ryan, L. (1989) *The HIV/AIDS Education and Young People Project: Report on Phase One*, Canterbury: HIV/AIDS Education Research Unit, Department of Educational Studies, Christ Church College.

Cockett, A.D., Skeldon, I., and Williams, R.J.W. (1990) 'Psychiatric services for adolescents in the South Western Region and their future in a changing Health Service', *South West Psychiatry* 4 (Spring): 5–11.

Coleman, J.C. and Hendry, L. (1990) *The Nature of Adolescence*, 2nd edn, London and New York: Routledge.

Court, S.D.M. (1976) *Fit for the Future. The Report of the Committee on Child Welfare Services*, DHSS, London: HMSO.

Department of Health and Social Security (1987) *AIDS – Monitoring Response to the Public Education Campaign February 1986–February 1987*, London: HMSO.

Douvan, E. and Adelson, J. (1966) *The Adolescent Experience*, London: Wiley.

Evans, J. and Acton, W.P. (1972) 'A psychiatric service for disturbed adolescents', *British Journal of Psychiatry* 120: 429–32.

Ford, K., Hudgens, R.W., and Welner, A. (1978) 'Undiagnosed psychiatric illness in adolescents; a prospective study and a year follow up', *Archives of General Psychiatry* 35: 279–82.

Freud, A. (1958) 'Adolescence', *Psychoanalytic Study of the Child* 13: 255–78.

Graham, P. and Rutter, M. (1985) 'Adolescent disorders', in M. Rutter and L. Hersov (eds) *Child and Adolescent Psychiatry: Modern Approaches*, 2nd edn, Oxford: Blackwell Scientific.

Hudson, P. (1978) 'Residential units for disturbed adolescents: can they be justified?', *Bulletin of the British Psychological Society* 31: 45–7.

Hurrelmann, K. (1990) 'Health promotion for adolescents: preventative and corrective strategies against problem behavior', *Journal of Adolescence* 13: 231–50.

Leslie, S.A. (1974) 'Psychiatric disorders in the young adolescents of an industrial town', *British Journal of Psychiatry* 125: 113–24.

Lewin, C. and Williams, R.J.W. (1988) 'Fear of AIDS: the impact of public anxiety in young people', *British Journal of Psychiatry* 153: 823–4.

Masterson, J.F. (1967) 'The symptomatic adolescent 5 years later: he didn't grow out of it', *American Journal of Psychiatry* 123: (11) 1338–45.

Masterson, J.F. (1968) 'The psychiatric significance of adolescent turmoil', *American Journal of Psychiatry* 124: 1549–54.

Millham, S., Bullock, R., and Hosie, K. (1978) *Locking up Children*, Farnborough: Saxon House.

Ministry of Health (1964) *In-patient Accommodation for Mentally Ill and Seriously Maladjusted Children and Adolescents*, HM(64)4, London: HMSO.

National Health Service, Health Advisory Service (1986) *Bridges over Troubled Waters*, London: HMSO.

Offer, D. and Offer, J.B. (1975) *From Teenage to Young Manhood. A Psychological Study*, New York: Basic Books.

Parry-Jones, W.L.E. (1984) 'Adolescent psychiatry in Britain: a personal view of its development and present position', *Bulletin of the Royal College of Psychiatrists* 8: 230–3.

Parry-Jones, W.L.E. (1990) 'Adolescent psychiatric services: development and expansion', in Royal College of Psychiatrists, *Child and Adolescent Psychiatry: Into the 1990s*, Occasional Paper no. 8.

Perinpanayagam, K.S. (1987) 'Organisation and management of an in-patient treatment unit for adolescents', *Journal of Adolescence* 10: 133–48.

Pichel, J.I. (1974) 'A long term follow-up study of 60 adolescent psychiatric out-patients', *American Journal of Psychiatry* 131: 140–4.

Place, M., Framrose, R., and Willson, C. (1985a) 'The difficult adolescents who are referred to a psychiatric unit. 1. Classification', *Journal of Adolescence* 8: 297–306.

Place, M., Framrose, R., and Willson, C. (1985b) 'The difficult adolescents who are referred to a psychiatric unit. 2. Clinical features and response to treatment', *Journal of Adolescence* 8: 307–20.

Royal College of Psychiatrists (1976) 'Memorandum on the psychiatry of adolescence', *British Journal of Psychiatry, News and Notes* September: 6–9.

Royal College of Psychiatrists (1978) 'The role responsibilities and work of a child and adolescent psychiatrist', *Bulletin of the Royal College of Psychiatrists* May: 12.

Royal College of Psychiatrists (1983) 'Providing a district service for child and adolescent psychiatry: medical manpower priority', *Bulletin of the Royal College of Psychiatrist* May: 94–7.

Royal College of Psychiatrists (1986) 'The role responsibility and work of a child and adolescent psychiatrist', *Bulletin of the Royal College of Psychiatrists* August: 202–6.

Royal College of Psychiatrists (1990) 'The role of the child and adolescent psychiatrist', *Psychiatric Bulletin* 14: 119–20.

Rutter, M., Graham, P., Chadwick, O.F.D., and Yule, W. (1976) 'Adolescent turmoil: fact or fiction', *Journal of Child Psychology and Psychiatry* 17: 35–56.

Steinberg, D. (ed.) (1986) *The Adolescent Unit: Work and Teamwork in Adolescent Psychiatry*, Chichester: John Wiley.

Steinberg, D., Galhenage, D., and Robinson, S. (1981) 'Two years referrals to a regional adolescent unit: some implications for psychiatric services', *Social Service Medicine* 15E: 113–22.

UK Government (1987) *The Law Relating to Child Care and Family Services*, Cmnd 62, London: HMSO.

UK Government (1988) *The Report of the Inquiry by Lord Justice Butler-Sloss into Child Abuse in Cleveland*, Cmnd 412, London: HMSO.

UK Government (1989a) *Caring for People. Community Care in the Next Decade and Beyond*, Cmnd 849, London: HMSO.

UK Government (1989b) *Working for Patients*, Cmnd 555, London: HMSO.

US House of Representatives (1988) *A Generation in Jeopardy: Children and AIDS, A Report of the Select Committee on Children, Youth, and Families*, 100th Congress 1st Session, Washington: US Government Printing Office.

Wells, P. (1986) 'Cut price adolescent units that meet all needs and none?', *Bulletin of the Royal College of Psychiatrists* 10: 231–2.

Wells, P.G., Morris, A., Jones, R.M. and Allen, D.J. (1978) 'An adolescent unit assessed: a consumer survey', *British Journal of Psychiatry* 132: 300–8.

White, R., Carr, P., and Lowe, N. (1990) *A Guide to the Children Act 1989*, London: Butterworths.

9 Empowerment and child welfare

Mike Stein and Nick Frost

INTRODUCTION

In recent years, in common with other areas of youth policy, welfare interventions with young people have undergone a series of profound changes and shifts. This chapter aims to analyse these developments by providing:

(1) a theoretical perspective on welfare interventions with young people;
(2) a historical overview of legal and policy development;
(3) an exploration of contemporary policy, looking specifically at the Children Act 1989; and
(4) a view of practice and policy directions for the 1990s.

Our central argument is that state interventions with young people can only be understood politically, and that the concept of 'empowerment' provides a useful theoretical approach to policy and practice development.

WELFARE INTERVENTIONS WITH YOUNG PEOPLE: A THEORETICAL PERSPECTIVE

Childhood and youth are socially created categories, historically and culturally variable (Aries 1985; Hoyles 1979), but which in contemporary Britain are strongly associated with powerlessness. Young people experience powerlessness through their status as young people – by exclusion from decision-making processes, for example in schools, or, on a wider basis, by their exclusion from the political process. However, this powerlessness is often overlaid by other categories, most notably social class, disability, ethnicity, and gender – which interact with generation to produce a matrix of power/powerlessness. This is a complex matrix which we go on to develop in some depth.

In the last two decades we have become used to understanding gender, ethnicity, disability, and to a lesser extent sexual orientation as indices of the unequal distribution of power in a stratified society. Equal-opportunities policies have become a familiar vehicle for attempts to tackle such inequalities. This conceptual framework has not been applied to generation in such a rigorous manner. In our analysis 'generation' is understood as a system through which young people experience negative attitudes, policies, and practices which act in an discriminatory manner against them. As with racism and sexism this is manifested in both individual practices and attitudes and in institutional forms.

Children and young people experience inequality according to social class, gender, ethnicity, and disability, but their experience cannot be fully understood unless generation is conceptualized as a comparable indicator. Judith Ennew (1986) has illustrated this using a matrix of power which indicates how poor, black girls are the most exploited and rich, white men are most likely to be the main exploiters (this is illustrated by Ennew from her work on child pornography, prostitution, and sex tourism as global phenomena).

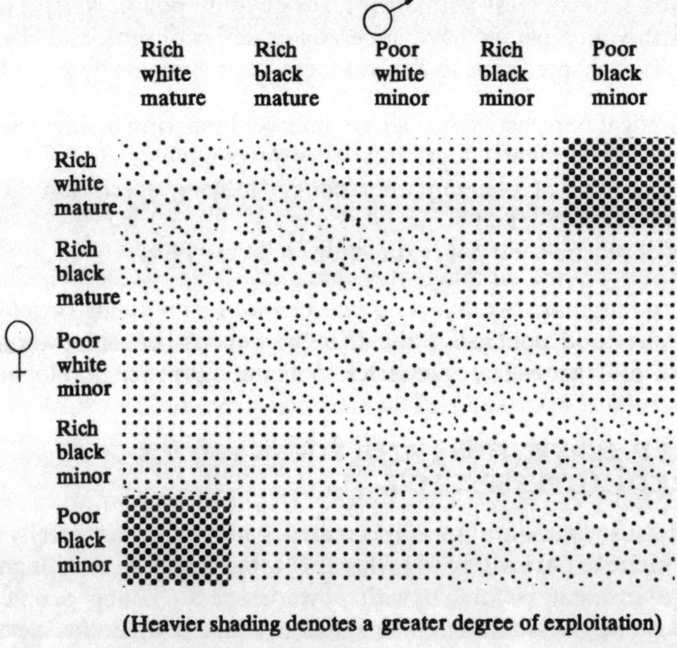

Figure 9.1 The dimensions of exploitation

Note: This graphic depiction of the relationship between age, gender, class and race shows exploitation shading the female half of the square most heavily. Equal relations may be thought of as possible between persons of the same age, sex, class and race, if personality factors are not taken into account.

Source: Ennew 1986: 3

Seen in this way generation becomes a crucial political field of play – comparable to those other fields we are more used to understanding as political. For this reason we find structuralist analyses, which are based exclusively on class, or feminist perspectives, which are based purely on gender, as inadequate in attempting to understand and construct a politics of childhood. The real challenge is to understand the complex interaction of different indicators of powerlessness and how they reinforce and interact with each other. As we have argued elsewhere:

> Children and young people should be perceived as an identifiable social group with their own set of interests . . . This point has rarely been recognised in either the literature on childhood, which tends to ignore class and gender, or the literature on inequality, which tends to disregard the separate experience of childhood.
>
> (Frost and Stein 1989:7)

Such an analysis should not privilege generation as *the key* political factor but simply attempt to put the issue centrally on the agenda. This political (as opposed to, say, a biological or psychological) understanding of childhood places power at the centre of our analysis of childhood and youth.

There are two important theoretical points to make about power, which are relevant to our discussion. First, power can only be understood as a relational concept. By this we mean that an individual or group is only powerless or powerful in relation to another individual or group. So the social position of people with disabilities, for example, only makes sense when understood in terms of their relationship with able-bodied people. Power becomes a material reality in the relationship between individuals, social groups, and institutions.

Second, power cannot exist without resistance. This resistance may be overt, as in, for example, demonstrations against governments or in the self-organization of consumers in the personal social services (Collins and Stein 1989). However, resistance may take more covert forms – in the field of child welfare, for example, the development of secret languages in residential institutions for young people. This gives us problems with the word 'powerlessness', as a display of resistance will indicate that even the most oppressed are not exactly powerless; they may maintain the possibility of resisting the demands of the powerful (see Clegg 1989).

We wish to argue, therefore, that young people are generally disadvantaged in terms of the distribution of power in our society. This perspective also helps us to understand the position of young people who are subject to welfare interventions, for they are often the victims of abuse of adult power. This may have been on an individual basis, say where a girl has been sexually abused by an adult male; or on a policy (or institutional) level where young people who have been abused are often removed into care, while perpetrators remain in the family situation.

If we begin to understand welfare work with young people through this theoretical framework, we would argue that this has profound implications for policy and practice interventions, which we will go on to explore in the last section of this chapter. Initially, however, we will summarize the development of child welfare through history and assess how this might inform our central argument.

HISTORICAL OVERVIEW

British welfare policy towards children and young people has a long and complex history, which will be summarized in this section. Our analysis leads up to a discussion of the Children Act 1989, which is the most recent and important policy development in the field of child welfare.

A major historical theme identifiable in the development of child welfare policy has been the attempt by the state to 'discipline' working-class children and young people (see Donzelot 1980). This disciplinary stance was taken initially to children as part of a class group, largely through the Poor Law, and later, in late Victorian times, to children as a group in their own right – demanding specific, age-related responses. Within this dynamic is contained a historically variable relation between the state and households, the nature of which is examined below.

In feudal Britain children who were homeless or illegitimate were often cared for informally within the locality where they originated. Heywood sums up the attitude to such children as follows: 'yet while he was nobody's child, he was also the child of the people, and some community obligation was felt toward him' (1978: 1). Babies and young children temporarily uncared for would stay in hospitals but this would often lead to their later being placed with wet-nurses or foster carers. This picture, however, should not be over romanticized. While communal approaches to child care provided a caring network there is also evidence of exploitation of children – physical and sexual abuse, and use as cheap or free labour.

As the old feudal order collapsed and with the beginnings of urban settlements, a new social group, the vagrant poor, was created and was perceived as a threat to the emergent social order: 'Flight out of feudal relations could only be flight into urban centres or into vagrancy. There was nowhere else to go' (Clegg 1989: 244). Both the urban poor and the vagrant were perceived as a social problem and an actual or potential threat to order.

As part of the response to this situation, in 1535 an Act of Parliament made compulsory the apprenticeship of all children aged 5–13 who were found to be begging. Of more significance, of course, was the passing of the Poor Law Act of 1601. The Act allowed church wardens to set the poor to work or to bind them as apprentices. This notorious piece of legislation was concerned almost exclusively with the discipline and regulation of the poor as a social group; it laid down the parameters of 'welfare provision' which were to remain with child welfare until the Second World War.

The rise of industrialism presented serious disciplinary problems for the state and for private capital alike. As the Industrial Revolution intensified and as the urban centres grew there were increased problems of poverty and cyclical unemployment, and hence groups of children and young people were impoverished, homeless, orphaned, or abandoned. The social relationships between rich and poor, increasingly between capitalist and worker, became instrumental and distant. Children and young people suffered greatly in the workhouses, on the streets, or in exploitative employment. Once those who survived their early years were weaned, they effectively became part of the adult world of work, unemployment, and poverty. Orphans and illegitimate children suffered particularly in the new social order (Rose 1986).

Philanthropic responses to these social problems began to emerge in the second half of the eighteenth century. Thomas Coram, for example, set up a foundling hospital for abandoned babies in 1747, and the Philanthropic Society developed a particular interest in young offenders. These and numerous other philanthropic initiatives were characterized by the fact that they were organized by the professional, landed, and emergent industrialist classes as their response to perceived social problems. These initiatives were often 'double edged' as far as the recipients were concerned. Philanthropy could offer immediate material relief, but reinforced the recipient as passive and often demanded a change of 'attitude' or life-style.

> Philanthropy is not simply a vocation, a moral choice; it is also an act of authority that creates a linkage of dependency and obligation between rich and poor. Of necessity, therefore, it is a political act, embarked upon not merely to fulfil personal needs but also to address the needs of those who rule and those who are ruled.
>
> (Ignatieff 1985: 153)

As philanthropic initiatives developed they began to respond more and more to children and young people as a specific social group – separating them out from the more general problem of poverty and disorder. During the nineteenth century the middle class developed a strong sense of childhood as a distinct stage of life, during which young people would be both protected and controlled. Reformers such as Mary Carpenter attempted to carry this conception of childhood into what she described as the 'perishing' and 'dangerous' classes. The child-saving movement grew throughout this period, and in the latter half of the century we find the origins of the National Society for the Prevention of Cruelty to Children, the Waifs and Strays Society, and the National Children's Homes aimed at developing specific interventions in relation to children and young people. Here too we begin to find the origins of social casework – which became crystallized in the form of the organized charity of the Charity Organization Society (COS). The key distinction for the Society was between the 'deserving' and the 'undeserving' poor; thus the poor were divided and responded to as distinct social groups requiring differential responses. This was a legacy which cast a long shadow over social work.

As the nineteenth century progressed the COS philosophy became increasingly anachronistic, with the existence of socialism as a political

alternative and as social disorder became more prevalent. In his classic analysis of the COS Gareth Stedman Jones has stated that it 'found itself a defender of what was increasingly coming to be regarded as an esoteric sectarian and anachronistic social philosophy' (1984: 313).

The political hegemony of the period passed to the Liberals who initiated a series of social-welfare reforms during the period between 1906 and 1914. These reforms codified child protection measures and attempted to alleviate some of the causes of childhood destitution through the provision of school meals and medicals. Significantly, the Children Act of 1908 created juvenile courts with jurisdiction over the rescue of needy children and the reform of offenders, thus creating the material base for the 'welfare' versus 'justice' debates which are still with us today (Tutt 1982). While the physical and social condition of children and young people was no doubt improved by these and related reforms, the tenor of the reforms, while minimalist rather than socialist, clearly accepted a role for the state as opposed to adopting a purely philanthropic approach. The straightforwardly disciplinary techniques of the Poor Law begin to develop a 'supervisory' aspect, an attempt to develop 'norms' through state initiatives (see Donzelot 1980).

In the years that followed the welfare approach to children was strengthened by the 1913 Poor Law Institutions Order which prohibited children aged 3–16 from being maintained in workhouses for more than six weeks. Children were to be boarded out or placed in children's homes.

The Children and Young Persons Act 1933 extended the grounds for young people being in need of care and protection, required the juvenile court to consider the 'welfare of the child', created approved schools and placed a duty on local authorities to board children out where possible.

The experience of the evacuation of children during the Second World War and the inquiry into the death of Denis O'Neill provided the stimulus for the Children Act 1948, which created Children's Departments, thus clearly separating out child welfare from the legacy of the Poor Law. This break was further emphasized by the duty placed on local authorities to further the 'best interests' of the child, contrasting with the 'less eligibility' principle of the Poor Law.

The Children and Young Persons Act of 1969 represented the high water mark of the welfarist approach to child welfare. The Act emphasized prevention and advocated a 'welfare'-based approach as opposed to a 'justice'-based approach by the juvenile courts. Courts were empowered to make care orders on children in need of protection, not attending school, or who had committed offences. Power shifted from the courts to social workers, who had increased responsibilities once the court had made the initial disposal.

The Children Act of 1975 is significant in this context as it contained for the first time an explicit recognition of the rights of the child. This was reaffirmed by Section 18 of the Child Care Act 1980:

> in reaching any decision relating to a child in their care, a local authority shall give first consideration to the need to safeguard and promote the welfare of the child throughout his childhood: and shall as far as practicable ascertain the wishes and feelings of the child regarding the decision and shall give due consideration to them, having regard to his age and understanding.

This section realizes that a potential conflict may exist between the professional's assessment of a child's 'best interests' and the wishes of the child. Perhaps more importantly the section can be used to encourage, develop, and legitimate a whole series of policies and practices which enable children and young people to participate in decisions affecting their future.

By the 1980s it became apparent that child-care legislation was in a highly unsatisfactory state, a realization which led to the passage of the Children Act of 1989, which is the keystone to the understanding of contemporary child welfare in England and Wales.

EMPOWERING YOUNG PEOPLE THROUGH WELFARE PRACTICE

How can we understand the implications of empowerment for policy and practice in child welfare? What sort of theoretical framework do we need in order to achieve change? What would a practice agenda look like?

For us it follows that empowerment acts as an effective framework for understanding policy and practice development with young people. In order to establish why empowerment is an important concept we will first have to argue that the emphasis on children's rights, often regarded as the 'radical' perspective, is an inadequate conception both theoretically and practically.

First, arguments for children's rights are often proposed in a legalistic and paternalistic manner – something that adults should legislate for *on behalf of children and young people*. In this sense children's rights are contradictory as they exclude children and young people from the process of improving their own lives.

Second, rights arguments have a tendency to stop once they have achieved the aim of reaching the statute book. The best example of this is the legislation designed to stop discrimination on grounds of gender or ethnicity. Such legislation, while a symbolic advance in its own right, has patently failed to eliminate such discrimination. In order to work, such legislative changes have to have an impact on material reality as well as on the statute books. To give an example from welfare practice, a social services department could introduce a policy that all children in care have a right to attend their statutory reviews. This policy might even be effectively introduced and young people may be attending for the full duration of their review. Such a right would be fairly meaningless, however, if the adults continued to use jargon, if numerous adults attended and 'swamped' the child, and if the young person was not allowed to take a friend or representative. Thus, the 'right' to attend in itself, while not undesirable, should not become an end in itself, but rather a trigger for major shifts in everyday practice.

Third, rights in relation to young people tend to be framed individually; 'the child shall have the right to. . . .' Effective change for children also requires collective action and organization. This is reflected, for example, in the National Association for Young People in Care (NAYPIC) (see further discussion below).

Therefore, while rights claims are no doubt a useful part of an effective programme, we would argue that 'empowerment' is a more useful, more thorough, and more theoretically defensible position, which goes beyond the limitations of the 'rights' schools.

If the above arguments hold water, then it is clear that welfare workers are intervening with children and young people who have been severely disempowered – the process of intervention should therefore be one which is empowering; that is, practice which attempts to reverse the flow of power away from young people. One advantage of using empowerment as a conceptual frame for intervention is that it immediately unifies different levels of practice. Welfare practice has traditionally been seen as:

(1) *individual* – casework or counselling or therapy;
(2) *group* – therapeutic, behavioural, or sharing;
(3) *collective* – youth work, community work, or working with organizations.

In welfare work these three levels of intervention, despite attempts to unify them, have remained fairly discrete and have drawn on different theoretical bases. Thus, individual work has usually been casework based and drawn on psychoanalytic or related theories. Groupwork has often been humanistic. Community work has drawn on more radical theories of political change.

Many existing dominant forms of practice exist in a tension with empowering practice; such practices can be variously identified by tendencies to individualize and pathologize explanations of social problems and to individualize the subsequent interventions. Thus, for example, forms of intervention drawing on psychotherapy often use pathological definitions of social events, some forms of family therapy decontextualize families as if they exist in splendid isolation, and behaviourally based interventions tend to respond to symptoms rather than causes. While such interventions display these tendencies they cannot be incorporated into an empowering framework. However, certain practices can be reframed and, by drawing from the principles of empowerment, can break with their more retrogressive features. Thus, we would argue, that radical therapies, drawing on feminism for example, can be understood as empowering practices which have distanced themselves from individualizing and pathologizing elements.

Let us go on to illustrate how empowerment can be used to evaluate practice at all the various levels.

Individual practice

Lisa is 15 and has been sexually abused by her father – he has been having intercourse with her over the past two years. Lisa has not been able to speak to anyone about this and has internalized all the guilt and self-blame which survivors often describe (Bagley and King 1990). In terms of our theoretical framework Lisa is a victim of adult and male power. She herself feels powerless to influence events – who can she tell, how can she tell, and what will happen if she does? Lisa is particularly close to her new form teacher and one day after school stays behind and decides to tell all to the teacher. The teacher maintains her relationship with Lisa through all the painful period that follows – social-work investigations, police interventions, court hearings, and the eventual imprisonment of her father. Thankfully Lisa's mother stays beside Lisa and the two make a new life without the father.

The teacher therefore empowered Lisa by;

(1) listening,
(2) believing,
(3) being there,
(4) giving Lisa choices.

This intervention allowed Lisa to make a decision and to start taking control over her own body and her own life.

This simplified case-study illustrates how 'empowerment', while a political concept, is also about sensitive one-to-one work with young people. In enabling Lisa to take some control she was empowered by an adult who did some very simple and straightforward things.

Group practice

A group of young people on a council estate have become labelled as a disruptive and criminal element. The local youth worker is able to gain access to a spare room in the local school which can be used as a base for these young people. They come together as a group and begin to generate their own solutions to their problems; they organize a weekly disco and a street hockey team to help overcome the boredom which they define as their primary problem. The youth worker supports them in doing this, but the agenda is set by the young people themselves. The success of these first two enterprises has spin-offs – they organize a play scheme for younger children over the summer and a volunteer scheme for working with elderly people on the estate. The project grows and becomes a fulltime activity for many of the young people. They form a good relationship with the local councillor and become influential in helping to frame and influence housing, environmental, and recreational policy on the estate. Thus, the group is empowered, more able to shape and influence events than they were as a disparate group of individuals.

Collective practice

The National Association of Young People in Care is an example of young people being empowered through self-organization. NAYPIC began in Leeds in the mid-1970s with a small group of young people meeting together to voice their experience as young people in care. A national movement began to emerge following a one-day conference organized by the National Children's Bureau. In 1979 NAYPIC itself was formed following a meeting of ten 'in care' groups. A management committee consisting of both young people and adults was formed. The initial aims of NAYPIC were to improve conditions in care, make information and advice available, to promote the views and interests of young people, and to develop local groups. The organization grew throughout the early 1980s and established itself as a major campaigning group on behalf of young people in care. While it has faced organizational problems in recent years, NAYPIC represents an important break with 'pathological' approaches to young people in care. NAYPIC thus illustrates how young people can be collectively empowered, with the support of adults who wish to organize with, and not on behalf of, young people.

Empowerment can therefore operate on a variety of levels with individuals, groups, or collectives. It can involve simple acts of practice – effective interviewing, sharing information, giving young people choices – or more dramatic clearly political acts, such as challenging local-authority policies. These acts are united by the fact of their attempting to transfer power to children and young people, to enhance their opportunity to influence their own lives.

The danger with this conception of empowerment is that it becomes seen as a panacea, an easy way of 'doing good' for young people. This would be a mistaken view. Of course in the three levels of practice we have described things go wrong – perhaps as a result of bad luck or misjudgement. What the utilization of the concept does, however, is to give practice a clear sense of direction. If one is attempting to move towards empowerment of young people as a practice goal then we can assess each aspect of policy and practice by asking the question: How does this empower young people?

CONCLUSION

In this chapter we have attempted to argue that empowerment is a significant concept which can illuminate both the theoretical and practical debate about child welfare. The creative use of empowerment can impact on all levels of welfare practice and offer a decisive break with paternalistic and pathological models of intervention.

REFERENCES

Aries, P. (1985) *Centuries of Childhood*, Harmondsworth: Peregrine.
Bagley, C. and King, K. (1990) *Child Sexual Abuse: The Search for Healing*, London: Routledge.
Brent, London Borough of (1985) *A Child in Trust.*
Campbell, B. (1988) *Unofficial Secrets: Child Sexual Abuse, the Cleveland Case*, London: Virago.
Clegg, S. (1989) *Frameworks of Power*, London: Sage.
Collins, S. and Stein, M. (1989) 'Users fight back', in C. Rojeck, G. Peacock and S. Collins (eds) *The Haunt of Misery*, London: Routledge.
Donzelot, J. (1980) *The Policing of Families*, London: Hutchinson.
Ennew, J. (1986) *The Sexual Exploitation of Children*, Oxford: Polity.
Frost, N. and Stein, M. (1989) *The Politics of Child Welfare*, Brighton: Harvester/Wheatsheaf.
Greenwich, London Borough of (1987) *A Child in Mind.*
Heywood, J. (1978) *Children in Care*, London: Routledge and Kegan Paul.
HMSO (1984) *Second Report from the Social Services Committee. Children in Care*, London.
HMSO (1985) *Review of Child Care Law*, London.
HMSO (1987) *The Law on Child Care and Family Services*, Cmnd 62, London.
HMSO (1988) *Report of the Inquiry into Child Abuse in Cleveland*, Cmnd 412, London.
Hoyles, M. (ed.) (1979) *Changing Childhood*, London: Writers and Readers Co-operative.
Ignatieff, M. (1985) 'State, civil society and total institutions', in S. Cohen and A. Scull (eds) *Social Control and the State*, Oxford: Blackwell.
Jones, G. Stedman (1984) *Outcast London*, Harmondsworth: Peregrine.
Lambeth, London Borough of (1987) *Whose Child?*
Parton, N. (1986) 'The Beckford Report: a critical appraisal', *British Journal of Social Work* 16.
Rose, L. (1986) *Massacre of the Innocents: Infanticide in Great Britain*, London: Routledge and Kegan Paul.
Tutt, N. (1982) 'Justice or welfare?', *Social Work Today* 14(7).

10 Juvenile-justice policy in England and Wales

John Pitts

The mid- to late 1960s saw a sustained attempt by a Labour government, radical social scientists, progressive Home Office civil servants, and members of the social-work profession to transform the juvenile-justice system in England and Wales.

In the run-up to what eventually became the 1969 Children and Young Persons Act (CYPA), the reformers attempted, among other things, to raise the age of criminal responsibility to 17, to transfer the control of juvenile justice from central to local government, and to abolish the imprisonment of children and young people. Three related principles informed their endeavour. They were:

(1) that social inequality, and the social disadvantages it engendered, were instrumental in propelling young people into delinquency;
(2) that the stigma involved in a court appearance merely compounded such social disadvantage by confirming the young offender's delinquent identity;
(3) that the state, through its social, economic, and criminal-justice policies, should play a central role in combating, and responding humanely to, both the causes and the consequences of social inequality.

The reformers wanted to replace a court-based system, founded upon the principle of 'just desserts', with a system based upon a scientific understanding of social inequality and its consequences. In justification they pointed to the fact that the juvenile court was first and foremost a mechanism for processing the most deprived working-class children and young people. How, they asked, could such a system, which responded only to the offence and ignored its ultimate social and psychological causes, deliver *just deserts* in an unjust society?

The reforms of the 1960s aimed to recast the image of the young offender as a victim of social deprivation and the psychological problems which such deprivation engendered. As such, the young offender needed the scientifically informed interventions of 'trained experts' rather than punishment. This attempt to decriminalize and depoliticize the juvenile-justice system encountered sustained resistance from the Conservative opposition and the legal and academic establishments (Pitts 1988).

Those sections of the 1969 CYPA which threatened the power and supremacy of the bench and the judiciary, although they had been passed by Parliament, were not implemented by the Conservative administration of Edward Heath which came to power in 1970.

With the advent of the 1969 CYPA we witnessed both the high water mark and the exhaustion of social-democratic reform in the post-war period in Britain. According to Booker (1980:9), these reforms had been based on 'the utopian belief that through drastic social and political reorganisation, aided by the greater use of state planning we should be able to create a new kind of just, fair and equal society'. It was an optimistic ideology, predicated on the belief that the intrinsic altruism and goodness of human beings could be realized if the fruits of a perpetually expanding economy could be scientifically targeted on social problems. When, in the late 1960s and early 1970s, the economy went into the kind of protracted recession which the dominant Keynesian explanations of economic life maintained were no longer possible, doubt was cast upon the entire reforming endeavour.

The 1970 Heath administration offered a new, harder version of Conservatism to match the starker economic realities which followed the economic boom of the 1960s. Heath entered government promising to control inflation, the unions, and crime, and this pledge ensured that the abolition of the imprisonment of young offenders, which only months before had seemed a possibility, was scrubbed from the political agenda.

Rather than abandoning the 1969 CYPA, the only parts the Heath administration failed to implement were those which placed limitations on the power of magistrates. Furthermore, it did not raise the age of criminal responsibility, thus ensuring that the supply of delinquents to be dealt with by the police and the courts was not diminished. Furthermore, it did not phase out the Attendance Centre and the Detention Centre in favour of the new community-based Intermediate Treatment (IT), as the Act had intended, but it placed no impediment in the way of the development of IT. It did not prevent young people under 17 being sentenced to Borstal Training by the courts, but it gave social workers the power to place these young people in the revamped approved school – the Community Home (with Education) (CHE). In doing so, it substantially increased the numbers of people who could decide whether or not a child should be removed from home.

The early 1970s saw the emergence of a juvenile-justice system which was not, as the 1960s reformers had hoped, transformed, but substantially expanded. Those elements of the system which had been brought into being by the 1969 Act were absorbed into a system which retained its traditional commitment to imprisonment as the ultimate disciplinary back-stop.

Social work, and the courts and prisons constituted the two, often antagonistic, faces of the new juvenile-justice system. The two elements grew out of very different assumptions about the nature of the problem of juvenile crime and the nature of the solution to it and so, perhaps inevitably, the scene was set for a struggle between the forces of 'welfare' and the forces of 'justice' for the body of the delinquent. This was a struggle which the forces of 'justice' won hands down. Between 1965 and 1977 the numbers of young people aged 14 to 17 entering detention centres rose from 1,404 to 5,757. In the same period the Borstal population remained fairly static but the proportion of 15 to 17 year olds in it rose from 12.3 per cent to over 30 per cent. In 1965 21 per cent of convicted young offenders aged 14 to 17 were dealt with in police-administered detention centres and prison-department administered detention centres and borstals. By 1977 this proportion had risen to 38 per cent. The period witnessed a parallel decline in the social-work presence in the juvenile-justice system. In 1965 18.5 per cent of convicted young offenders were being supervised in the community by social workers or probation officers; by 1977 this had dropped to 13.5 per cent. These developments occurred, moreover, in a period in which recorded serious juvenile offending was fairly static and in some instances, in decline.

The renaissance of imprisonment, the failure to effect significant social change through social-work intervention, and cuts in the resources of local-authority social services departments (SSD) caused many people working in social welfare, academic commentators, and reformers to rethink the ideas which had informed their practice and the strategies for social change and penal reform which they had adopted. Gradually a new theoretical and ideological orthodoxy began to emerge, the tenor of which contrasted sharply with the optimism of the 1960s.

LEAVING THE KIDS ALONE

'Radical non-intervention' told workers in the juvenile-justice system that in their attempts to act in what they presumed to be a young offender's best interest they could actually be disadvantaging them further (Schur 1974). It enjoined them instead, wherever and whenever possible, to 'leave the kids alone'. The argument ran thus:

(1) Juvenile offending was a more or less universal phenomenon and an inevitable by-product of growing up.
(2) Whatever its causes, criminologists and social scientists had yet to devise an effective response to, or treatment for, juvenile offending.
(3) Attempts by agents of the state to do good to disadvantaged young people on the pretext of an assumed relationship between social circumstances and offending behaviour was an infringement of their rights and liberties serving to spoil their identities and so project them deeper into a deviant career.

Only through a reversion to due process of law, the demystification of welfare professionalism, an embargo on 'prevention', and a repudiation of 'need', it seemed, were the rights and liberties of young offenders to be defended (Morris *et al.* 1980). The attempt to do 'more good' was to be rejected in favour of doing 'less harm'.

In 1979 the Personal Social Services Council published *A Future for IT*. In many ways this brief book was a manifesto for a 'minimalist' practice in the juvenile-justice system. Whereas the people who had drafted the 1969 Act had envisaged IT as a means whereby the needs of youngsters in trouble might be more effectively met, the practice which emerged from *A Future for IT* suggested only programmes and regimes which magistrates would believe were tough enough to serve as alternatives to custody (Pitts 1979). Meanwhile, the Lancaster Centre for Youth Crime and Community was developing the technology which would operationalize the minimalist approach to juvenile justice articulated in *A Future for IT*.

SYSTEMS MANAGEMENT

The 'systems management and intervention' exercises developed by Lancaster in the late 1970s and early 1980s were popular with hard-pressed SSDs as they attempted to reduce the enormous costs of holding young offenders in CHEs. Systems management and intervention is the attempt to change the behaviour of key decision makers in the juvenile-justice system in order that penalties imposed upon young offenders be minimized and, as a result, the number of children and young people committed to care and custody reduced. In the longer term, residential establishments for young offenders are closed and community-based alternatives are established to respond to their erstwhile populations. The system is monitored and a computerized analysis reveals the points at which the 'wrong decisions' are being made. 'Gatekeeping' procedures, aimed at exerting control over maverick decision makers, are then instituted in order to iron out the anomalies and return the system to a state of rationality (cf. Thorpe *et al.* 1980).

This approach to problems in the juvenile-justice system has been fairly effective in reducing the numbers of juvenile offenders referred to residential establishments by social workers but, until the mid-1980s, it was having a much less significant impact upon decisions made by the police and the juvenile bench who, as Parker *et al.* (1980) have noted, hold substantially more power in the juvenile-justice system than social workers. One of the products of early systems management was the alternative tariff.

THE ALTERNATIVE TARIFF

If juvenile-court magistrates were to use the community-based alternatives, established in the wake of systems-management initiatives, as a sentencing option, it was argued, the alternative had to offer a programme and a regime which acknowledged their concerns. These concerns were assumed to coalesce around the importance of the child or young person being made to confront their offending in a situation which offered a heightened level of discipline, control, and surveillance. It was these assumptions which set the scene for the introduction of 'tracking' and the 'correctional curriculum'.

Tracking is a method of intensive surveillance in which the young offender agrees to a contract which specifies where they will be, and when they will be there, for the duration of their programme. The tracker then appears, usually unannounced, at places where the young offender is supposed to be to make sure that they are there. Beyond this the tracker will keep in touch with parents, teachers, and other interested adults in order to check on progress in the areas of education, relationships, and recreation. Should the young person not be where they are supposed to be or not be making progress in the specified areas, they can be taken into the tracking HQ for a more intensive day-care programme which will address the problems they are having in behaving correctly.

Tracking was developed in the USA as an alternative response to serious offenders who would otherwise have spent long periods in jail. One of the criticisms of tracking schemes in Britain has been that in applying the approach to less serious offenders tracking actually increases rather than decreases the level of control to which they would otherwise be subjected.

The correctional curriculum is another US import. Based on theories of human motivation developed within behavioural psychology, it comprises a set of techniques which strive to enable the offender to identify the moments in the behavioural sequence, which culminated in the delinquent act, when they might have acted differently. Through role-play, 'cartooning', and video feedback, young offenders are encouraged to become attuned to those features of social situations which evoke a criminal behavioural response from them. The programme then attempts to desensitize them to these stimuli while inculcating alternative behavioural triggers which evoke non-criminal responses to criminogenic situations. In its pure form the correctional curriculum, like tracking, will have no truck with questions of social need or educational or emotional deprivation. To do so, it is claimed, would be to engage in the kind of spurious 'needology' so beloved of conventional social work (Thorpe *et al.* (1980)).

Whether tracking or the correctional curriculum will be shown to have made a greater impact upon offending behaviour than any other intervention is less significant than the fact that they offer the juvenile bench a set of alternative penalties designed, in terms of duration and content, to replicate existing institutional penalties. Ultimately it is as strategic initiatives which aim to change the behaviour of juvenile court magistrates and as cost-effective responses to individual offenders, that they should be evaluated.

THE INDIVIDUALIZATION OF PRACTICE

The emergence of systems management and the alternative tariff are examples of the way that the advent of minimalism marked a change in the level at which social phenomena and social problems were analysed and the kinds of theorists who were doing the analysis. During the 1960s and early 1970s in Britain and the USA social policies in the sphere of juvenile crime and justice were profoundly influenced by the opportunity theory of Richard Cloward and Lloyd Ohlin (1960). Cloward and Ohlin's analysis of the relationship between socio-structural disadvantage and juvenile crime provided the theoretical rationale for the British and US poverty programmes during this period. What the theorists strove to identify and what governments strove, through their social policies, to address were the ultimate causes of crime and social deprivation. By the mid-1970s a new breed of theorists and policy makers was rejecting such optimistic endeavours and opting instead for what they described as 'realism'. The New Realists maintained that while the investigation of the ultimate causes of social phenomena was a legitimate academic endeavour, it could contribute nothing to policy making because, as James Q. Wilson (1978:50) observed, '. . . ultimate causes cannot be the object of policy efforts precisely because being ultimate, they cannot be changed'. The New Realists advocated policies in which the minimum amount of state intervention would make the maximum quantifiable impact.

It is not difficult to see why the analytical individualism of New Realism came to establish the boundaries of the discourse on crime and justice in the 1980s. In practice this meant that agencies and professional workers with young offenders were required to justify their activity in terms of its contribution to the eradication of crime rather than its contribution to neighbourhood resources or the social and psychological well-being of offenders. In short, workers and agencies were under increasing pressure to offer 'hard-headed' 'no-nonsense' responses to children and young people in trouble irrespective of their needs or, indeed, what might actually work.

In practice this meant that neighbourhood strategies based around clubs or adventure playgrounds, detached (street) work with natural groups of young people, and community-work initiatives which attempted to enable the children, young people, and adults who lived in high-crime inner-city areas to gain more power and control over their lives were called into question. These relatively expensive attempts to address criminogenic social conditions, and their consequences, through compensatory programmes and interventions in social and political structures had largely run out of steam and funding by the mid-1970s (Smith *et al.* 1972; Robins and Cohen 1978). In 1976 an entire phase of 'Urban Aid' funding, a major element in the British poverty programme, was redesignated to assist local authorities to establish IT centres. This was one of many signals that central and local government were getting out of the 'social-compensation' business and into cost-effective social reaction.

THEORETICAL INVERSION

In the decade between 1970 and 1980, policy, theory, and practice in the juvenile-justice system in England and Wales was transformed. The concern with meeting social need was supplanted by a concern to defend legal rights. Social-work intervention was replaced by radical non-intervention. If, before, the threat to young offenders came from the juvenile bench and their defenders from the SSDs, now the roles were reversed. If before, delinquency was a symptom of poverty and deprivation, now it was classless and normal.

The central irony of the minimalist, or non-interventionist, project was that its growing influence in Britain paralleled a massive rise in youth unemployment and heroin addiction, unprecedented levels of urban civil disorder, and the rediscovery of child abuse and racism in all areas of social life. Radical non-intervention notwithstanding, juvenile-justice workers could not easily ignore the reality that they were dealing with children and young people whose chances and choices were increasingly limited by their rapidly worsening social, economic, and personal circumstances.

By a process of inversion a very complex social reality was drastically simplified. It was not that the advocates of minimalism were wrong to criticize the theories which had informed social-work interventions with young offenders or the unintended consequences of those interventions. It was that in their attempts to distance themselves from these theories and practices, rather than taking what they had to offer and moving on, they simply advocated their opposites. What was needed was a set of ideas and practices which were informed by both the achievements and the mistakes of the past and confronted the complexities of the present.

THATCHERISM AND JUVENILE JUSTICE

In September 1990 David Waddington, Home Secretary in the third Thatcher administration, responded to the announcement of an unprecedented rise in the crime rate by enjoining motorists and householders to be more careful about locking their doors. In hindsight it may well be that the greatest U-turn of the Thatcher years was in the area of juvenile justice. In October 1979, in stark contrast to David Waddington's low-key response, William Whitelaw, Home Secretary in the first Thatcher administration, was announcing that the streets of Britain would be made safe once more by the application of 'short sharp shocks' to thieves and hooligans.

Although the right-wing Conservative account of crime and civil disorder is somewhat lacking in intellectual refinement, it is an article of faith and a more or less failsafe rallying cry for the Conservative Party's rank and file in periods when other government policies are faltering. It locates juvenile crime as a manifestation of the deeper problem of moral decline which is seen to generate not only law-breaking but industrial strife and inflation as well. This moral degeneracy is a consequence of misguided government welfare initiatives of the past and the relaxation of standards which they have fostered. These policies, it is claimed, result in the disruption and dislocation of the moral order and:

> the spread of what could be called a delinquent syndrome, a conglomeration of behaviour, speech, appearance and attitudes, a frightening ugliness and hostility which pervades human interaction, a flaunting of contempt for other human beings, a delight in crudity, cruelty and violence, a desire to challenge and humiliate but never, but never to please.
>
> (Morgan 1978: 13)

For right-wing Conservatives, delinquent 'youth' is an ideological device with a dual significance. On one hand the 'bad' behaviour of the young is a consequence of the mistakes made by the parental generation, while on the other it indicates the reprehensible direction in which our society is moving. In this account the moral and economic spheres are one, and economic success is both a consequence and a manifestation of moral worth. The task for government is to turn back the clock to a time when the natural economic disciplines of the free market and the natural moral discipline of common sense ensured that the industrious and the thrifty reaped their just rewards while cheats, thieves, and idlers received their just deserts.

The policies which flow from this account of events are inevitably contradictory. Home Secretaries as vote-conscious politicians must demonstrate their toughness yet, as cost-conscious managers of the justice and penal apparatus, they must conserve their resources. 'Law and Order' governments are almost invariably also committed to reducing public expenditure, yet more law and order inevitably costs more money. This problem was particularly acute in the 1980s as the prison system quite literally teetered on the edge of collapse and the costs of expanding it to accommodate the subjects of a Tory law-and-order campaign threatened to put the Home Office in the red until the twenty-first century. The juvenile-justice policies of the early Thatcher years were primarily ideological, the caveats about reducing the numbers of juveniles in custody seemed to have been framed more in hope than expectation. From the middle of the decade, however, pragmatism had clearly triumphed over ideology.

Juvenile-justice policies and strategies developed by the Thatcher Government in the early 1980s were constructed in the face of research evidence which indicated that the intended changes would either contribute nothing to the achievement of the Government's stated objectives or would actually make the problem, to which the legislation was the Government's intended solution, worse.

At the Conservative Party conference in 1979 William Whitelaw announced the introduction of a new experimental regime, the 'short sharp shock', at New Hall and Send detention centres. The centres were opened in 1980. In March 1981 the experiment was extended to another two centres. In 1984 the Home Office Young Offender Psychology Unit which evaluated the effectiveness of the new centres published *Tougher Regimes in Detention Centres*. The purpose of the experiment had been, it said, to see whether young offenders could be effectively deterred from committing further offences by spending a period of weeks in a detention centre with 'a more rigorous and demanding regime'. The report noted however that: '8.21 The introduction of the pilot project regimes had no discernible effect on the rate at which trainees were reconvicted' (Home Office 1984: 243). On 5 March 1985 the new regime was extended to all detention centres in England and Wales. In 1988 detention centres were absorbed into the national system of Young Offender Institutions and the tougher regimes were abandoned.

The case of the short sharp shock is one of many examples of a government implementing a juvenile-justice policy which, according to research evidence and the opinions of its professional advisers at the Home Office and the DHSS, was destined to fail. David Farrington, reflecting upon the contribution research has made to the formulation and monitoring of government juvenile-justice policies, observes that: 'It is tempting to think that the government, the Home Office and the Department of Health and Social Security do not want an adequate evaluation of their juvenile justice activities' (Farrington 1984)

The 1982 Criminal Justice Act, the flagship for the Thatcher administration's law-and-order campaign, was similarly ill-fated. The Government's stated commitment to reducing custody did not square with the increased power it had given magistrates to imprison young people in Youth Custody Centres (YCCs). The Government had hoped that by reducing the minimum period a child or young person could spend in the newly toughened detention centre (DC) to three weeks, magistrates would be encouraged to use the relatively inexpensive DC in preference to the more costly YCC. The Home Office organized a public-relations blitz which purported to demonstrate that if young offenders were subjected to the new, tougher regimes for shorter periods the deterrent effect would be greater. It encouraged magistrates to make greater use of this 'new' sentencing option and, in anticipation of the success of its initiative, it warned the governors of DCs, in vain as it turned out, to prepare themselves for a 40 per cent increase in throughput.

Rather than reducing the number of young people who entered custody and the time they spent there, in the first two months after the implementation of the Act the YCC population rose from 5,892 to 6,839 (approximately 16 per cent). By the end of the first full year of operation this had increased to 65 per cent. Clearly more young people were entering the system and many more than anticipated were receiving maximum YCC sentences of six months or two consecutive six-month sentences rather than the three-week DC sentences for which the Government had hoped.

It became evident to the government that the magistrates were making excessive use of their new sentencing powers, in many cases simply ignoring the safeguards against the profligate use of custody which were built into the Act (Burney 1984). This was in turn feeding an already serious crisis of overcrowding within the prison system. Clearly a new strategy was needed.

THE DHSS IT INITIATIVE

In 1983, Home Secretary Leon Brittan announced an investment of £15 million in the *New Initiative in Intermediate Treatment*. The Initiative aimed to create 4,500 'alternatives to custody' for persistent young offenders. Brittan had changed tack, and he was now trying to persuade magistrates to divert the relatively serious young offenders who attracted the longer and more expensive YCC sentences, and who constituted an important element in the 'prison crisis', to alternatives to custody. Local Authority Circular (LAC) (3) (83) which launched the IT Initiative stated that the £15 million would be spent over three years to establish 111 alternative-to-custody projects for juveniles throughout England and Wales.

Having, in 1979, thrust the problem of juvenile crime to the centre of the political stage and developed policies which were irrational symbols of political grit, by the mid-1980s the Government was attempting to deflect political attention from juvenile crime in order to release some of the pressure in the penal system. In any rational calculation the trial and imprisonment of juveniles was an obvious target for reform but for such reform to be possible the political issue of juvenile crime had to be depoliticized. The Government realized that it had to be moved from the political arena to one in which outcomes were determined largely on the grounds of economic rationality and administrative pragmatism. Ironically the Thatcher administration had come to the same conclusions, albeit for substantially different reasons, as the left-of-centre radicals in the Wilson administration who, fifteen years earlier, had attempted to abolish the imprisonment of children and young people.

To all intents and purposes, by the late 1980s juvenile justice had been depoliticized. The ideological struggle over social disorder and the socialization of the young was being conducted elsewhere. It had moved on to a different terrain: to the debate about the teaching of history, the national curriculum, responses to poll-tax resisters, the 'war against drugs', and the regulation of football fans.

THE IMPACT OF THE IT INITIATIVE

The IT Initiative appears to have been the most successful innovation in the criminal justice system in the post-war period. Between its commencement in 1984 and 1989, the numbers of juvenile offenders entering custody fell from 6,800 to approximately 2,000. The alternative projects were provided by voluntary organizations, some of which were brought into being for the purpose, and the programmes they provided resembled the time-limited offence-focused work already referred to. The technology developed initially by Lancaster offered a timely solution to a government which was in a mess on the law-and-order front and was in the market for a solution. Thus it was that radical 'abolitionist' social-welfare practitioners and left-wing and liberal academics found themselves in an alliance with the toughest law-and-order government of the post-war period. Their objective was to curb the excesses of the lay magistrates who wielded power over the juvenile courts and who were responsible for the erratic and punitive sentencing which had led to Britain being the European country with a pro rata prison population second only to that of Turkey.

Evaluating the precise contribution the IT Initiative made to the dramatic changes in sentencing during the period is no easy task, however. We know that the level of juvenile custodial sentencing, as a proportion of all sentences imposed in 'Initiative' areas, was in most cases two to three percentage points lower than the national average. Most commentators have suggested that this lower rate testifies to their effectiveness, and this may be the case. It could also be the case, however, that a disproportionate number of Initiative projects were established in areas which already had lower rates of juvenile custody. One of the conditions for funding Initiative projects was that magistrates and the police should be involved in setting them up and managing them. It would therefore not be wholly surprising if, in an area where a commitment to alternatives to custody by police and magistrates already existed, the rate of custodial sentencing was already below the national average. Nor is it the case that reductions in custodial sentencing were achieved only in the 111 project areas.

Another factor which brings into question the centrality of the IT Initiative in achieving reductions in custodial sentencing is that the biggest change in the juvenile-justice system during the period was the reduction in the numbers of children and young people entering juvenile courts. Whereas in 1980 71,000 boys and girls aged 14–16 were sentenced by the juvenile courts in England and Wales, by 1987 this figure had dropped to 37,300, a reduction of something over 47 per cent. Cautioning, and other forms of pre-court diversion, were starving courts of juvenile offenders. The cautioning rate for girls aged 14–16 rose from 58 per cent in 1980 to 82 per cent in 1987. For boys the figures were 34 per cent in 1980 and 58 per cent in 1987. It is arguable that the dramatic reductions in youth imprisonment may have been achieved in part by initiatives taken by the police and social workers to prevent magistrates from dealing with young offenders, and not simply by the provision of alternatives to custody.

The courts were being starved of cases. Indeed, in what came to be called the 'custody-free zones' of Northampton, Southend, and Basingstoke, the juvenile courts almost went out of business. Yet what was happening inside the court during this period was paradoxical. If large numbers of petty offenders are being diverted from court we might reasonably expect two things to happen: namely, a proportionate decrease in the number of low-tariff penalties imposed by the court and a proportionate increase in high-tariff penalties. During the period the use of the low-tariff penalties of absolute and conditional discharges, rather than falling, increased for young men, from 18 per cent of disposals in 1980 to 24 per cent in 1987. At the other end of the scale, we might reasonably assume that if trivial offenders are diverted from the court then only the most serious, custody-prone young people will enter it. Yet in fact, the proportion of juveniles sentenced to custody in juvenile courts rose only slightly during the period, from 11 per cent to 12 per cent.

These figures are perplexing but they could suggest not only a change in sentencing practices but a change in sentencing culture in which lower-tariff sentences are imposed upon the more serious young offenders entering juvenile courts. If this is the case then the Government and juvenile-justice reformers can congratulate themselves on having persuaded magistrates to sentence both more leniently and more rationally. There is, however, a significant body of evidence which suggests that magistrates cannot be constrained to sentence 'rationally'. This evidence suggests that some of the young people who entered juvenile courts and were eventually imprisoned were not, on any objective assessment, particularly custody-prone (Parker *et al.* 1989).

Beyond this, it is clear that the requirements upon courts, specified in the 1982 and 1988 Criminal Justice Acts, that certain conditions must obtain before a custodial sentence can be imposed are routinely ignored by magistrates (Burney 1984; Parker *et al.* 1989). In an experiment conducted in Kent between 1984 and 1987, 18 per cent of custodial sentences were appealed against on the basis that they had been made without regard to these conditions. Some 86 per cent of these appeals were successful (NACRO 1988).

There is also evidence that black young people with relatively modest antecedents are more likely to be remanded or sentenced to custody than their white counterparts (Pitts 1988). Wendy Taylor (1982) discovered that homelessness, joblessness, and a previous care order were the factors which led to black young people in Crown Courts being twice as likely as whites to attract a custodial sentence.

Box and Hale (1986) have observed that unemployed young people are sentenced more harshly than those in employment. Young people entering the Youth Custody Allocation Centre in Rochester in the early 1980s had a far higher level of unemployment than pertained in the youth populations in the areas from which they came (Guest 1984).

Thus far, most commentators have assumed that the reductions in juvenile custody have been achieved by the provision of alternatives and that further reductions, or at least a stabilization around this lower level, will occur. There is some evidence, however, that the reductions are 'bottoming-out' and that in some areas, the North West in particular, levels of custody are now beginning to rise again. This may be attributable to a 'backlash' in which magistrates, having now seen the subjects of previous 'alternative' disposals returning to court, are less willing to use them. Were this to emerge as a medium to long-term trend it would once again raise questions about whether reform based on influence alone, and not enshrined in statute, can be sustained.

THE IT INITIATIVE AND YOUNG ADULT OFFENDERS

In *Crime, Justice and Protecting the Public* (1990) the Government was clearly optimistic that the apparent success of the IT Initiative could be replicated in work with Young Adults aged between 17 and 21, a group which constitutes 25 per cent of all known offenders, accounts for 21 per cent of all court appearances, and whose level of imprisonment has risen steadily in recent years. If this were possible then the major component in the 'penal crisis' could be addressed. Chris Stanley (1989) expressed the prevailing view about the lessons the IT Initiative has to teach the adult system when he wrote:

> So what successful ingredients used to reduce the custodial sentencing of juveniles could be used for the young adult (17–20-year old) offender? . . . The Probation Service can establish inter-agency partnerships. These partnerships could include employment agencies, voluntary organisations, representatives from housing and the police, the courts and the community.
>
> Alternative to custody schemes with a backing of inter-agency groups can sell their schemes to the courts and other agencies. . . .
>
> (ibid: vii)

The notable omission from this comprehensive list is diversion from court. A strategy for young adult offenders which emphasizes alternatives to custody and ignores diversion from court could misfire very badly. But even if the Government were to change tack and promote pre-court diversion it would face an uphill struggle. At present only 10 per cent of Young Adult Offenders are cautioned, and it is a moot point whether a political strategy which has been effective with children and young people aged 10 to 16 can be applied to young men in their late teens and early 20s who are, by and large, responsible for a disproportionate amount of the most serious crime committed in Britain.

Beyond this, of course, there is less evidence than is usually supposed that courts can be made to act rationally. Such evidence as exists about the behaviour of magistrates and judges suggests that their continued erratic custodial sentencing is serving to compound the predicament of the already disadvantaged.

THE PROBLEM OF CRIME

The central preoccupation of the IT Initiative and the apparatus which is being developed to deal with young adult offenders is the cost-effective management of adjudicated offenders. As we have seen, these preoccupations have led to reductions in custodial sentencing but their focus upon reaction to crime has served to obscure the problem of crime itself.

In 1981 and 1985 the inner cities of Britain witnessed events variously described as riots, disturbances, or uprisings. After a decade in which the pursuit of the causes of juvenile crime had been eclipsed by a preoccupation with the management of the juvenile-justice system, the relationship between social deprivation, status frustration, and juvenile crime was rediscovered. Once the issue of race, crime, and justice forced its way on to the political agenda it became clear that not only were black young people treated differently, and in most cases, far more harshly, than their white counterparts in the juvenile-justice system, they were also far more likely to be the victims of crime (Lea and Young 1984).

This resonated with the concerns of women working in the justice system and criminology who discovered inordinately high levels of victimization of working-class women and children. It was clear that the victims of socially disadvantaged young offenders tended to be socially disadvantaged themselves. The person most likely to be attacked and robbed by poor young men was a poor young man. It was the poorest pensioners and women living on the poorest council estates who were effectively imprisoned in their flats through fear of attack or burglary (ibid.).

In a situation in which victims, perpetrators, and agents of control are all locked into a social drama which unfolds in patterned ways over time, irrespective of the characters playing the roles of offender, victim, or police officer, it was no longer adequate to assert as the authors of *Out of Care* had in 1980 'that we must make a moral and ethical choice to take the side of the young offender' (Thorpe *et al.* 1980). If the situation was to be resolved then the resolution would have to be social and preventive rather than individual and reactive.

SOCIAL PREVENTION

The worsening political fortunes of the Thatcher administration in the late 1980s steered it away from the Reaganite 'survival of the fittest' social policies it had favoured earlier in the decade. Try as the Thatcher

Government might, it has been unable to impose an American-style political culture upon the British public. According to the opinion polls, the public persists in the belief that the state should intervene not only to rectify the most obvious injustices but also to create, and guarantee, the conditions which make for a decent life for all citizens irrespective of wealth or ability.

Margaret Thatcher's decision to designate the 1990s as the 'caring decade' and her pledge to increase public expenditure may have indicated that, at last, she was beginning to learn this lesson. It is certainly indicative of a growing disenchantment amongst Conservative politicians with Reaganite approaches to social problems. This disenchantment has been fostered, in part at least, by the obvious failure of British and American criminal-justice strategies to reduce crime and the obvious ability of some European governments, the French in particular, to reduce both crime and youth imprisonment.

In the summer of 1981 there were violent disturbances in the ghetto suburbs of Lyon, Marseilles, and other major French cities. Most of those involved were poor young people whose families came from what were once the French North African colonies. Fearing that the situation might reach the crisis proportions it had in Britain in the spring of that year, the socialist government of President Mitterand established the Bonnemaison Commission to devise a response. The Commission's report observed that because of poverty, racism, and the absence of opportunity many of the young people involved in the disturbances were on the social and economic margins of French society. Any attempt to repress crime, it argued, must therefore involve a concrete expression of 'solidarité' with them. The problem to which the Bonnemaison Commission addressed itself was, in Bellow's phrase (1982), 'how this population might be approached'.

In the event the approach was made by community workers who, in turn, engaged older adolescents from the North African community as youth workers in a programme of sporting, educational, and cultural activities, the *étés-jeunes*, developed with, and in large part directed by, the children and young people in high crime neighbourhoods. In 1983, its second full year of operation, 100,000 children and young people participated in the programme. Alongside the *étés-jeunes* the Government created a nation-wide 'social prevention' programme chaired by the deputy Prime Minister. At town level Delinquency Prevention Councils, chaired by the mayors, were established and they worked with local youth groups, tenants associations, politicians, planners, the police, and architects to develop new initiatives in areas where there were high levels of crime, poverty, and racial tension.

In Les Minguettes, a high crime estate on the outskirts of Marseilles, consultation with residents led to the demolition of high-rise blocks and the refurbishment of the remaining housing. Youth and community facilities were built and job training schemes created. As a result the drift away from the estate was reversed and the rate of recorded delinquency fell from 7,200 cases to 4,500 and continues to fall. From 1985 France has witnessed a national decline in the types of offences likely to be committed by young people. There has been an overall fall of 10.5 per cent during this period with a fall of over 8 per cent between 1985 and 1986 (King 1988).

Contrary to the claims of right-wing Realist social policy the French experience suggests that escalating levels of crime and civil disorder are not an inevitable corollary of economic change if the political will exists to consult and work alongside marginalized people to create a decent environment, effective public services, and real educational and vocational opportunities. Where this approach has been tried in Britain the results have been similarly promising. In the late 1970s the NACRO Safe Neighbourhoods Unit, building upon Environmental Crime Control experiments on high crime estates, introduced tenant consultation exercises. By 1984 their Youth Activities Unit was utilizing techniques derived from Community Organization and Community Action along with the development of informal social, educational, and recreational interventions with young people in 'dangerous' neighbourhoods. It made them safer. In the wake of an initiative on a housing estate in West London, previously the scene of persistent racial attacks, the crime rate dropped by 77 per cent (NACRO 1987).

By the late 1980s, throughout Britain, local initiatives, known variously as youth social work, youth advocacy, detached youth work, outreach, empowerment, community action, community organization, or Intermediate Treatment were working on the problems of crime and victimization with socially deprived people in impoverished neighbourhoods (Blagg and Smith 1989).

Douglas Hurd, Home Secretary in the same British Government which was initially so enamoured of Reaganite toughness and non-intervention, was by the end of 1989 offering 'social prevention' to the victims of crime. This offer was no doubt inspired, in part at least, by solid evidence that the essentially ideological changes prescribed in *Crime, Justice and Protecting the Public* (1990) will do nothing to make the inner cities safer. The Labour Party general election manifesto is likely to include a commitment to social prevention, but one which moves beyond the present government's heavy reliance on the voluntary sector and establishes it as a responsibility to be discharged by local authorities supported by the Departments of Education and Science, Health, Employment, the Environment, and the Home Office.

In the sphere of crime and justice, the 1980s was the decade of simple solutions and increasingly complicated problems. It started with a 'short, sharp shock' and, thanks to the introduction of the ill-starred tagging experiment in 1989, ended with an electric one. By the end of the decade many politicians, criminologists, and senior police officers were agreed that more policing and the seemingly endless manipulation of penalties could do little to contain what was essentially a social and economic problem.

The social-prevention initiatives developed in France, and to a lesser extent in Britain, offer no simple solutions to the problems of crime, justice, and the inner city. Their promise lies in their willingness to explore responses with, and learn from, victims and offenders. They are diverse, hard to pin down, and so harder to incorporate into a political dogma. But perhaps their major strength is that they move beyond the individualism of minimalism, placing the plight of both the perpetrators and victims of crime back within their shared social and economic predicament.

REFERENCES

Bellow, S. (1982) *The Dean's December*, Harmondsworth: Penguin.

Blagg, H. and Smith, D. (1989) *Crime, Social Policy and Social Work*, London: Longman.

Booker, C. (1980) *The Seventies*, Harmondsworth: Penguin.

Box, S. and Hale, C. (1986) 'Unemployment, crime and the enduring problem of prison overcrowding', in R. Matthews and J. Young (eds) *Confronting Crime*, London: Sage.

Burney, E. (1984) *Sentencing Juveniles*, London: Hutchinson.

Cloward, R. and Ohlin, L. (1960) *Delinquency and Opportunity*, London: Routledge & Kegan Paul.

Day, L. (1979) *A Future for IT?* Personal Social Services Council.

Farrington, D. (1984) 'England and Wales', in M. Klein (ed.) *Western Systems of Juvenile Justice*, London: Sage.

Guest, C. (1984) 'A comparative analysis of the career patterns of black and white young offenders', unpublished MSc thesis, Cranfield Institute.

Home Office (1984) *Tougher Regimes at Detention Centres*, London: HMSO.

Home Office (1990) *Crime, Justice and Protecting the Public*, London: HMSO.

King, M. (1988) *Making Social Crime Prevention Work – The French Experience*, NACRO.

Lea, J. and Young, J. (1984) *What Is to Be Done about Law and Order?* Harmondsworth: Penguin.

Morgan, P. (1978) *Delinquent Fantasies*, London: Temple Smith.

Morris, A., Giller, H., Szued, M., and Geech, H. (1980) *Justice for Children*, London: Macmillan.

NACRO (1987) *The Golf Links Project*, NACRO.

NACRO (1988) *Diverting Juveniles from Custody*, NACRO.

Parker, H., Sumner, M., and Jarvis, G. (1980) 'The production of punitive juvenile justice', *British Journal of Criminology* 20 (3).

Parker, H., Sumner, M., and Jarvis, G. (1989) *Unmasking the Magistrates*, Milton Keynes: Open University Press.

Pitts, J. (1979) 'Doing your bird on the HP', *Howard Journal*, December.

Pitts, J. (1988) *The Politics of Juvenile Crime*, London: Sage.

Robins, D. and Cohen, P. (1978) *Knuckle Sandwich*, Harmondsworth: Penguin.

Schur, E. (1974) *Radical Non-Intervention*, New York: Free Press.

Smith, C., Farrant, M., and Marchant, H. (1972) *The Wincroft Youth Project*, London: Tavistock.

Stanley, C. (1989) 'The lessons of the IT initiative', *Community Care*.

Taylor, W. (1982) 'Black youth, white man's justice', *Youth in Society*, November.

Thorpe, D., Smith, D., Green, C.J., and Paley, J.H. (1980) *Out of Care*, London: George Allen & Unwin.

Wilson, James Q. (1978) *Thinking about Crime*, New York: Basic Books.

11 Leaving home

Housing and income – social policy on leaving home

Damian Killeen

INTRODUCTION

Technically speaking, with the exception of those circumstances where young people are directly in their care, central and local governments do not have and have no need of a policy concerning that essentially private process of transition from dependence to independence commonly referred to as 'leaving home'. Other than the legal definition of the age below which a young person must have his or her parents' permission before establishing a separate household (18 in England, Wales, and Northern Ireland, 16 in Scotland), there are no enforceable rules which require that young people and their parents must either separate or stay together. However, there is an increasing concern that this area of apparently personal decision making is becoming ever more circumscribed by social policy developments in other areas of government responsibility. Among these, housing, social security, and Community Charge policies are the most prominent.

THE CRISIS OF YOUTH HOMELESSNESS

One focus of this concern is the apparent increase in the numbers of young people who are becoming homeless; both in the sense of those living in insecure accommodation and, most dramatically, in the self-evident destitution of those who have taken to living on the streets. Voluntary organizations estimate that 200,000 young people experience acute homelessness each year in Britain. The extent of the problem is highlighted by the observations of the Foyer des Jeunes Travaileurs (a French organization which provides hostel places for young people), that Britain has the most acute problem of youth homelessness of all European countries, and by the observations of Childhope (which concerns itself with the welfare of street children in the Third World) that the numbers of young beggars to be found in London and other major British cities would not disgrace some parts of South America and Africa.

These international comparisons are encouraging some policy makers to shift their perspective from a parochial, personalized approach to the question of youth homelessness towards a more comprehensive appreciation of the historical trends which are leading to a widespread social and economic exclusion of young people, trends which require a reassessment of traditional attitudes towards the process by which young people leave their parental homes. This issue takes on an especial relevance with the birth of a 'Europe without frontiers' from 1992, when young Europeans dissatisfied with their prospects in their area of origin will be able to leave not only their home but also their home country in the search for better job and housing opportunities. The prospect of homeless young people from other member countries of the EC presenting themselves to local authorities in Britain will require the untangling of a complex web of national and supranational legislations concerning the protection of young people and the rights and responsibilities of those who are not able to support themselves which the current protocols for the 'harmonization' of social policies (such as those on social security) and the systems for ministerial co-operation on specifically national responsibilities (such as housing) have yet to begin to address. The need for a fresh overview of the condition of young people leaving home is nowhere more apparent than in Britain where government persists in the view that the problem of youth homelessness is little more than a question of the individual responsibility of young people and their parents and a matter of little relevance to the state.

PROTECTION FOR HOMELESS YOUNG PEOPLE

While Britain's homeless persons' legislation is in advance of that offered by many other countries, it is significant that protection for homeless young, single people is more limited than that provided for other groups. Essentially, discretion is left to local authorities to decide whether or not a young person is 'vulnerable' as a consequence of their homelessness and will, therefore, qualify for rehousing. One reason for this might well have been a lesser profile for the issue of youth homelessness when the legislation was passed. But a reading of the relevant parliamentary debates demonstrates that the idea of giving additional rights to homeless young people was seen as likely to stretch too far the willingness of local authorities to implement legislation towards which may of them were already unsympathetic.

Despite increasing pressure on successive governments to strengthen protection for homeless young people, changes in the law have consistently been resisted. The present Government's response to the weight of lobbying and media pressure on the subject of youth homelessness during 1989–90 was to accuse young people of leaving home unnecessarily over trivial disputes about their parents' unwillingness to provide them with the desired new car or new coat and to make a financial provision for opening additional hostel places for homeless young people in London and the South East when the weather deteriorates beyond a critical point. Otherwise, Government has declined to intervene for fear that additional provision might encourage increased numbers of young people to leave home.

HOUSING YOUNG PEOPLE

If homeless young people sleeping in Cardboard City represent the tip of an iceberg, the main body of the problems faced by young people leaving home are less easy to quantify but no less pervasive in their effects on young people and their families. In order to form a separate household from their parents, young people need both a range of housing options from which they can select the one most suited to their needs and adequate resources with which to both acquire and maintain the housing of their choice. The evidence is that both the opportunities and the resources available to young people are increasingly out of step with their needs.

Even those young people who have the resources with which to provide themselves with housing are under stress, as evidence from the Building Societies Association (BSA) in 1985 showed. In an international comparison of housing tenure by age, the BSA found 'an unusually high level of owner occupation amongst younger households [which] reflects the lack of available rented housing rather than natural tenure preference'. As the BSA explained, young people, who are normally more likely to be transient, would wish to avoid the high transaction costs (and, more recently, the escalating interest rates) associated with owner-occupation. Britain's continued commitment to home ownership and public subsidy of owner-occupiers via tax relief on mortgage-interest payments was also identified by the Duke of Edinburgh's Enquiry into British Housing conducted in 1987, the International Year of Shelter for the Homeless, as a major source of housing stress for young people who would prefer to rent.

Rented housing is the preferred accommodation for the majority of single-person households including young people but the supply has failed to keep step with the increase in demand. Demographic trends suggest that, despite an overall decrease in the numbers of young people in the population, the numbers of young single-person households are set to continue to increase, with a major element of this increase being due to a growth in the number of widowed and divorced people under the age of 30. These people are also competing for single-person accommodation with growing numbers of divorcees in older age groups and, more recently, with the increased demand for single-person accommodation resulting from the Government's policies on care in the community.

The main providers of rented housing have traditionally been local authorities, whose priorities in the past have not greatly assisted young single applicants, although they constitute some 20 per cent of demand.

The other major provider has been private landlords who have housed the majority of young single people in a wide range of types of small flats, bed-sits, and so on. Changes in housing policy and related subsidy policies have created a dramatic reduction in supply from these sectors just at the time when demand is set to increase. Government policy on the provision of social housing – to diminish the role of local authorities and enhance the role of the private sector – has inhibited district councils from meeting the demand from young people. The private sector, on the other hand, while it has responded to demand from upper income groups, has demonstrated that it does not see sufficient potential for profit in the provision of mainstream social rented housing. Housing Associations, which are also perceived by Government to be in the private sector, do not have the experience of operating on the scale required to meet the total demand and are limited in what they can do by the amounts of subsidy available to them from Government via the Housing Corporation and its equivalent in Scotland, Scottish Homes.

Something of the scale of young people's experience of housing problems was provided by an opinion poll conducted throughout the UK for Shelter by MORI in November 1987. This demonstrated that 24 per cent of the 15–25 year olds had personally experienced difficulty in finding housing. A further 24 per cent knew another young person who had experienced this problem. Of the 24 per cent who had found it difficult to acquire housing, one-third were still living with their parents. Some 13 per cent of young people had left home by the time they were 17 and 39 per cent by the age of 20. Some 27 per cent had left home to marry or share with a partner; 22.5 per cent lived singly after leaving home; and 9.5 per cent of the age group was in receipt of Housing Benefit. The young people interviewed had high hopes of living independently and of leaving home at the latest by the age of 21 or 22. But they were also realistic about the financial difficulties. Many gave the main reason for living with their parents as their inability to afford to move. This stressful situation could apply to as many as 1.5 million young people in Britain. Youth homelessness is one of the consequences which occurs when families can no longer tolerate this stress.

There is, therefore, a crisis in the supply of housing opportunities to young people which current policy does little to address. This crisis is compounded by government policies on housing benefits and social security which affect the ability of young people to pay for accommodation and to maintain an acceptable standard of living once they have acquired it.

THE NEW PATTERN OF YOUTH WELFARE

In April 1988 the Government initiated a new scheme of welfare support consisting of three main elements: Income Support, Housing Benefit, and the Social Fund. The new scheme is administered by a new Department of Social Security which, together with a new Department of Health, replaced the old DHSS. In their planning to introduce the new system, the main effect of which was to 'target assistance on those in greatest need', the Government gave specific consideration in its consultations to the position of young people within the welfare system.

Income Support replaced Supplementary Benefit as the basic welfare payment for those unemployed people who are not entitled to Unemployment Benefit. Previous distinctions between the householder and non-householder rates of benefit (which provided additional support for those who were responsible for running their own homes) were replaced by different levels of benefit entitlement (applicable amounts) based on the claimant's age. While the level of benefit payments to people aged 25 and over continued in line with the general uprating of benefits, lower rates of Income Support were determined for people aged 18–24 and under 18. This new structure of Income Support constituted a clear case of age discrimination against young people since it became possible under the new rules for three people who have identical accommodation and living costs to receive different levels of benefit depending on their age.

The Social Fund, a system of grants and loans, was introduced as the replacement of Single and Exceptional Needs payments to which Supplementary Benefits claimants were previously entitled. The Social Fund is an entirely discretionary scheme operating within cash limits. This puts young people into competition for assistance with other groups who are seen to be in greater need. Other than those leaving care or prison, who might be eligible for a Community Care Grant from the Social Fund, most young people are likely to be offered assistance in the form of an interest-free loan. Given that they are already subject to lower levels of Income Support than older people, young people are less likely to be able to afford the repayments and are, therefore, less likely to be eligible for a loan. Previously, Single Needs Payments were of assistance to young people setting up separate households, in the form of deposits to secure accommodation and grants for basic furniture requirements. For the majority of young applicants, this assistance is no longer available.

Housing Benefit, the third plank of the Government's new welfare-benefits regime, takes the form of a 100 per cent rent rebate for anyone whose net income is below or at the relevant 'applicable amount' under the Income Support regulations. For those with incomes above the applicable amount, the rebate is reduced by 65p for every additional pound of income. Again, the age-related banding of the applicable amounts discriminates against younger people who are in employment or in receipt of a training allowance. These young people can find that they are required to pay a larger proportion of their income on rent than another person whose income and outgoings are the same as their own and who only differs from them in age.

One additional factor introduced more recently by Government contributes to the ability of young people to afford independent accommodation and relates to the new welfare-benefits scenario. The Community Charge (or Poll Tax) requires that everyone over the age of 18 must pay at least 20 per cent of their charge. For those earning more than their 'applicable amount' this is increased by 15p for each additional pound earned. Again, because their applicable amount is lower, those aged under 25 will pay a larger proportion of the Community Charge than those over this age. A particularly disturbing aspect of the Community Charge – in addition to the failure of many young people to pay it – is the increasing failure of young people to register as electors for fear that this will make then more easily traceable by the authorities. The consequences of this trend in terms of future participation in democratic processes are not difficult to predict.

The poverty trap (by which the penalities on increased income are so severe that the incentive to earn extra is diminished or removed) is not unique to young people, but, combined with the lower levels of benefit to which young people are entitled, it creates a considerable disincentive to young people to leave their parents' home and set up an independent household. The fact that young people continue to attempt to live independently on the incomes now available is an acknowledgement of the fact that, for the majority, there is no other choice.

However, harsh as these discriminations against young people may be, the most significant action of the Government with respect to young people has been the withdrawal of a right to Income Support for unemployed young people aged 16 and 17. During the 1987 parliamentary election campaign the Prime Minister gained public support for her view that young people who refuse a place on the Youth Training Scheme (YTS) should not have the option of claiming state welfare payments. In September 1988, the existing legal entitlement to Income Support for all unemployed 16 and 17 year olds was withdrawn whether or not the young people were YTS refusers. Instead, the Social Security Act 1988 provided the Secretary of State for Health and Social Security with a range of discretionary powers which he was able to implement without further detailed scrutiny by Parliament. In Scotland where young people are competent in law from the age of 16 to marry or live away from parents' homes without their parents' consent, this measure has a greater significance than elsewhere in Britain.

This exclusion of 16 and 17 year olds from the social-security system ran contrary to the previous trend of policy which entitled all unemployed young people to Income Support and which also allowed for Income Support to be paid to school pupils or YTS trainees if they were 'estranged from their parents'. According to the Department of Health and Social Security (DHSS Guide to Young People and Social Security), estrangement means 'you are not living with your parents and are not being kept by them and either you are not in touch with them or they are separated from you for reasons which can't be avoided'. Turning its back on the precedents and principles which had retained this category of vulnerability in social-security legislation, the Government stated that in future it did not intend that estrangement from parents would result in entitlement to Income Support. In arriving at this decision, the Government ignored a large body of advice supporting the view that estrangement from parents is the common experience of the majority of young people who are homeless or in housing crisis. The Government's failure to recognize this reality has exposed it to much adverse publicity and has been the cause of considerable controversy. Since the original rules were introduced the Government has made a number of concessions; in particular, they have accepted that some restricted groups of young people who are deemed to be 'estranged' from their parents should be entitled to a higher level of Income Support for limited periods.

DEPENDENCY CULTURE

On each occasion in recent years when young people's welfare benefits have been reduced or their entitlement removed, the action has been accompanied by a ministerial comment criticizing young people's use of these benefits. In 1984, Dr Rhodes Boyson asked 'are they to be freeloaders evermore?' In 1986, introducing the new regulations governing the payment of board-and-lodgings payments, Norman Fowler referred to young people 'abusing and exploiting the welfare state'. Responding to parliamentary questions about one of Centrepoint's annual reports on the service the agency provides for the increasing numbers of homeless young people in London, Margaret Thatcher retorted that young people should not leave their parents' homes before they were able to afford to provide themselves with somewhere else to live: 'there are a number of young people who voluntarily choose to leave home and I do not think we can be expected – no matter how many there are – to provide units for them'. In a world of full, or nearly full, employment where income bears some relationship to the cost of living, this simplistic response might have some merit; but, in a world of limited employment opportunities for young people, where minimum wage controls have been abandoned and the levels of allowance for trainees and benefits for the unemployed have been consistently depressed, the former Prime Minister's response failed to acknowledge the additional stress which the target of economic independence places on young people and, especially, on those whose parents do not have spare resources with which to assist their children to leave home.

FAMILY POLICY

What is remarkable about the present Government's 'family policy' is that it runs counter to most people's understanding of the role of families with regard to adolescents. It is also a major aggravation of the problems of family friction and family breakdown which result in youth homelessness and increased youth housing demand. This was demonstrated in research conducted for the Department of Health and Social Security in 1985 into the 'Attitudes of Beneficiaries to Child Benefits for Young People'.

The researchers' findings spell out the importance of separate welfare benefits for young people at levels which enable them to progress along the 'steps to independence' which are available to the employed. They specifically challenge the proposition that young people are encouraged to leave home because of the availability of additional welfare benefits. The findings reinforce the traditional role of parents in preparing young people for independent life. Most parents stress the importance of allowing children to develop responsibility through gradual steps to independence which allow both parties to come to terms with the changing nature of their relationship. In families where the pace of relationship was forced either by the parents or the young person, it generally created tension and conflict within the family.

> Perceptions of dependency appear to vary quite markedly with the post 16 activities of young people. Those starting work are felt to be more independent from their parents than those who remain at school, while those who remain at school or those employed on ET schemes have a semi-dependent status. These perceptions seem to be rooted in the relative financial dependency of young people on their parents. Benefits for the 16–19's appear to enable young people to gain some independence from their parents.
>
> (Hedges and Hyatt 1985)

But this view of the family is not consistent with the view of Government and its advisors. Taking its lead from American ideology, which regards the family as the best form of social services department and as a 'caring, competent little organization', government policy has sought to stress the dependence, as opposed to the independence, of family members. In particular, parents have in recent years been required to take greater financial responsibility for the housing and maintenance costs of unemployed young people and those on low incomes. The cutting, in 1983, of a weekly £3.10 Housing Addition from the benefit of unemployed young people living with their parents was the most clear early step in this direction. The gradual delaying of the point at which school-leavers can claim unemployment benefits also served to shift responsibility for unemployed young people from government to parents.

Beginning in 1985, the Government has also been consistent in seeking to limit financial support for young people living away from their parents' homes. The Board and Lodgings Regulations, for example, introduced limits on the length of time for which unemployed young people under the age of 25 could receive financial assistance to stay in bed-and-breakfast hotels. Additional criteria were introduced for young people wishing to qualify for this support in addition to the basic requirements for qualification for Income Support.

With these new 'exceptional categories' for qualification for Income Support, Government also marked a distinct move away from entitlement by law towards entitlement by regulation of the Secretary of State. The Government has defended this shift by arguing that it introduces flexibility into the process of providing assistance, thereby assuring that 'real need' is properly met. Experience has shown that 'flexibility' in fact means more bureaucracy, less sensitivity, and no right of appeal against increasingly centralized decision-making procedures.

The Government's own study of the implementation of the Board and Lodgings regulations in Scotland demonstrated that the Department of Health and Social Security lost contact with 25 per cent of its study sample and that 17 per cent of claimants were required to use other benefits in order to pay for housing. A joint monitoring exercise by Shelter and the Scottish Council for Single Homeless in one month in 1985 found fifty-seven young people who had become homeless as a consequence of the introduction of the new rules. Despite this and similar evidence from elsewhere in Britain, the Government has persisted in claiming that no hardship was caused to young people by the Board and Lodgings measures.

In 1984, *The Economist* described the welfare state with regard to young people as 'a game of snakes and ladders'. More recently it has been said that:

> The benefits and allowances which currently exist are, in some cases, grossly inadequate to perform their designated function, inequitable between groups in largely similar circumstances, have little in the way of coherent underlying principles or view of the position of young people in society, in the sense that the objectives of one part of the system are subverted by another.

These views were echoed by the government-appointed Social Security Advisory Committee, which stated in its 1986–7 report:

> We remain concerned about the problems surrounding benefit in general and young people in education in particular. Young people from the age of 16 now face a range of choices including continuing in education, perhaps as far as higher education, or leaving to find a job, join the Youth Training Scheme or some or other form of training, or become unemployed. We believe that the benefits system is not fully geared to helping young people make the right choices in this area.

Regrettably, the only discernible principle underlying recent government policy on youth incomes and support has been one of financial expediency, summed up in the one word 'cuts'. The extent to which the Government has been prepared to put young people at risk in an attempt to cut the costs of what it describes as a 'dependency culture' was clearly demonstrated in the parliamentary debates surrounding the withdrawal of welfare-benefit entitlements from 16 and 17 year olds. Wishing to limit payments only to those young people whose lack of income would expose them to 'severe hardship', the Minister resisted appeals to soften his policy at least by removing the word 'severe' from the legislation. He replied,

> Severe hardship is clearly a more parlous state than hardship. It means something more than a mere tightening of the belt or doing without certain items which are normally part of a person's existence. It means that the hardship must be of such a degree that there is a real risk to health or indeed life itself. I should include in that category, sleeping out on the streets. To leave out the word 'severe' could give entitlement to income support to a far greater number of our young persons than is intended. The overall intentions of the Government in relation to young people and their dependence on the benefit culture would be put at risk in that many could claim hardship, while very few are likely to be entitled on account of a risk of severe hardship.

The Charity, Youthaid, calculated that between 1979 and 1986 the Government saved at least £50 million in youth welfare-benefit cuts alone. Ironically, the Government has sought to justify these cuts, particularly the withdrawal of benefit entitlement from 16 and 17 year olds, by reference to the findings of the Beveridge Report which is commonly regarded as providing the ground plan for today's 'welfare state'.

William Beveridge's report on Social Insurance, published in 1942, shares many principles in common with those of today's social policy makers. Clearly the concept of the 'state handout' or 'something for nothing' had no place in his thinking. It was William Beveridge who wrote that 'for boys and girls (under the age of 18) there should, ideally be no unconditional benefit at all; their enforced abstention from work should be an occasion for further training'. There is little doubt that Beveridge would have been an admirer of the Youth Training Scheme. But, in one respect at least, Beveridge would have been deliberately out of step with current government policy. He did not propose that 16 and 17 year olds should be excluded from the Social Insurance scheme; indeed, he proposed rates of payment for young people which were between one-third and a half of the current average level of adult wages.

This allowance for 16 and 17 year olds was regarded as possible because there was more to Beveridge's proposals than a simple system of Income Support. The White Paper on Social Insurance was the spearhead of an attack on 'the five great evils of post war Britain; Want, Disease, Ignorancc, Squalor and Idleness'. According to Beveridge, the Social Insurance system was just one element in the social and economic reconstruction of Britain. In addition to his own scheme, Beveridge assumed the existence of a system of child allowances, comprehensive health and rehabilitation services and an avoidance of mass unemployment. The maximum level of unemployment which he felt could be tolerated by his Social Insurance scheme was 10 per cent in any one sector of the labour market and an average of 8.5 per cent overall.

With high rates of employment and retraining for those who lost their jobs, unemployment was not envisaged as a long-term experience. As a consequence, everyone, except those incapable of work, could be regarded as a potential contributor to the Social Insurance scheme and in time of need, everyone could be a potential recipient of aid. This was the central unifying feature of Beveridge's scheme, that it is a scheme 'in which it is right for all citizens to stand in together, without exclusions based upon differences of status, functions or wealth'. In the Social Insurance scheme which he envisaged, all would participate, regardless of their resources at any particular point in time and any person could derive assistance regardless of the contribution they have made before the need occurs. Beveridge identified this as the main feature which differentiates a compulsory, government scheme from other kinds of private insurance. It was these considerations which, despite his views on young people and training, led Beveridge to include 16 and 17 year olds as potential beneficiaries of his scheme. Of course, at a time of very low youth unemployment, it was not anticipated that there would be very many calls on this aspect of the budget.

Since 1946 the question of the entitlement of 16 and 17 year olds to Income Support has been considered by the DHSS and by other bodies reviewing the social-security system under both Conservative and Labour administrations. They have all come to the view that, while everything should be done to minimize the dependence of young people on welfare benefits, the basic entitlement should be retained as a matter of justice and prudence, in order to protect those in the age group who are not able to protect themselves and who have no one to provide for them.

Bearing in mind, no doubt, William Beveridge's remarks on training and benefits, the Government proposed in 1981 that Supplementary Benefit entitlement should be replaced by the guarantee of a training place for all unemployed 16 year olds. This was opposed by the Manpower Services Commission (MSC) Youth Task Force. The MSC persisted in opposing the withdrawal of benefit from young people, fearing that such a move might undermine the voluntary nature of the scheme.

The Social Security Advisory Committee has also been consistent in opposing the withdrawal of benefit from young people and research, such as that from Social and Community Planning Research, has underlined the importance of independent access to benefits entitlement by young people. Parents identify the independent income of unemployed young people as a central feature in their role as trainers for their children's eventual independence from the family.

YOUTH UNEMPLOYMENT

The rise in youth unemployment has been well documented elsewhere but the impact of increasing youth unemployment is more than statistical. A report from the Commonwealth Secretariat summarizes the personal impact of unemployment on young people. Taken together with the insecurity which stems from a lack of suitable housing and the increasing risk of homelessness, these factors delineate the growing vulnerability of those young people in Britain who are excluded from the 'traditional' patterns of taking up employment and leaving home.

An immediate impact of unemployment on the individual young person is the loss of livelihood and – in the absence of family or state support – the onset of poverty. Isolation, the absence of status and a sense of future, loss of self-esteem and self-confidence, alter a young person's sense of identity and can breed a sense of hopelessness. Independent living and family life becomes or remains beyond the economic means of unemployed young people. Diminishing or static prospects of stable meaningful employment throw them into or keep them in chronic dependence on the financial and cultural resources of others – especially parents. Loss of independent leisure and the strains of overcrowding subject individuals and families to enormous problems.

For some this can result in severe mental illness and there appears to be a widespread recognition of the effects of unemployment on mental health in general and on young people's mental health in particular. In Australia, for example, it appears that unemployment raised the chances of young people having a psychiatric disorder by a factor of six. Canadian evidence suggests that the young unemployed have more psychological distress in relation to unemployment than do older individuals. Suicide and deliberate, self-inflicted injury are closely associated with unemployment. In Scotland, for example, nearly half the attempted suicides in one survey were unemployed and those attempting suicide are predominantly young people.

The Commonwealth report also highlights the economic costs of youth unemployment in terms of the loss of direct and indirect tax revenues consequent on a reduction in the incomes and expenditures of unemployed young people, together with the increases in costs associated with welfare payments and the costs of special measures to combat unemployment. Moreover, unemployment diminishes the capacity of young people to make an effective economic contribution to the future since unemployed young people, at the crucial formative stage of a career, will not be getting the development and learning experiences from working which affect future skills and attitudes to work. The prospect for unemployed young people would seem to be one of continuing poverty with all the personal stress entailed and a preparation only for the least-skilled work which is associated with low levels of pay and which promises only continuing poverty for the future.

YOUNG PEOPLE IN THE MARKET

For the past twelve years, young people involved in the process of 'leaving home' have constituted a form of laboratory for the social policies which governments of the time have begun to introduce more slowly and cautiously to other sections of the population: the removal of wages-council protection and reductions in legal protection for those in work; an increase in discretionary welfare payments and a reduction in basic benefits; a continued resistance to the idea that the state has a primary duty to protect the most vulnerable – such as the homeless. As the years have passed, Government's agenda has become increasingly transparent; that once a person leaves the support of their parents' home their survival should be linked entirely to their playing an economic role within the market-place. Those who remain unemployed are criticized for pricing themselves out of work, for failing to be sufficiently mobile ('getting on their bike'), and for missing the opportunities provided by the education system to adapt themselves to the requirements of employers. Those who choose to study rather than to be in employment can expect, in most cases at least, to have their teaching costs met, but must increasingly look to parents or to part-time and temporary employment for the money to pay for food and housing. Taken further along the social continuum, this is consistent with the increasing emphasis on health insurance rather than health service and on the personal rather than the state pension.

The outcome of the Government's social experiments with youth, its attack on the so-called 'dependency culture', have not been too promising. Homelessness and youth unemployment (especially long-term unemployment) have increased, young people's incomes have decreased or failed to keep pace with inflation, and, by all reports, the level of stress on individual young people (for example, threats of suicide) and their families has increased. There is little prospect of an improvement, with both the Government and employers haggling over who should be responsible for training young people to meet the needs of the economy.

Young people leaving home rarely do so to invite dependency on the state. For most people, the first flat and the first job or the college or university course are significant steps towards independence. For the fortunate or for the well resourced, these initiatives will lead, with relatively little difficulty to the stabilities of steady jobs and new families but the economic realities of fundamental recession throughout the 'developed' world mean that increasing numbers of young people do not have these opportunities to achieve stability and do not have parents and families with the necessary resources to support them unaided. The truth is that young people were never totally 'dependent' or 'independent' but that we are all, increasingly, interdependent. This is what the failure of a 'market' approach to young people making the transition from the parental home to adult life ultimately reveals.

A lack of a positive investment in young people in training, and also in the social services which they need in order to develop fully as adults, is a sign of weakness rather than strength in our society and betrays a deeper sense of insecurity. As individual parents we are less confident that there is a real prospect of a full participation in society for our young people when they leave our doors. It used to be said that young people are important because they are the future. We seem to hear this said less often these days.

There are many practical measures which will need to be taken to provide young people with a more positive scenario for 'leaving home' which run across the full gamut of social policy. They all have their costs and would have to be battled for against the other social priorities. But there is one – cost-free – measure which could be taken today and which would introduce a greater sense of a communal responsibility for the social welfare of young people. If we began to adopt in Britain the system which is already in action in Denmark and Sweden of subjecting all social-policy proposals to the discipline of a 'youth-impact report' which attempted to indicate the likely consequences on young people of the proposed measures, we could begin to move towards a society which shows fewer signs of treating unemployed and poorly housed or homeless young people as mere burdens on those who are better off. Our society could become more demonstrably accountable to young people for the actions it takes which affect them and we could begin the process of decreasing the undoubted alienation of these young people who, in failing to make the 'perfect' transition from parents' home to the wider world, are made to feel that, through their failure, they have become excluded from that society.

REFERENCE

Hedges, A. and Hyatt, J. (1985) *Attitudes of Beneficiaries to Child Benefit and Benefits for Young People*, London: Social and Community Planning Research.

12 The adolescent as consumer

Fiona Stewart

INTRODUCTION – THE HISTORICAL CONTEXT

'The post-war period has witnessed the emergence on an unprecedented scale of "youth" in all its manifestations and subgroupings, as a distinct, highly visible and much remarked upon social entity' (Davis 1990: 18–19).

According to John Davis the term 'teenager', and its equation with a distinctive pattern and style of consumption, can be traced back to 1945 in the United States. In Britain the discovery of the 'teenager' and the emergence of a youth market did not really feature until the mid-1950s. The factors underpinning the projection of youth or 'teenagers' as a distinct consumer group relate to the booming post-war economy. Full employment meant relatively high wages for the youth worker, which was in marked contrast to the employment situation in the pre-war period. According to Davis, by the late 1950s average teenage earnings had increased by more than 50 per cent in real terms from pre-war levels.

Not surprisingly the situation spawned growing commercial interest in the sector and by the end of the 1950s an array of goods and services, from fashions and entertainment to food and drink, was specifically aimed at satisfying the needs and aspirations of the youth consumer. Although the overall spending power of the youth population was not that significant in comparison with other consumer groups, young people tended to have a much greater 'discretionary' element to their spending power. Consequently their spending tended to be concentrated in the 'non-essential' sectors and this made them a particularly attractive target to the burgeoning 'leisure' economy. Furthermore, the newly found affluence of the post-war teenager was boosted by and inextricably linked with the rising affluence of their parents. While young people remained in the parental home they were effectively sheltered from the financial burden of having to provide for life's necessities. They were unlikely to have dependents, and the rising levels of affluence among their parents meant that in relative terms their contribution to maintenance had fallen.

Undoubtedly, the possibility of capturing the teenage pound was the major factor spawning initial commercial interest in the youth population and this has remained important in maintaining interest ever since. There has however been another factor at play fuelling the sustained commercial interest in adolescents and youths. In the post-war period, rising real affluence has given rise to an explosion in consumer markets with an enormous proliferation in the consumption choices available to people. Inevitably, competition within and between sectors of spending has intensified. One outcome has been the development of what might be termed the 'Jesuit School of Marketing', the basic aim of which could be summarized as getting them young and keeping them.

In some markets, financial services being a good example, experience indicates that once that initial decision is made, loyalty, albeit grudging, is maintained. In other rather more fashion-led and fickle areas the rationale is that even as we pass through the life cycle, we remain to some extent 'prisoners of our youth'. Attitudes and values developed during this crucial formative period will not be altered by life-stage events. Thus, we respond to certain images throughout our lives that play to these fundamental attitudes and values.

So pervasive has been this youth orientation that it has spilled over into more mainstream culture, with dominance given to images of youth in the media and the market-place. As David Downes (1966, quoted in Davis 1990: 123) has noted, the market has played a considerable role in the provision of new youth-oriented products, in the spread of youth styles, and therefore ultimately in keeping the category of youth in one form or another in its position of high visibility throughout the post-war period.

A great deal has been written about images of youth, both with the way in which they view themselves and the way they are viewed by the rest of society. It is undeniable, however, given the nature of the increasingly consumer-oriented society we inhabit, that the commercial influences on young people's lives have grown and that this has had a profound impact on adolescents and young people. As Gardner and Sheppard (1989: 3) have noted

> . . . consumption has ceased to be purely material or narrowly functional – the satisfaction of basic bodily needs. Today consumption is both symbolic and material. It expresses, in a real sense, a person's place in the world, his or her core identity.

This has influenced the way young people choose to spend their money and time, the images they respond to, and their values and motivations. A wider social ramification has been the impact of the commercialization of adolescents and young people on those who are increasingly excluded from full participation in this consumption process. They are bombarded with the same images and subjected to the same peer-group pressures as their more fortunate counterparts, without the means to satisfy, in a material sense, their aspirations.

So what of the future? The 'baby bust' of the 1970s will feed through into an absolute decline in the numbers in the youth population over the next few years. In itself this will profoundly shape the experience of this generation. One view is that the situation will bring about the demise of the intense youth orientation we have witnessed during the post-war period, others see the spotlight intensifying. Either way there are broader ramifications.

The aim of this chapter is to examine the factors impacting on the 'life-styles' of young people. Starting with an examination of trends and forecasts in the size of the adolescent population, the following three sections will address the spending power of the adolescent and youth populations, their spending preferences, and their time use. The chapter will then go on to address the values and motivations of young people, whether and in what way they are changing, and the key influences on young people. The implications arising from the exclusion of some groups from the consumption process will be considered. The chapter will conclude with a perspective on the future, examining the issues arising in the 1990s.

A brief mention needs to be made of the data boundaries used in the chapter. In broad marketing terms, the youth market is usually taken to comprise the group of consumers between the ages of 16 (sometimes 15) and 24. The rationale is that most will, at some time during the decade when they are members of that group, make the important transition from dependence on the family and the state to independence. Aside from the profound psychological ramifications, this process also results in a change in young people's material circumstances. On occasions the group is split further into two groups: the first comprising those between the ages of 16 and 19 and the second, those between the ages of 20 and 24. This reflects the differing material circumstances affecting the two groups. Where possible data on the slightly younger 'adolescent' age groups (14 to 16) have been included.

THE SIZE OF THE ADOLESCENT AND YOUTH POPULATIONS

Currently there are 3.9 million 15–19 year olds and 4.6 million 20–24 year olds in the United Kingdom. Together they comprise almost 15 per cent of the population. Males outnumber females in both groups. Although this factor is not of particular concern now, it does have significant implications when these age cohorts reach the family formation stage.

It is evident from Figure 12.1 that the proportion of the population comprised of 15–24 year olds has changed fairly dramatically over the course of the century. Taking a historical perspective, it is clear that the proportion of 15–24 year olds in the population fell steadily during the first half of this century, reaching a low point in the 1950s, before rising steadily throughout the 1960s and 1970s, and plateauing during the 1980s. This age group will decline as a proportion throughout the 1990s, although remaining above the figure for the 1950s.

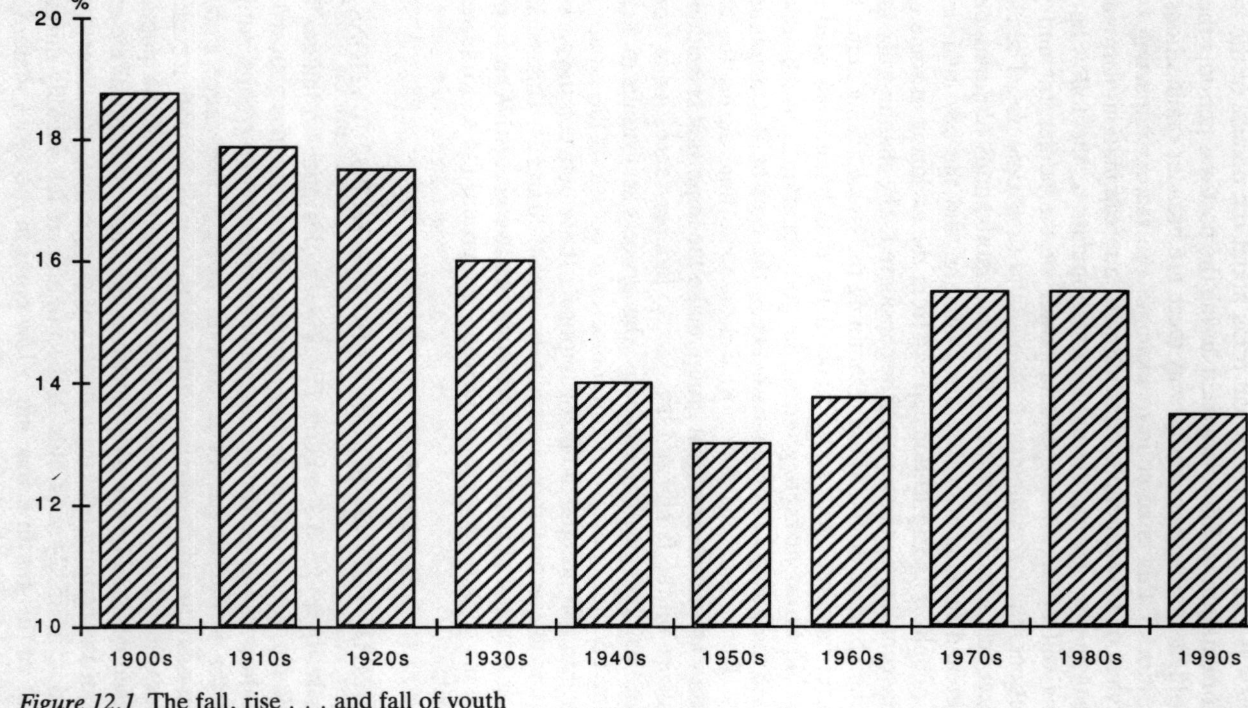

Figure 12.1 The fall, rise . . . and fall of youth
Source: Annual abstract of statistics

The actual number within the age group has an important bearing on their economic circumstances. The increasing prosperity enjoyed by this age group in the post-war boom in large part related to their relative scarcity. During the 1930s, by contrast, a time of economic depression, the relative number of young people was high. Similarly, the spending power of the youth population was adversely affected in the early 1980s when rising numbers of young people (the products of the 1960s 'baby boom') coincided with a period of economic recession. This was reflected in the high youth unemployment figures in the early 1980s.

The 1990s will again be a period of relative scarcity in the numbers of young people. The numbers in the 15–19 age group will fall by 17 per cent between now and 1995 and the numbers within the 20–24 age group will fall by 12 per cent. Although the fall in the number of 15–19 year olds will bottom out in 1994, the number of 20–24 year olds will continue to fall. By the turn of the century there will be 3.7 million 15–19 year olds and 3.5 million 20–24 year olds (Figure 12.2), 1.3 million fewer than now.

Already the implications of the shortfall in the number of young people are evident. As Ermisch (1990) has noted, the annual entry of young people into the labour market has been declining throughout the 1980s, but the fall during the next four years is particularly steep. While the number of entrants will start to rise again after 1993, and continue to increase into the next century, the influx of young workers will remain at much lower levels than during the period between 1975 and 1985. As a result their earnings potential is likely to receive a boost. Thus, the overall decline in the number of young people will be offset to some extent by an increase in their per capita spending power, although it will be insufficient fully to compensate for the shrinkage in the size of the group overall.

Some social commentators have indicated that the decline in the number of young people will result in more profound commercial and cultural shifts away from the youth population. In considering this suggestion, it is worth setting changes in the size of the youth population within the context of changes in the age structure of the population overall. From Figure 12.3 it is evident that while the number of young people is falling, the number of families with children will be growing, as will the numbers within the 'middle-aged' group of 45–59 year olds.

As a result of these demographic shifts it is argued that the commercial and cultural centre of gravity will shift up the age spectrum to the middle age group, whose numbers are not only growing rapidly but whose spending 'discretion' will be very powerful due to a combination of factors. The implications of this situation will be discussed more fully below. It is to the subject of the spending power of young people that the next section turns.

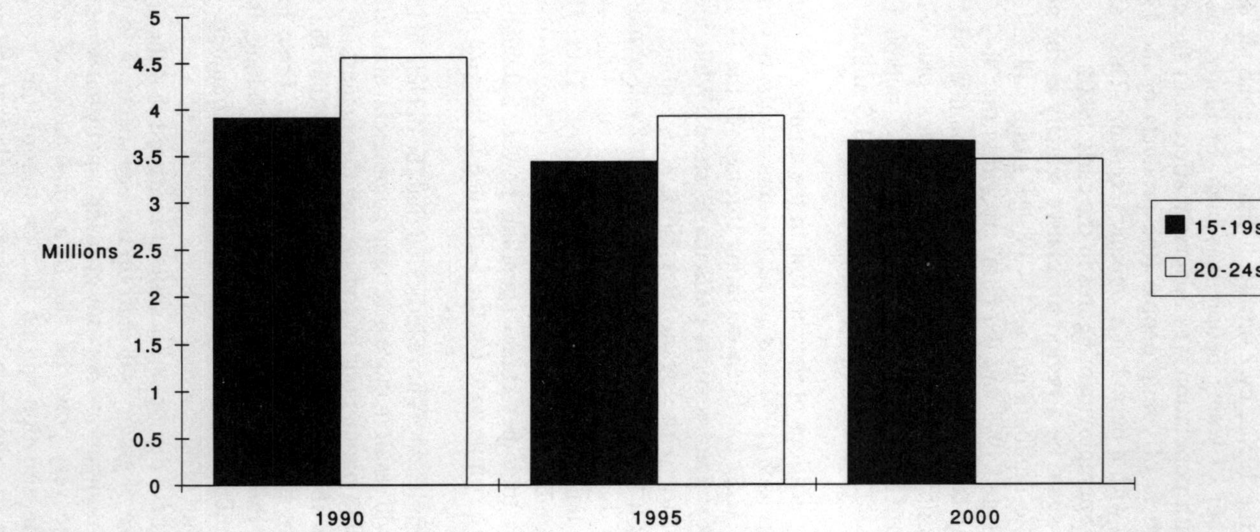

Figure 12.2 The youth population
Source: Mid 1988 based OPCS

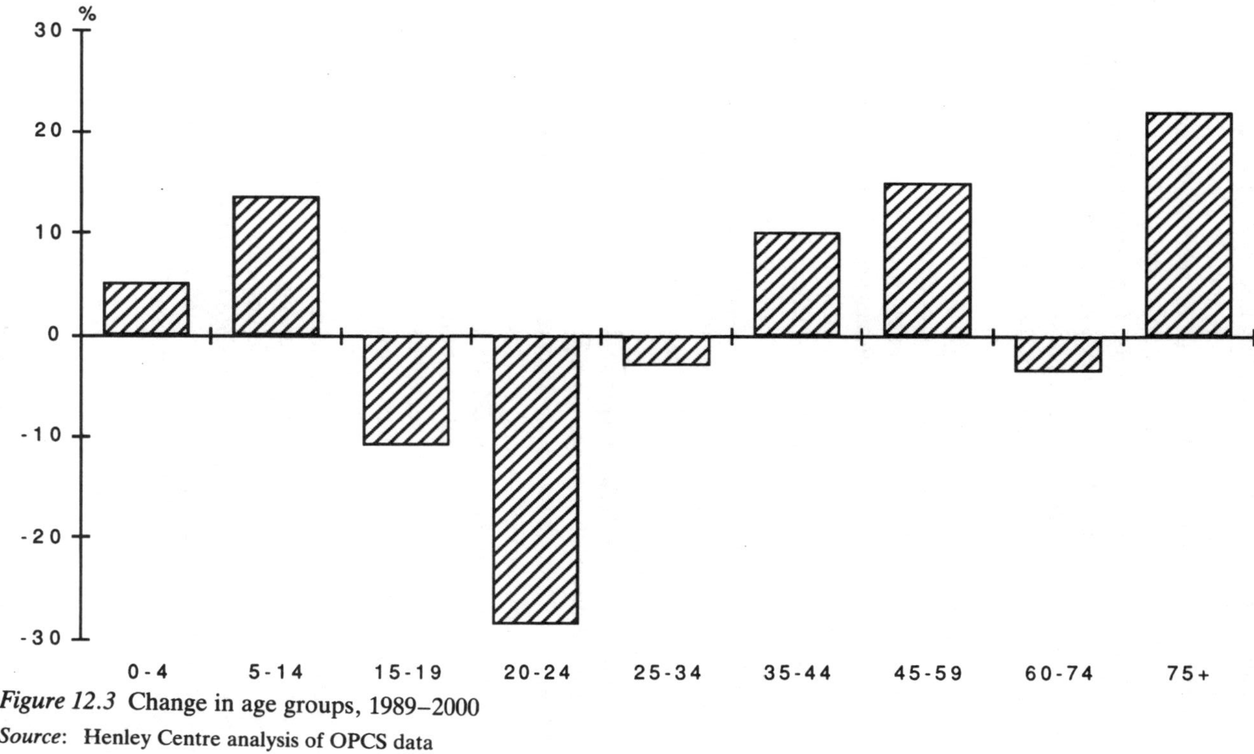

Figure 12.3 Change in age groups, 1989–2000

Source: Henley Centre analysis of OPCS data

MONEY IN THEIR POCKETS: THE ECONOMIC DISCRETION OF YOUNG PEOPLE

A major reason why much of the marketing information available on young people starts at the age of 16 is that their spending potential is actually fairly limited before this age. While still at school adolescents tend to have three major sources of income: first, parental pocket money; second, wages from Saturday jobs, paper rounds, and other casual employment; and third, 'hand-outs' and gifts from family and friends. These sources may be supplemented by 'leakage' of money designated for other items, such as fares or school 'dinner' money, although the sums involved are small.

A large-scale pocket-money survey conducted annually on behalf of Wall's Ice Cream (Birds Eye Walls 1990) provides some useful data on the average spending power of the 14–16 year old age group. Figure 12.4 shows that, in 1990, the average weekly total income for 14–16 year olds was £9.16 (a startling 51 per cent increase on 1989). Of this, earnings account for about 40 per cent, parental contribution for a further third, the balance being accounted for by 'hand-outs' from friends and relations. This gives 14–16 year olds an average annual per capita income of £476.32. Multiplying this figure by the number of 14–16 year olds in the population suggests that overall, average annual spending power is some £1 billion – not an insignificant sum, particularly given its concentration into a limited number of spending sectors.

Data from the 1988 New Earnings Survey, shown in Figure 12.5, provides a breakdown of earnings among the 'youth' age groups for both men and women. Among the under 18s the differential between men and women is not very marked. Average gross weekly earnings for men were £89.30, and among women it was £87.40. Even at this age a more marked differential exists between manual and non-manual workers. For manual workers under 18 average gross weekly earnings were £87.4, whereas the corresponding figure for non-manual workers was £94.4.

Between the ages of 18 and 20, the differential between men and women becomes more marked, with women earning on average £21.30 less than men per week. Interestingly, among this group the differential between manual and non-manual workers appears to work marginally in favour of manual workers whose earnings are £1.20 more than non-manual workers in the same group. By the 21–24 age group, average gross weekly earnings for men have increased to £179.60 and for women to £143.20.

Taking a composite measure to provide spending-power figures which are comparable with the rest of the data used in the chapter indicates that the total spending power of the 15–19 age group is £10.7 billion, while that of the 20–24 age group totals £34.6 billion. Together this accounts for 15 per cent of the total income of the population.

One of the factors limiting the spending power of this age group is

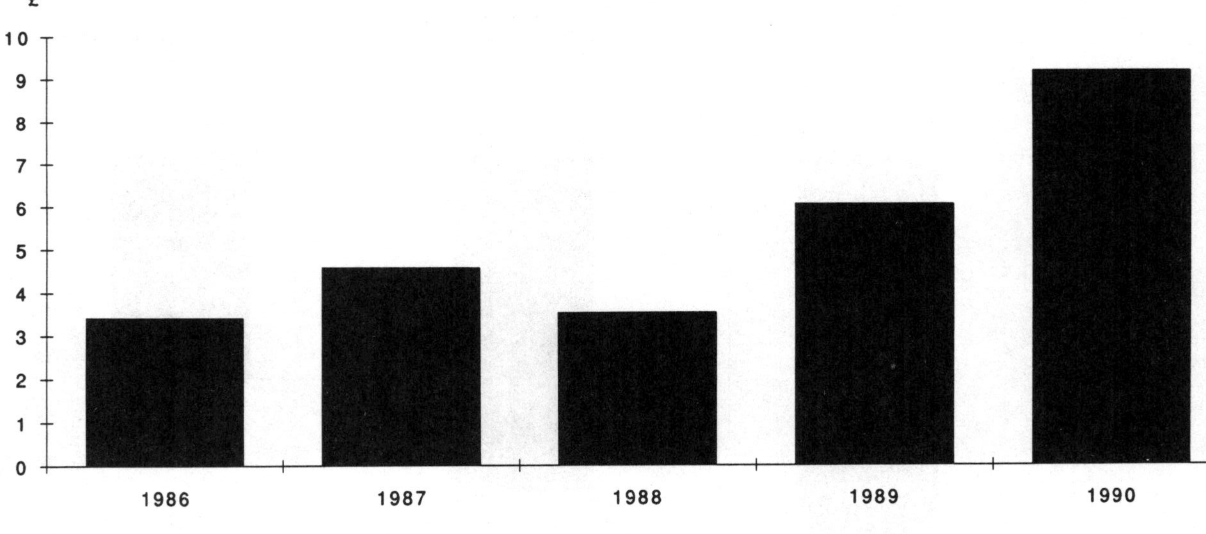

Figure 12.4 Average weekly total income, 14–16 year olds
Source: Wall's pocket money monitor 1990

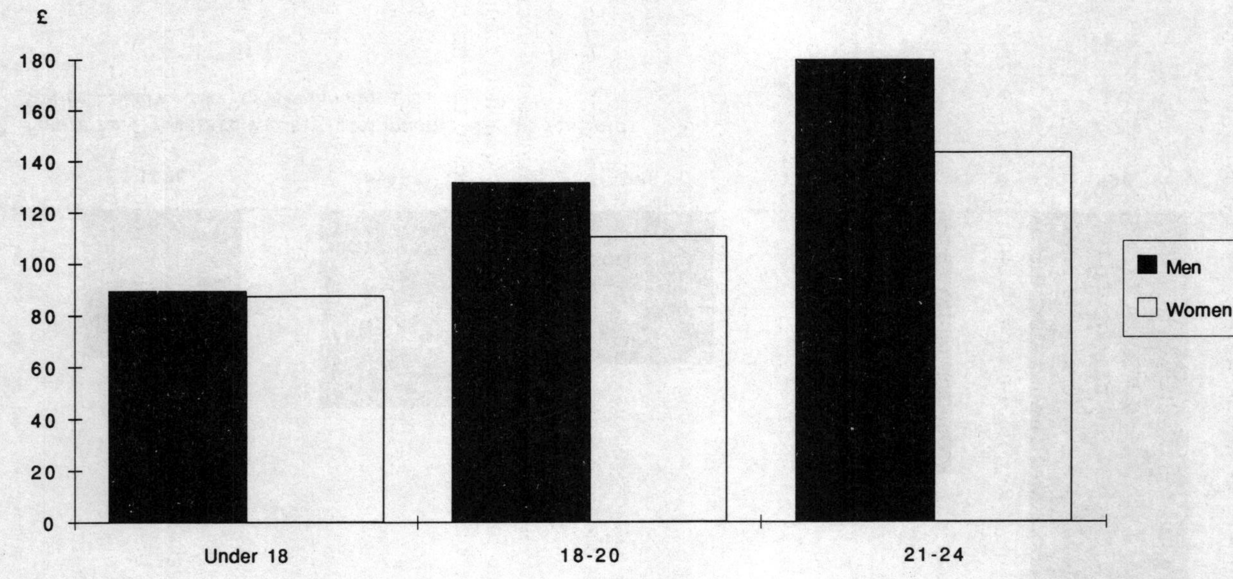

Figure 12.5 Average gross weekly earnings
Source: Department of employment new earnings survey

that increasing numbers are choosing to remain in full-time education. In 1988, 32 per cent of 16–18 year olds were still in full-time education. Among 18–24 year olds, a quarter were participating in further or higher education.

In the short term this trend will exacerbate the labour-market situation, given the anticipated fall in the number of school-leavers available for employment. As Ermisch (1990) has pointed out, the 'baby bust' generations have a strong incentive in terms of a higher expected future return to continue their education. This is likely, therefore, to moderate the fall in the number of students in full-time education implied by changes in the population aged 18–21.

Thus, for employers requiring school-leavers, there is considerable and mounting competition for available labour. Earlier this year both Tesco and Sainsburys announced substantial increases in the wage rates being offered to 16 year olds, 22 per cent at Tesco and 40 per cent at Sainsburys. Similarly a shortage of recruits for clerical and other white-collar jobs is resulting in incentives, not just of higher salaries and good training prospects, but also entertainment allowances or season tickets.

Although many of the identified trends point to the increasing spending potential of young people, certain recent and forthcoming developments will serve to depress their spending power. First, the introduction of individual poll-tax assessments has had a negative impact on the spending potential of young people. Second, the phasing in of student top-up loans will lower the spending power of the student population; and repaying the loan will eat into the income of available graduates. Given the continued shortage in the number of appropriately qualified graduates, however, employers are likely to offer starting salaries to take account of the pay-back factor.

Over the next few years, the demographic time bomb will have an adverse impact on the aggregate spending power of the youth population, and the situation will be exacerbated by the increasing propensity for young people to remain in further or higher education. The gap in the per capita earnings power of this group compared with older workers is likely to narrow, however. This high per capita earnings potential, combined with the high level of spending discretion enjoyed by this age group, means that they will be an attractive target for the commercial sector. Similarly, financial-service companies such as banks and building societies will be offering even greater incentives to students, as 'sweeteners' in order to attract their custom in an increasingly competitive market-place and safeguard their future customer base.

WHO GAINS: WHAT DO ADOLESCENTS AND YOUNG PEOPLE SPEND THEIR MONEY ON?

Among younger adolescents their *own* money tends to be spent on such predictable items as: sweets and snacks; magazines; records and tapes; and stationery. The research also indicates that quite a lot of weekly money is saved, presumably, as with the older age group, to spend eventually on a major item.

Clearly, however, what these adolescents purchase with their own money is very small in comparison with what parents purchase for their children. The limited evidence available here indicates that adolescents show much greater commercial awareness and have an ever greater degree of autonomy in choosing what they want to wear, eat, and do. Parents are urged to buy not just a particular product but a particular 'brand'. This seems an inevitable outcome in a society in which individuals' 'perceived' identities are created increasingly on the basis of consumption choices.

In addition to facing these exhortations, parents may also be independently encouraging the process. The forementioned situation means that parents themselves create identities, not just on the basis of their own choices, but also those of their children. Children are increasingly viewed as a reflection of the parental 'life-style'. Many of the expenditure priorities among slightly older young adults are likely to be evident among the adolescent population. It is clear that children are becoming active in more adult markets at an ever younger age.

Those in the 16–24 year old age group clearly have a greater degree of autonomy to purchase exactly what they want. Table 12.1 reproduces the results of a recent survey by the British Market Research Bureau (BMRB)/ Mintel (1990) on the spending priorities of this age group. Respondents were asked how they would spend a hypothetical £50. Teenagers within this group are most interested in spending on clothes, records and tapes, and cosmetics, while those in their early 20s are more likely to spend their money on entertainment or to save up for a specific item.

Table 12.1 The spending priorities of 16–24 year olds, 1990

Item	%
Clothes	68
Records/tapes/music	34
Going out/drinking	21
Save towards holiday/special purchase	20
Something for car/motorbike	13
Cosmetics/haircare products	8
Books	7
Sport	7
Hobbies	7

Source: BMRB/Mintel (1990: 33)

As would be expected, marked differences are evident in the spending preferences of men and women. It is interesting to note that in some areas their interests appear to be converging. Although young women are still more likely to buy clothes, the gap is narrowing. The Centre's own research reaffirms the increasing fashion consciousness of young men as their sense of identity is achieved increasingly through their outward appearance.

Technological developments and the falling real price of durables have made the duplication of entertainment durables a key feature of many households. Young people today probably spend a higher relative proportion of their income on records and tapes because they have the hardware available on which to play them. Generally, however, it is striking that the overall spending priorities of young people have changed relatively little over time. Back in the 1950s the key youth markets were fashion and entertainment and their dominance has continued. The main difference is that today's young have relatively more to spend.

The greater financial discretion enjoyed by young people is reflected in the more widespread penetration of financial products among this group. Even among the teenage groups there has been a proliferation of 'card'-based bank accounts over the past few years, such as Midland's Livecash, to rival the old post office savings account. Research carried out by the BMRB (quoted in Mintel 1990: 41) indicates that about two-thirds of 15–19 year olds have some form of current account and this rises to 80 per cent among those in their early 20s.

There has been a long-standing debate as to whether easy access to financial service products encourages debt accumulation among young people. Generally, it is recognized that consumer debt is a growing problem facing society, but the key question is whether young people are more likely to get into debt. Certainly, access to a wider range of financial services does give young people a greater degree of flexibility in purchase decisions and may lead to a greater temptation to overstretch themselves. On the other hand, the proliferation of more mainstream financial products means that the young are less likely to be at the mercy of unscrupulous loan sharks.

Spending priorities are to some extent a reflection of the way in which young people choose to spend their time, and time use and activity patterns are the focus of the next section.

TIME USE AND ACTIVITY PATTERNS

The amount of 'free' time available to different groups in the population depends on the amount of time left after the time spent on paid employment; travel to and from work; essential activities such as housework, food preparation, and necessary child care; and sleep have been accounted for.

It is generally true that the young and the old have more free time available than the age groups in the middle, who are likely to have greater work and domestic commitments. Within the youth population, it is those within the 16–19 age group who have relatively more free-time potential than those in their early 20s. Those in the 20–24 age group spend more time on paid employment, they also spend more time on household chores, such as cooking and cleaning. This reflects their higher likelihood of having moved out of the parental home into a separate household. The 16–19 year olds have sixty-seven hours of potential free time and 20–24 year olds have sixty-three hours.

The ability to participate in a wide range of leisure activities is constrained not just by time considerations but also financial ones. This is particularly so given the increasing commercialization of leisure. Those in the 20–24 age group may have less time overall, but as they are more likely to be in paid employment, they have more money available to spend on leisure activities.

If the overall amount of 'leisure space' is taken as the measure, signifying a balance between money and time availability, then 16–19 year olds have a smaller overall leisure space than 20–24 year olds. The better overall balance achieved by 20–24 year olds means that they have a greater choice of activities. Moreover, a further major factor that has important implications for leisure time use is mobility. Here it is significant to note that one-third of those in their early 20s drive a car or van on a regular basis.

Essentially, there are three features which characterize young people's activity patterns: first, they are relatively time-intensive; second, they are socially oriented; and third, they are physically active. It is not surprising that time-intensive activities show much higher levels of participation and frequency among the young and the old relative to the family and middle-aged groups. This situation is particularly the case among the teenage group, given their high time discretion relative to money. For example, watching television is consistently high across the whole 16–24s age range, 16–19s watch about twenty-two hours a week and 20–24s, on average just over three hours less. Likewise, participation and frequency of watching videos is high but is biased towards the teenage group. The same is true of listening to records and tapes: the teenage group spend about twenty-one hours a week and those in their early 20s four hours less. Young people also spend a fair amount of time reading magazines, particularly those relating to their hobbies and interests.

The social orientation of young people's activity patterns is of little surprise given their spending priorities outlined above. A lot of young people spend their leisure time at the pub, particularly those in their early 20s. The lower participation among the younger age group, still 72 per cent, in part reflects the significant proportion of the age group who are legally 'under age'. This group spend time eating out in fast food restaurants, with the older group eating out in smarter restaurants. They spend time at friends' houses, particularly the teenage group. They frequently go to discos and the cinema and are more likely to go to fairs and theme parks.

Their generally high participation in away-from-home activities is easily explained. As has been noted above a relatively high proportion of the younger age group are still living in the parental home and even though the majority of the older age group will have 'flown the parental nest' their living conditions are likely to impose a number of constraints.

Many of these socializing venues provide a haven of privacy and, sometimes, anonymity.

Young people show much higher levels of participation in physically active leisure pursuits: well over a third of the 16–24 age group regularly take part in individual sports; over a third of 16–19 year olds and a quarter of 20–24 year olds regularly play team sports and about half regularly visit a sports centre. Sports centres also operate as socializing venues for young people. Young people are also more likely to jog, and do aerobics, keep fit, and other forms of home exercise.

There thus appears to be a close correlation between the way young people spend their time and their expenditure priorities as outlined above, and this seems to square with conventional views about the life-styles of young people. It is to the underlying values and motivations of young people, crucial in understanding their time use and spending priorities, that the discussion now turns.

WHAT MAKES THEM TICK? THE VALUES AND MOTIVATIONS OF YOUNG PEOPLE

A great deal of hyperbole surrounds images of youth, much of it suggesting the existence of a distinctive 'youth culture'. The notion of youth culture is that of a distinct set of values and motivations which unites young people, cutting across class or gender boundaries and separating them from other groups in the population. The sociologist Talcott Parsons, writing in the United States in the early 1950s, noted four distinctive features which characterized youth culture: first, 'irresponsibility' and an emphasis on 'having a good time'; second, the prominence of sport as an avenue of achievement (in contrast to adult occupational achievement); third, a vague antipathy towards the adult world; and finally, physical attractiveness as a source of peer-group status.

All these characteristics have tended to feature in popular stereotypes of young people throughout the post-war period. It has been argued that the easier economic conditions of the period pre-1974 may have been responsible for the more uncompromising attitudes of young people of that era. The generally harsher economic climate since then has resulted in a reappraisal in the values of young people. The previous idealized cult of youth has become a luxury that young people can no longer afford.

As Davis (1990), among others, is at pains to point out, however, empirical evidence tends to refute the notion of the existence of a rebellious and resistant youth culture. Rather more striking is the essentially conventional nature of the majority of young people. More recent observations have noted the increasingly fragmentary nature of youth groupings, which underpins the breakdown of the notion of some unifying youth culture. In the Centre's view this is a reflection of the generally more individualistic nature of society.

There are two elements to this individualism, both of which have had an important impact on the values and behaviour of young people. First, rising overall affluence and changing production methods have provided both the desire and the means to move away from mass-produced products and hence mass consumption. In this environment less status accrues from the simple ability to buy goods and services, but more from what specifically is bought and how that is different from what others buy. This has resulted in the increasingly fragmentary nature of consumption. This attitude comes across from the Centre's research. For example, young people are even more likely than the population as a whole (67 per cent compared with 55 per cent) to endorse the idea of buying things that not many other people will have.

Second, individualism is taken to describe the changes in the way individuals arrange and organize their social lives and achieve their life goals. In this sense, individualism is taken as the dialectic opposite of collectivism and has manifested itself in the reduced importance of both traditional collective institutions like trade unions and other formalized methods of social representation. Indeed, Stuart Hall (quoted in Gardner and Sheppard 1989: 45) argues that the radical social transformations that have taken place have resulted in 'greater fragmentation and pluralism, the weakening of older collective solidarities and block identities and the emergence of new identities associated with 'greater work flexibility and the maximisation of individual choices through personal consumption'. Following on from this Gardner and Sheppard (1989) see that the weakening or loss of received identities has left a gaping hole where class, association, or region once was. Consumption has filled this perceived gap. The way young people view themselves and their attitudes needs to be seen against this background. Their essentially material aspirations are reflected in Table 12.2.

Table 12.2 'Which of these things do you think that you will want to have before you are 40 and which do you think you will able to afford?'

	Want		*Afford*	
	15–19	*20–24*	*15–19*	*20–24*
House of own	83	81	72	70
Private pension	60	52	47	48
Private health care	30	31	18	17
Private education for children	14	15	7	7
Stocks and shares	14	10	10	9
Enough money to eat out with family 1+ a week	44	49	51	47
Two holidays abroad a year	44	48	33	37
A luxury car	41	34	23	18
A second home	10	11	3	4

Source: MORI (1989)

Further evidence that the enterprise culture has set root in the minds of the young is found in the fact that almost half of 15–19s and 20–24s agreed that they would like to run their own business. More significant was the finding that almost one-third of 15–19 year olds expected to run their own business at some point in the future. This greater sense of individualism is reflected in their attitudes to wider political issues. For example, in research specially commissioned for the programme 'Ten Years On', to mark the tenth anniversary of Conservative Government under Mrs Thatcher, the more individualistic and instrumental attitudes of young people comes across strongly.

Respondents were questioned as to whether they felt they would get a better or worse service if certain services were run by a private company rather than the state. With the exception of coal, young people were less likely to think services would be worse than the population as a whole. In certain areas, such as 'care for the elderly' and the 'provision of leisure centres and swimming pools' young people were much more likely to favour private provision. While over 50 per cent of young people preferred the notion of a country which 'emphasises the social and collective provision of welfare', over a third favoured the opposite notion of 'a country where the individual is encouraged to look after himself'.

The research indicates that in some respects young people's attitudes and values conform to certain general social stereotypes, while in other areas they appear to contradict them. Table 12.3 gives some indication of the current priorities of the 16–24 age group. Again the instrumental and individualistic outlook on life is evident. More widespread concern over health is evident across all ages, but what is interesting is the extent to which it has assumed importance in the minds of the young. In many respects attitudes appear to be running ahead of behaviour given the evidence with respect to alcohol consumption and reliance on fast food. On the highly topical issue of the environment, over three-quarters of 16–24 year olds feel that it is important to buy products that do not harm the environment, yet this is a much lower level of response than that found among the population as a whole.

The essentially conventional attitudes of young people are reflected in much of the survey research. A recent survey carried out by market analysts Mintel (1990) found that young people would like to be described as sensible/responsible, sensitive/caring, and intelligent. The picture has remained remarkably steady over the last few years, although being thought of as creative/artistic and wild/unpredictable had grown in popularity. The relative ranking of the responses and the change since 1987 is shown in Table 12.4.

The picture that emerges is essentially one of incorporation into the mainstream. Although in certain respects young people emerge as more hedonistic and more idealistic than older age groups, overall the most striking feature is the apparent degree of consensus with the rest of the adult population.

A further explanation for the way young people's attitudes and values appear to be changing relates to the notion of 'post-modernism'. One way of considering the impact the phenomenon of post-modernism is having on individuals' lives is along the following lines. Life in the past could be interpreted much more as a 'package deal'. Once an individual acquired certain real features, in terms of age, sex, and so on, then the expectation was that they would acquire a fairly narrow set of values which 'limited' their behaviour. Increasingly, as society has become more affluent and the old social mores, relating to age, class, and gender, have broken down, it seems evident that we are free to 'appropriate' meanings into our lives from just about wherever we choose.

Table 12.3 'How important is it for you, at the moment, to do something about each of the following?'

% agreeing essential/very important	*16–24s*	*Total sample*
Earning more money	64	46
Improving my health	62	69
Enjoying myself more	61	47
Improving my knowledge	61	52
Improving my confidence	54	53
Fulfilling obligations to others	54	57
Making myself feel safer	52	61
Getting more free time	50	38
Getting more control over life	48	43
Getting people to respect me more	41	29
Making more friends	38	31
Helping a good cause	36	39

Source: Henley Centre 'Planning for Social Change' Survey, 1988

Table 12.4 How young people would like to be described

	1987	*1990*
Sensible/responsible	50	42
Sensitive/caring	42	37
Intelligent/thoughtful	30	32
Amusing/extrovert	21	22
Creative/artistic	12	18
Up and coming/successful	11	15
Wild/unpredictable	10	15
Romantic/impulsive	8	11
Cool/streetwise	9	10
Sophisticated/stylish	10	6

Source: BMRB/Mintel (1990)

Again, this is having an important impact on the attitudes and values of young people. It also essentially finally breaks down the notion of a united and rebellious youth because it means that for the majority there is little left to rebel against. Following through this augurs for the further absorption of youth into the mainstream of society.

KEY INFLUENCES ON YOUNG PEOPLE

Much of the literature relating to young people focuses on young people's susceptibility to influences during these formative years. Implicit in what has been written is the perception that such influences and pressures are in some way damaging because of their potential impact on behaviour. Of particular concern is the role of the media and particularly advertising, both of which are often deemed to exploit adolescents and young people for commercial purposes. As Davis (1990: 166) has noted, '. . . the entertainment media, or indeed the whole flourishing youth culture industry, served simultaneously to create the teenager and thus to exploit the young'.

The notion is that the media 'manipulates' young people into buying things they do not want, perhaps cannot afford, and even possibly should not have. Moreover, clearly the media, through advertising, exposes adolescents to a large number of messages for products which are not aimed at them. The focus for much of the criticism is over advertisements for cigarettes and alcohol, which are seen to glamorize, making these harmful products desirable to young people.

Clearly, the behaviour of adolescents and young people is determined by a complex and interconnected network of influences. Much of the evidence on young people and advertising suggests that over the years, as adolescents and young people have become more experienced consumers, so their attitudes to advertising appear to be much closer to those of adults. Taking the cases of drinking and smoking, data collected for the Health Education Council indicate widespread trial of both cigarettes and alcohol. Isolating the extent to which such behaviour is due to advertising is difficult, however, and much of the available research emanates from Advertising Associations, who inevitably may be selective in the research they present. A multinational study conducted by the International Advertising Association purported to show that (by comparable definitions), four times as many 15 year olds smoked regularly in Norway, where a complete ban on tobacco advertising has been in operation since 1975, than in the much less restrictive environments of Argentina or Hong Kong.

The conclusion is that a myriad of other influences, such as the smoking behaviour of parents, siblings, and peers in addition to an array of socio-cultural factors, must have played a part. Some have argued that the behaviour of screen idols is more likely to result in emulatory behaviour in respect to smoking, for example, than a piece of slashed purple fabric. Certainly, research conducted by Mintel indicates that young people are more likely to be influenced by the endorsement of products by personalities.

The Centre's research shows that in general young people tend to feel they are influenced by those with whom they generally agree, as is evident from Table 12.5. From this one would conclude that the major influences on young people are their friends, followed by their parents. Other major influences include 'partner' (this figure is considerably lower among young people, as many, particularly in the younger group, do not have a partner) and employers. Again such figures tend to reinforce the notion of the conformity of young people, with 68 per cent generally agreeing with their parents. The results underpin the importance of the 'peer group' in influencing behaviour.

Table 12.5 How much you agree with various people and how much influence they have (base: 16–24s)

	Agree with	*Influenced by*
Friends	81	59
Parents	68	58
TV news	70	32
Work colleagues	53	32
Partner	49	46
Employer	45	39
Brother/sister	44	22
Newspaper read	40	40
Other relatives	39	14
Royal Family	36	6
Manufacturers	30	14
Retailers	25	10
Adverts	24	17
Government	24	14
Church/religious leaders	23	12

Source: Henley Centre, 'Planning for Social Change'

Young people are much less deferential towards traditional figures of authority, such as the Government, Church, and religious leaders, the Royal Family, and manufacturers. In each case less than 15 per cent feel such figures have influence over them. This seems to be more a reflection of a pervasive breakdown of hierarchical authority structures, given the responses of other population groups, than any particular anti-establishment feeling among the 'youth' population.

Also worth noting is the low level of influence the commercial sector is felt to have. The media, in the form of TV news, is felt to be an influence by almost one-third, but newspapers are felt to have a low level of influence. Again other research from the Centre would tend to support this. Young people feel they are less likely to be influenced by nationally advertised and well-known brands than older groups, who in general are much less confident consumers.

Although essentially conformist, young people emerge as being increasingly independent of mind, and at an increasingly younger age. Clearly, however, a myriad of influences is at work on young people. Certain cynics might argue that the fact that young people do not feel they are being influenced by advertising tells us merely of the subtlety and power of such commercial messages and their ability to 'manipulate' the peer-group mentality.

THE EXCLUSION ZONE

It seems undeniable, to casual as well as empirical observers, that Britain is becoming an increasingly divided society. Income distribution has become more heavily skewed in favour of the more affluent households. While between 1979 and 1986 the top fifth of households saw their share of total household income increase from 38.1 to 42.2 per cent, those in the bottom fifth witnessed a decline from 7.3 to 5.9 per cent. This situation is not totally political, for the gap started widening again in 1976, three years before Mrs Thatcher began her term of office.

It is well known that those in poorer households have fared relatively worse, caught in the vicious spiral of the poverty trap, or reliant on benefits indexed to prices rather than wages (the latter of course having risen much faster over the past few years). The Henley Centre has calculated that some 11 million people constitute this 'second nation': a core 'group' of 7.3 million and a fringe group comprising a further 3.7 million.

Thus, although the range of market choices available to young people has increased exponentially, a substantial minority find themselves increasingly marginalized and excluded. The situation is exacerbated by the widespread diffusion of technology, bombarding these young people with images of what they cannot have. Inevitably this results in resentment and tensions. In America, the so-called 'trainer wars' provide an extreme example of the way in which the desire to conform to the latest fashion has resulted in violence and even murder. In the summer of 1990 a 13 year old boy was murdered by another young teenager for a pair of fashion trainers.

Of course it is dangerous to make cross national and cross-cultural comparisons. 'Trainer wars' need to be seen in the context of life in the urban ghettos, where violence has long been a feature of everyday life. They do, however, provide a chilling reminder of the lengths to which those excluded from the process of consumption will go in order to obtain the 'symbols' of acceptance.

AN UNCERTAIN FUTURE: ADOLESCENTS AND YOUNG PEOPLE AS CONSUMERS INTO THE 1990S

The 1990s will mark a 'new' period in the economic and cultural significance of young people, the experience of which will have an enormous impact on their attitudes and values. A key issue will be the way in which the construction of an internal market in Western Europe, the sustained expansion in world trade, and the increasing globalization of the media will condition the experiences of young people. Certainly one outcome is likely to be that the individual experiences and the influences individuals are exposed to are becoming increasingly homogeneous.

Given the perceived commercial opportunities that arise out of such a situation there is mounting interest in understanding the extent to which the lives of young people, in terms of their aspirations and life-styles, are converging across national boundaries. Certainly, many of the structural factors impacting on young people in this country, such as the 'baby bust', changing household structures (smaller families and increasing incidence of divorce), rising affluence and more widespread access to higher education are evident across much of Europe. Such trends serve to increase the 'shared' experience of young people.

One of the most powerful influences cementing the 'shared' experience of Europe's young consumers has been the pervasiveness of American cultural norms and commercial brands. American brands such as Coke and Levis, or cultural icons such as Michael Jackson or Madonna, have established an almost universal appeal among young people the world over, to such an extent that they have become synonymous with youth and fully integrated into more mainstream culture.

As the barriers to internal trade come down it is likely that a stronger sense of European identity will result. Within youth markets this will impact on the dominant cultural forces and there may well be a decline in the prolonged hegemony of American imagery and symbolism. Over half of 15–19 year olds (52 per cent) considered themselves to be European as well as being British, which is higher than among the population as a whole. Equally striking, however, is the fact that 39 per cent of these teenagers did not consider themselves to be European.

As in Britain, the forces of greater fragmentation and pluralism are evident across much of Europe. Thus, just as the attitudes and behaviour of adolescents and young people are becoming more individualistic, so too across Europe. What this means in effect is that 'subgroups' found in the UK are likely to be found in other European countries too. Thus, although one could argue that general convergence will take place, there will however remain certain differences in behaviour based on factors such as national cultural identities, habit, and climate, and these factors will take far longer to break down.

Finally, there remains the issue of the wider impact of 'youth' on society in the 1990s. Some observers are suggesting that a decline in their numbers will have widespread cultural as well as commercial implications. The decline in the numbers within the youth population coinciding with an increase in the numbers and, more importantly, spending power of the middle-aged population will result in the 'mantle' of commercial and cultural leadership passing from the former to the latter group. Such a scenario implies that 'young people' will no longer be the drivers of change that they have been perceived to be over the past thirty years. Rather than parents seeking to 'keep up' with their children, we could see a return to the historical norm in which young people emulate the values and behaviour of their parents.

An alternative, and more disturbing outcome could be that adolescents and young people feel they have been 'expelled' from the position of cultural dominance. Such dominance has meant that in large part, youth culture has been absorbed into the mainstream. Exclusion may result in the opening up of 'new hostilities' between adolescents and older groups with the possible development of subversive youth cultural phenomena. Given the generally conformist nature of young people's views as expressed above, and given the increasingly fragmentary nature of social groups, it is difficult to envisage a 'unified' culture taking hold of the nation's youth.

An alternative scenario altogether is that the commercial pressures on young people intensify, due to their increasing scarcity. Significantly fewer young people in absolute terms alongside the anticipated expansion of the proportion of the group in education will affect their labour-market status. The number of 16–19 year olds in the British work-force will decline from 2.5 million to 1.9 million, a reduction of 23 per cent.

It is already evident, as mentioned above, that appropriately qualified young people are finding themselves much courted by potential employers, with the result that their per capita spending power increases accordingly. In the Henley Centre's view they may find themselves even more in the spotlight, as they were in the 1950s (when a relative fall in their numbers intensified the demand for their labour), with the commercial sector aiming to maintain their share of the increasingly affluent youth market.

Whatever happens in the wider social sphere, the centrality of the consumption ethic as a governing factor in young people's lives will remain. It is important for those involved in all areas of adolescents' and young people's lives to understand the impact consumption has, and be able to cope with its wider ramifications.

REFERENCES

Birds Eye Walls (1990) 'Pocket Money Monitor', produced by HCPR Ltd for Birds Eye Walls, Walton on Thames, Surrey.

Davis, J. (1990) *Youth and the Condition of Britain – Images of Adolescent Conflict*, London: Athlone Press.

Ermisch, J. (1990) *Fewer Babies, Longer Lives*, York: Joseph Rowntree Foundation.

Gardner, C. and Sheppard, J. (1989) *Consuming Passion – The Rise of Retail Culture*, London: Unwin Hyman Ltd.

Henley Centre, The (1978) *Planning for Social Change*, London: The Henley Centre for Forecasting.

Henley Centre, The (1988) *Planning for Social Change*, London: The Henley Centre for Forecasting Ltd.

Henley Centre, The (1989) *Planning for Social Change*, London: The Henley Centre for Forecasting Ltd.

Mintel (1990) *Youth Lifestyles 1990*, London: Mintel Publications Ltd.

MORI (1989) 'Ten Years On', research conducted on behalf of Juniper Productions, MORI, London (unpublished).

Wolfe, A. (1990) *Children and Advertising: An Advertising Association Monograph*, Henley: NTC Publications.

Name index

Subject index